D0886625

BOB HOPE

PORTRAIT
OF A SUPERSTAR

Charles Thompson

ST. MARTIN'S PRESS
NEW YORK

Library of Congress Cataloging in Publication Data

Thompson, Charles.
  Bob Hope.

  1. Hope, Bob, 1903–   2. Comedians – United
States – Biography.   I. Title.
PN287.H63T5   792.7′028′0924 [B[81–5799
ISBN 0–312–08724–1   AACR2

'I feel so much better after a show than I do before. Because, when you get into a room full of people and they're laughing, it does something to everybody. I know it does something to my tax man – he just loves it . . .'

Bob Hope
21 November 1977

List of illustrations

1

Chicago in the winter of 1928 was no place for the faint-hearted. The prairie wind howled through its narrow streets, threading between the skyscrapers, chilling all before it and lashing against the unprotected faces of the crowds hastening home from work.

But at least one young man was in no hurry that dank and dismal November afternoon. He had no job and nowhere in particular to go – except perhaps home to the invitingly warm fires of Cleveland, and Mum and Dad. Lester T. Hope, former song-and-dance man and now would-be comedian, was at the end of his tether.

'My God! No wonder they call this the Windy City,' he thought sourly, as he pulled his overcoat more tightly around his freezing body and angrily tugged the faded derby further down towards his tingling ears. The coat, like the hat, had seen better days. But then so too had their owner. As he shuffled along, apparently oblivious of the crowds bustling around him, the broad shoulders slumped even further and the air of despondency heightened visibly.

A deserted park bench provided the ideal spot for a much-needed review of the situation: in one coat pocket, a dime – his last; in the other, a packet of peanuts – also his last; inside his crumpled suit, he knew already, lurked a sheaf of IOUs and bills amounting to $400.

'I'm finished,' thought Lester. 'So far ... so near ... for so little ...'

Cleveland was but a day's bus ride away – if only he had the price of the fare. Thoughts of ending it all were quickly thrust aside, as an ever-active mind tried to come up with a joke about a man who had spent the last 48 hours staying alive on just two tiny bags of peanuts. No punch line came. But by the time the last of the peanuts had brightened the life of a pigeon or two, Lester T. Hope was on the road to success again.

Charlie Cooly, an old school friend from Cleveland, happened by chance upon the dejected figure. With him was Charlie Hogan, a Chicago booking agent.

'You any good, Hope?' asked Hogan suspiciously, after Lester had poured out his tale of woe.

'You bet,' retorted Hope, with barely a pause for thought.

'Okay. I'll give you a break,' said the agent.

He offered Lester three days at Chicago's West Englewood Theatre and the princely (to Hope) sum of $75. It wasn't much. But when you are 25, broke and on the verge of quitting the business you love, it was a lifesaver – and Lester grasped it firmly.

That was the turning point. It marked the dawning of a new age of comedy; the first real step in a career spanning five decades; the making of the man who, as Bob Hope, would travel ten million miles to give the world a billion laughs.

2

Bob Hope got his first chuckle on 29 May 1903, when he became the fifth of seven sons born to Avis Townes Hope.

Avis Hope, the daughter of a Welsh sea captain, was a diminutive brown-eyed woman with boundless energy and an unshakable belief in the future. As she prayed that her latest offspring would be blessed with the family trait of earnest endeavour, her English husband, William Henry, shrugged off the birth of yet another son by taking a few pints in the local public house.

Pa Hope came from a long line of master stonemasons and builders. His father James was a stone-carver of considerable ability and determination – he once walked the hundred miles from Bath to London to help build the Royal Courts of Justice in the Strand. He was also in Paris for the carving of the more intricate parts of the Statue of Liberty. In the mid-1800s James went into business with his friend Percy Picton and they formed the building firm of Picton and Hope, basing themselves at Hitchin in Hertfordshire. Son William had little option but to follow the family trade as a master stone-cutter. When he married Avis Townes the couple moved into 44 Craigton Road – one of a row of modest homes built by Picton and Hope.

The latest addition to the Hope family was christened Leslie Townes at the Church of England in the New Hall district of Eltham. The name Leslie was given to him in honour of a local soccer hero of the era. Little Leslie – it would be many years before he acquired the name the world would know him by – spent the first three years of his life in the house at 44 Craigton Road. During that time the family fortunes fluctuated dramatically. The Picton and Hope partnership had been dissolved at the turn of the century, but William's skills continued to command top money. Then along came the brick – and for the Hopes the hard times began. The death of Queen Victoria in 1901 coincided with the end of a golden age of British architecture. With it went the insatiable demand for craftsmen such as William Hope. The bricklayers became the new elite of building and the prosperity that Leslie was born to turned to near poverty by the time he was a toddler. As jobs became scarcer William spent less and less time on the scaffold, and more and more time on the racecourse or in the nearest public house quaffing pints of ale.

With the coffers dwindling rapidly, Pa Hope sold Craigton Road and moved his family to Bristol. The entire Hope clan turned out at Eltham's Well Hall Station to see them off. The Hopes moved into a rambling house near the centre of Bristol, and Father began scouring the city for work. Meanwhile young Leslie turned his attentions to nearby St George's Park.

'My only two real memories of England concern that park,' says Bob. 'Once I was bitten by a dog there, in that place you don't talk about, and another time I was clonked on the noggin by a rock while defending my dog from a gang of Bristol kids. I carry both scars to this day . . . and I've been leery of dog acts ever since!'

Bristol failed to provide the fresh start Leslie's father was banking on. His drinking increased and the atmosphere at home reached an all-time low. His brothers, Frank and Fred, had emigrated to Cleveland in Ohio some years before. Frank had built up a thriving plumbing business and it was he who persuaded William to seek a better life in America. In 1907 William packed his bags, kissed his wife and sons goodbye, and boarded a liner bound for New York.

'I'll send for you when I've made good,' William promised his wife. 'It won't be long and things really are going to get better.'

Pa Hope was as good as his word. The rare skills of an English master stonemason were in great demand in Cleveland

and the dollars flowed into his bank account. For once they stayed there.

Christmas 1907 brought good news from Cleveland – they would be reunited with Father within a few months. William was not on the dock to greet his brood when they landed at New York's Ellis Island, after a rough voyage in steerage, in March, 1908. But the immigration formalities were speedily dealt with and Ma Hope herded her boisterous boys into New York City, where they boarded the train for Cleveland.

One of the first sights they saw in Cleveland was a beautiful church built by Father – the Newkland Avenue Presbyterian. According to Bob the building had a profound effect on mother and sons; 'When we arrived we were Episcopalian. Then we saw the church! We liked it so much we turned Presbyterian.'

After an emotional reunion at Uncle Frank's house, the Hope boys were bedded down with various relatives. They remained separated until Avis found a home on Euclid Street in East Cleveland.

Young Leslie was enrolled in the nearby Fairmount Junior School where he became an instant hit. During a lesson break on his first day a classmate asked his name.

'Hope ... Leslie,' was the very English reply.

From then on the whole school dubbed him 'Hopelessly', although they later shortened it to 'Hopeless'. But many a Fairmount pupil quickly learned that the robust 'Hopeless' was both fast on his feet and firm with his fists.

Life was not only tough at school, though. Pa Hope's new found enthusiasm for hard work soon waned and he began to drown his sorrows again. 'The United States,' he told his wife, 'is a fine place for women and dogs. But it's a poor place for horses and men.'

The business set-backs and drinking placed a severe strain on relations at home. William, a violent and irrational disciplinarian at the best of times, paid less and less attention to his seven sons. Fortunately for the boys, as their father grew more remote, their mother took a greater interest in their upbringing.

Avis Hope was a remarkable woman. Moods of depression would soon be dispelled with a flash of her brown eyes and a frank lecture. She was honest with her brood about the dire financial straights they were in and instilled into them a fierce determination to succeed against all odds. None of the Hope children took this more to heart than Leslie. The lesson in optimism stood him in good stead in the hard years to come.

When he moved from Fairmount to East High – a more senior school – Leslie, like all the Hope boys, started to hustle for money. Mum and Dad couldn't afford to give them pocket money, so the only way to get some was to earn it. Leslie had two principal sources of income – singing and shooting pool. By the time he was eight years old he had already developed a distinctive voice – 'halfway between high tenor and soprano' – and an awareness that it could be put to very good use.

'It just seemed natural that I should sing,' recalls Bob, 'so when Sunday rolled around, and we were broke, a bunch of us would board a streetcar for Luna Park (the local amusement park) and begin singing popular songs. 'I'd sing a solo. Then we'd give with a quartet. And then, just before getting to Luna, we'd pass the hat and split the proceeds!'

The youngsters spent their earnings at the park. Before going home, the group would pick up a few dollars more singing on street corners. 'The net always went into Ma's family treasury,' says Bob proudly.

Shooting pool provided less of an income. Although Leslie was a familiar figure around the Cleveland pool halls by the age of 12, and an acknowledged expert with the cue, the friends he hustled were as poor as he was. But the few cents he managed to win were enough to satisfy his great love – the movies. After a few hours in the pool hall Leslie would scurry off to the Alhambra or Park cinemas.

'I sat in the dark for hours,' says Bob, 'watching the flickering shadows on the screen. I could see myself as Rudolph Valentino . . . racing over the sands on horseback with Agnes Ayres in my arms.'

Nobody seemed to mind how many hours young Leslie spent gazing at his film idols, but the family did object to the time he spent hanging around the pool halls.

'Your son Leslie's spending too much time around that billiard place,' a worried Aunt Louise told his mother. 'He's turning out to be a loafer!'

'Not at all,' retorted Avis Hope. 'The poolroom is just part of growing up. Don't worry about Leslie. He'll turn out fine.'

When it came to making a fast buck, though, Leslie was far from a loafer. Each summer the big firms in Cleveland would hold huge weekend picnics for their employees in the many public parks around the city. The highlight was always the sprint racing. And Leslie, remarkably fleet of foot, would enter as many events as he could. Often he was seen at two or three picnics each Sunday.

'In those days,' recalls Bob, 'the prize was five dollars for first and three for second. I had a buddy I used to run around with – a boy called George Jennings. And we used to win all the races. We had tricks how to win 'em and everything.'

The tricks (Leslie never called it cheating) often involved his brothers: if he was up against a really fast opponent another Hope would enter too, but would stumble at a crucial point in the race. The faster boy was put off his stride and Leslie, or George, could then take the winner's prize.

Although Leslie was basically an honest child there was a time when he briefly flirted with crime, fell foul of the law and ended up in jail. One hot summer Sunday he and some pals decided to ease their boredom by breaking into a local sporting goods shop, and 'borrowing' some tennis racquets and balls. Unfortunately the gang was caught red-handed within hours – happily playing with their ill-gotten gains in a nearby parking lot. A very frightened Leslie spent a few uncomfortable hours locked up before being rescued by his angry parents. The promise he made to 'go straight' was never broken.

Leslie then turned his hand to a variety of part-time jobs: he delivered bread for a bakery: served milk shakes at a soda fountain; chopped meat in his eldest brother's butcher shop; sold shoes; caddied for the well-to-do at a local golf club; ran a flower stall and, at the age of 12, sold newspapers to the then richest man in the world – John D. Rockefeller Senior.

'The newspaper was two cents and he used to stop at this corner where I stood,' says Bob. 'He gave me a dime one day and when I found I couldn't change it, I said, "I'll trust you till tomorrow." He said, "No! Get change..." So I had to run about fifty yards, probably losing around ten sales while I got the change! I came back, gave him eight cents and he said, "Always deal in cash." That was all about two cents and it taught me a lot about money.'

Leslie's childhood earnings were increasingly spent on his great passion for the silver screen. Charles Chaplin, the clown genius came from the same part of London as the Hopes, had become the rage of the age and an irresistible draw.

'He was my idol,' says Bob. 'I'd never miss a picture. It amazed me that one little guy with a funny moustache, derby, baggy suit and cane could evoke so much laughter.'

Leslie reasoned that if Chaplin could do it, so could he. He scrounged an old suit from a brother, some scruffy shoes and a battered derby from Dad, smudged his top lip with charcoal, hacked a stick from a handy tree and waddled off duck-legged down Euclid Street twirling his pseudo-rattan cane as he went. The amazing sight brought roars of laughter from brothers and neighbours alike. It was enough to persuade Leslie to enter some of the many Charlie Chaplin imitation contests that were popular at the time. His finest hour came in Luna Park one Sunday when the judges overwhelmingly declared Leslie T. Hope to be the 'Champion Chaplin'. The first prize, a new stove, was proudly taken home to Mum and put to good use for many years.

The influence of Charlie's silent-screen antics was lasting and more than just a childhood fantasy. 'In about 1927,' says Bob, 'he was in New York and somebody told me that his car was standing in front of the Forty-Fourth Street Theatre. And I went over, and stood in the doorway for an hour and a half – just to see him leave!'

Charlie Chaplin clearly gave the young Hope a taste for show business, but it was his mother who actively fostered it. Even when the family finances were at an all-time low she found money to buy a second-hand piano so there would be music in the house.

'My mother was always singing,' says Bob. 'In fact she was a concert singer when she was younger. And so I think that's where we all inherited our voices because all we did was sing around the house.'

Leslie's father also played his part. When the mood was right he would entertain the boys for hours with jokes and amusing tales. 'He was quite a funny guy,' recalls Bob. 'We have a picture of him with a high hat and cigar, when he was acting jolly.'

The records of Cleveland's East High School show that Leslie Townes Hope was far from being its most brilliant scholar, even though he was one of the brightest pupils. Leslie found the lessons boring and a chore, and could see little merit in staying on to 'pass examinations for the sake of passing them'. So, at the earliest opportunity, he left East High to seek fame and fortune elsewhere.

3

The smoke had hardly cleared along the Western Front when the Armistice was signed on 11 November 1918. The Great War was over at last. Leslie Hope heard the tremendous news when he started his first steady job as a night shift parts clerk in a Cleveland car plant – the Chandler Motor Company. He had been eagerly accepted by the firm because so many young men were away at war. But it was not to be a long-term career.

'I had a great job,' he recalls, 'until we found out there was a dictaphone in the office. We had a quartet and we used to sing into this dictaphone, and then listen to the playback. Then one morning the boss came in and pushed the button. We'd forgotten to erase this song and he heard us singing! That was the end of us at the Chandler Motor Car Company.'

Leslie then tried to make a name for himself as a newspaper reporter. His hero was Damon Runyon – widely considered to be one of the greatest reporters of all time – and Hope believed he could emulate the master. He didn't, and soon retired from journalism.

His efforts to earn pugilistic fame were equally short-lived. The tough youngster who had few problems holding his own at school found semi-professional boxing a wholly different proposition, even fighting under an assumed name.

'I had a buddy who called himself Packie West,' says Bob. 'So I strolled down the next day and registered as Packie East ... which was a big laugh for all the guys around. I had about four fights!'

10

Fifty years later Hope had a string of one-liners to recall his days in the ring:

I used to fight under the name of Rembrandt Hope – I was on the canvas so much . . .

There was one sports writer who said I was the only fighter in Cleveland history carried both ways – in and out . . .

I was really a very colourful fighter – I wore blue trunks with a yellow streak down my back . . .

I was the only fighter in Cleveland who wore a rear-view mirror . . .

Leslie's boxing ambitions gave way to an earnest desire to get into show business and become a vaudeville entertainer. But first he had to learn to dance. He already knew a few basic steps, taught to him by the black vaudevillian King Rastus Brown, and was able to add to those quickly by enrolling in the local dance school run by another former vaudevillian, Johnny Root. After only six months, though, Leslie was called to see Johnny and told that the school must close.

'Over my dead dancing pumps,' said Hope.

'Well, what are you going to do about it?' asked Root.

'Take it over – pupils and all,' replied the impetuous teenager.

So Hope became the proud proprietor of a bankrupt Cleveland dance school. He even had business cards printed: LESLIE T. HOPE WILL TEACH YOU HOW TO DANCE – BUCK AND WING, ECCENTRIC, WALTZ-CLOG AND SOFT SHOE.

1922 was a year of mixed fortunes for Leslie: his dance school finally folded, but his romance with a local beauty, Mildred Rosequist, blossomed. He managed to persuade her to become his first dance partner, and to try for a career in vaudeville. To begin with, they developed their act by appearing in small Cleveland variety theatres each Saturday night, collecting four dollars each for their trouble. Hardly a king's ransom, but it was a start. As Leslie's confidence grew so did his enthusiasm for a career in vaudeville. Part-time bookings in Cleveland, he decided, were not for him. There was a big world out there – somewhere.

The only problem, he soon realized, was going to be persuading Mildred's mother to allow him to take her teenage daughter on tour. Mrs Rosequist refused. But despite losing

Mildred, Leslie, still only 20, was confident of making the big time. Before long he had teamed up with a boyhood friend, Lloyd Durbin.

Once again he used the local Cleveland theatres as a rehearsal ground for the new act. Then, just as it seemed that they were doomed to spend the rest of their lives in Ohio, they secured a booking at one of the city's biggest vaudeville houses, the Bandbox Theatre. It was 1924 and, despite only getting a few paltry dollars for the appearances, Leslie had good reason to begin celebrating his 21st birthday early. Topping the bill at the Bandbox was the legendry silent-screen star Fatty Arbuckle. Roscoe Arbuckle had been another of Hope's childhood film idols, but in 1921 the bulky comedian had been charged with the manslaughter of a prostitute in San Francisco. Though he was acquitted, the scandal finished him in puritanical Hollywood and he was forced to tour vaudeville houses to stay alive.

Hope and Durbin had a very small part in the production; they tap danced and soft-shoe-shuffled around the stage, sang 'Sweet Georgia Brown', and struggled through a pantomimed Egyptian comedy dance routine. The pair regarded it as their show business debut and it was a success. Arbuckle was impressed and sent for them. Neither had ever met a movie star before and were greatly over-awed. 'I was thrilled to be on the same bill,' Bob said later.

'You boys are pretty good,' said Arbuckle, trying to put them at their ease.

Fatty promised them an introduction to Cleveland tab show producer Fred Hurley. He kept his word and the pair were booked for a road show called Hurley's Jolly Follies.

The tab shows – musical and comedy tabloids – were the lower echelons of the rapidly dying art of American vaudeville. Radio and film had brought about dramatic changes in entertainment, and vaudeville was fighting a losing battle. Small variety houses were fast being replaced by bigger theatres with facilities for both live performances and motion pictures where there was room and money only for the major stars. So impresarios concentrated on the remaining low-budget theatres away from the large cities where up-and-coming and has-been vaudevillians combined to present cheap novelty shows for between 10 and 30 cents a seat. Each tab company would have a permanent troupe of around 16 people, including entertainers and chorus girls, but there were no top-billers or separate acts. Everyone worked together in a series of fast-moving skits aimed at keeping the audience awake for around 90 minutes.

For Leslie it was a whirlwind introduction to vaudeville: he would be singing one moment, dancing the next, then having to play a straight man, then an Irish comedian or an Italian gigolo – he even played the saxophone. And all for $40 a week.

'That's a lost art today,' says Bob. 'Any young fella who was fortunate enough to get on a tab show really appreciated it in later years because it was a great school. It was a great place to pick up a lot of experience in doing different things. And it did more for me, as far as stage presence and confidence on the stage was concerned, than anything else.'

That first year on the tab circuit was tough for Hope and Durbin. To begin with, they worked the Spiegelberg group of theatres pounding out one-night stands through Indiana, Kentucky, the Virginias, the Carolinas and down into Georgia in the Deep South. Money was short and the rickety tour bus was far from comfortable, but not even that or the seedy rooming houses and cheap hotels could dampen young Leslie's spirits. This was the life. Even the cold and cramped nights spent curled up on the bus seats did little to dispel his enthusiasm.

Then the pair graduated to the more prestigious Gus Sun Circuit. Hope and Durbin were beginning to make an impact and the future looked rosy. Then, in 1925, Lloyd Durbin collapsed after a meal complaining of severe stomach cramps. He died of food poisoning, and Leslie had lost both a friend and a partner.

Hope realised that he was not yet ready to go solo so he teamed up with dancer George Byrne. It was a more adventurous partnership altogether. Hope and Byrne began to experiment seriously with comedy routines.

Their big moment came in McKeesport, Pennsylvania, when they were allowed to present a straight comedy revue called *The Blackface Follies*. Unfortunately it got more laughs offstage than on. No one thought to tell the inexperienced pair to use burnt cork and not black greasepaint when 'blacking up'. Hope and Byrne were the glossiest blackface comedians ever seen in McKeesport. But worse was to come: cork washes off in seconds, but the greasepaint took hours of painful scrubbing – much to the amusement of the others in the troupe. With the laughter still ringing in their smarting ears, the duo decided to give blackface a miss in the future.

1926 saw them expanding their comic talents in an act billed as *Smiling Eyes* at an increased salary of $50 a week. By now Hope was earning enough to send money home each week. *Smiling Eyes*, however, did little to enhance Leslie's reputation as a comedian – he played stooge while George cracked the gags. Byrne would be crossing the stage holding a hanger with a woman's dress on it.

'Where are you going?' Hope would enquire.

'Down to get this filled,' Byrne would reply, to raucous laughter from the audience.

Then George would amble back – this time with a long plank under one arm.

'Where are you going?' Leslie would again ask.

'To find a room,' George would explain. 'I've already got my board.'

Leslie's three-year connection with Fred Hurley finally ended amicably early in 1927 when a Detroit booking agent secured him and Byrne an engagement at the city's State Theatre. They were offered $225 a week – more money than they had ever dreamed of. They jumped at the chance.

Detroit was less than 200 miles from Cleveland, across Lake Erie, but to the boys it seemed like another planet. To them the State Theatre was the big time and to be celebrated. By the time they opened, and well before first pay day, they had blown their savings and were flat broke.

They stayed at the State long enough to replenish their bank accounts and collect some mild reviews. These led to more bookings in Detroit, before they were lured to Pittsburgh by the pledge of a $75-a-week pay rise for a season at the Stanley Theatre. Now that they were $300-a-week men, Leslie and George felt ready to take the really big step – to New York. Both were tiring of the constant travelling from city to city. They reasoned that the Big Apple, with its thousand vaudeville houses, could offer them a comfortable living without ever having to move outside the area. When their stint at the

Stanley came to an end, they bought a set of new costumes – smart red-and-white striped Eton jackets, high-waisted trousers, big hats and flashy black canes capped in white – and caught a train to the East Coast.

A series of auditions and one-night stands in a few slum-like theatres resulted in a booking with the Keith and Orpheus Circuit. They even developed a new act, including a slapstick dance number that had them dressed as firemen squirting water all over the stage. The work, though, was irregular and Leslie, crammed into a 'shoe-box-sized' sleazy hotel room with his partner and their luggage, began to lose heart for the first time in his relatively short career. Dollars were flowing out far more quickly than they were coming in, and the depression and worry forced his weight down to 140 pounds. Hope and Byrne talked long about quitting and heading back to the greener pastures of Cleveland. But the bright lights of Broadway were beckoning.

4

Broadway in 1927 was at its peak. The 80 theatres crammed near its centre would boast an all-time record of 286 new productions in the coming season. And Hope and Byrne would be part of it – of that they were sure.

Broadway was a colourful and awesome sight for a 24-year-old, made even more so by the famous names of the twenties: George M. Cohen, Eddie Cantor, Ruth Etting, Jimmie Durante, and Fred and Adele Astaire – the 'darlings of Broadway' since their 1924 hit by George Gershwin, *Lady Be Good*. There were the songsmiths like Cole Porter, Rogers and Hart, Irving Berlin, and Jerome Kern – whose classic musical *Show Boat* would become the smash hit of the 1927–28 season.

The audition for the Eddie Dowling production, *The Sidewalks of New York*, was a heady experience. Awaiting them in the stark rehearsal room just off Broadway were Dowling, Kate Smith, Dick Keene (of the top vaudeville team Keene and Williams) and 18-year old Ruby Keeler (soon to marry the self-styled 'greatest entertainer of all time', Al Jolson). Leslie and George hurried through their usual song-and-dance act, and then waited nervously as the group went into a whispering huddle. 'You've got the job,' Dowling informed them tersely after what had seemed like a lifetime.

The pair were teamed with Ruby Keeler and given a simple song-and-dance number set in a laundry. They worked hard to perfect their small part, but on opening night they knew they were doomed. The show itself got fair reviews – Hope and

Byrne did not.

It was an inauspicious Broadway debut. Dowling didn't wait long to cut their act, and once again they were out of work. Leslie had learned the hard way that even the most lavishly financed Broadway efforts could not survive unless critics and audiences pronounced them immediate hits – something attained by only one show in five.

The revamped *Sidewalks* went on to enjoy a long run, but Leslie had witnessed the end of an era, although he didn't know it at the time. The halcyon days of Broadway were over – the movies had learned to talk. Al Jolson, hailed a few years before as the 'king of Broadway', was ad-libbing 'You ain't heard nothin' yet' in the Warner Brothers motion picture *The Jazz Singer*. From 1928 onwards Broadway would experience an irreversible decline – but not before Leslie returned, as Bob Hope, to triumph, to add his name to the long list of stars who established themselves on Broadway.

First, however, there were four more years of apprenticeship to serve back on the road. A friendly agent had warned them that they wouldn't get anywhere until they left town, changed their act and started from scratch somewhere else. The pair decided to try Chicago. While they raised money for their trip by featuring at the then renowned B.S. Moss Franklin Theatre, Hope asked Mike Shea, a Cleveland booking agent, to find them some work between New York and Chicago.

Shea booked them for three days at a small variety theatre in New Castle, Pennsylvania. It was a momentous date and another turning point in Leslie's career. The money wasn't good – only $25 each for the three performances – but at least they were the 'star' act, going on last. There was also an added bonus: the manager needed someone to announce the following week's attractions at the end of the show; Leslie T. Hope got the job. Never one to miss an opportunity, he decided to turn the advertising slot into a comedy routine:

Ladies and gentlemen ... next week Marshall Walker will be here with his Big Time Revue. Marshall is a Scotsman ... he got married in the backyard so the chickens could get the rice ...

That line gave Hope his first laugh as a solo artist. He followed it up with a gag about a Scotsman who killed his wife by buying her vanishing cream. Both audience and management loved it.

'They laughed,' recalls Bob, 'and the manager said "That's very good. Do that. People like that." So I kept adding to it and before I finished I was doing about eight minutes of this announcement with a lot of jokes in it. And that's where the germ sort of started.'

After the final performance, Hope and Byrne sat down in their dressing room to have an earnest talk.

'Our act has got tired and stale,' George said to his younger partner. 'And I'm tired too. You're getting bigger laughs on your own. The double-act just doesn't work any more. I vote we split right now.'

Leslie, who had been thinking along the same lines himself but was loath to hurt his friend, went through the motions of trying to dissuade him. 'Nope, I've made my decision,' Byrne insisted, 'and it's final. I'm going to retire!'

And so Leslie Hope became a stand-up comedian – by accident.

Cleveland was only 50 miles from New Castle, so an excited Leslie returned home to Euclid Street and once again contacted Mike Shea. The agent wasted little time in booking him on a tour of one-nighters throughout the city. America's newest comedian celebrated by developing a new act. He realised he needed a gimmick to hide his lack of fresh comedy material and opted for the blackface technique he and George Byrne had tried with such disastrous consequences two years previously. This time he made sure he used burnt cork!

Decked out in a huge red bow tie, white cotton gloves and brown derby hat, Leslie quickly established himself as a colourful jokester around the halls of Cleveland. Then came an enforced change in his act and appearance. Running late as usual, he missed his regular streetcar and by the time he got to the theatre it was too late to black up. Much to Leslie's surprise, the new 'white' Hope made little difference to the audience. In fact, if anything, they seemed to be laughing harder and more often.

'If I were you I'd leave that cork off your face,' said Mike Shea as his protégé bounced off stage. 'Your face is funny enough the way it is!'

Within weeks of dropping blackface Hope made another

fundamental alteration – Leslie T. Hope became Lester T. Hope. 'I thought that was a little more manish,' said Bob. 'I found a lot of girls would call me Leslie and I'd call them Leslie, and there was a sort of conflict of interests there so I changed it to Lester.'

By then Hope had concluded that he had exhausted the possibilities of Cleveland, even though Mike Shea still had bookings by the score for him. Remembering his aim to try Chicago, he once more headed west. He regretted the trip almost immediately. Auditions were few and far between, and wholly unproductive. Even the local papers produced little of interest. All they seemed to be interested in was the success a young crooner from Spokane, Washington, was having with the Paul Whiteman Orchestra at the city's Tivoli Theatre. 'Bing Crosby's version of 'Wistful and Blue' is a smash hit,' said a review. For Lester Hope, comedian, there was little comfort in such news. He couldn't even find a lousy job, much less a smash hit.

Then came the chance meeting with Charlie Cooley and Charlie Hogan, and three days at the West Englewood Theatre. His short appearance didn't bring glowing reviews from the critics, but it did attract the attention of the manager of the Stratford Theatre. He had just fired his popular emcee and was looking for a replacement to hold the show together.

'How about it?' he asked Hope. 'I'm prepared to give you a one-night try-out.'

Lester thought hard for a while, recalling the advice a musician once gave him to 'cut the dancing and corny comedy routines' and become a 'master of ceremonies', before giving a hesitant nod of approval. He was nervous that first night, but gave a competent debut performance. The manager was impressed enough to rebook his discovery for a further two weeks at $300 a week. Six months later Lester was still there – free of debts and with a faithful following of his own.

It was at the Stratford that Hope first experimented with the quick-fire brand of humour which would become his trade mark in later years. Before that he opened his vaudeville act with a technique favoured by Jack Benny.

Good evening ladies and gentlemen ... a funny thing happened to me on the way to the theatre tonight. Dropped into a local restaurant for a meal. When I'd eaten it I found I'd left all my money here at the theatre. So I told them. And the cashier said, 'That's all right. We'll just write your name on the wall and you can pay it the next time you come in.' 'But,' I said, 'I don't want my name on the wall where everybody can see it.' She said, 'Don't worry – your overcoat will be hanging over it . . .'

'Then I used to stand and just stare at the audience,' says Bob, 'and defy them to laugh. And that was a kind of funny idea; that you would just demand a laugh.'

As an emcee, though, Hope greatly increased his pace and poured out a succession of short jokes (known as one-liners) without leaving an obvious place for the audience to laugh. It soon earned him a reputation – for it was a distinctive style he was to adopt for life.

'It's a sort of pseudo-sophisticated delivery,' explains Bob, 'and it's a way to time an audience, and make them enjoy it more. You try to disguise and hide the joke. . . . An audience enjoys that very much because it keeps them on their toes. Whereas, if you came up to the joke and said "There's the joke . . ." they'd get sick of that pretty fast.'

The six-month Stratford run also taught Hope the value of having a constant supply of new jokes. He found that out the hard way – a gag which raised the roof one night would get only polite laughter a few performances later. He discovered that, despite the size of Chicago, he was performing to substantially the same audience; most would visit the theatre at least seven or eight times a month.

In those days he couldn't afford writers and was forced to poach whatever fresh material he could. A popular magazine of the day was *College Humor* and Lester found it a rich source. Then there were the constantly changing out-of-town acts. 'Heard any new gags on your travels?' Hope would ask as he plied them with drinks in one of Chicago's speakeasies.

The strain of constantly renewing his own material eventually got to Lester and he quit the Stratford. He persuaded his girlfriend at the time, Louise Troxell, to join him in touring the Keith Western Circuit, with whom he had been offered a job. Keith Western was a step down, but at least it supplied some interesting venues – including a date in Cicero, a Chicago suburb annexed by the mob of the slum-bred Italian delinquent Alphonse 'Scarface' Capone. 'Bottles', as he was also known, was effectively the ruler of – as one newspaper put it – 'the only completely corrupt city in America'. Prohibition, which would last until 5 December 1932, was pouring six million dollars a week into the pockets of Capone and his henchmen. In Cicero, Al's hoods freely roamed the streets by day and packed the variety theatres by night.

For Lester and Louise it was a frightening experience, but one he put to good comic use in later years:

If they liked you they didn't applaud – they just let you live . . .

They used to have an intermission – to give the audience a chance to reload . . .

They were really tough – they used to tie the tomatoes on the end of a yo-yo, so they could hit you twice . . .

Having decided to 'get out of Chicago fast', Hope and Troxell signed with the Keith Western Circuit. They stomped the small towns of America's Midwest, before ending up in Fort Worth, Texas, as part of Bob O'Donnell's Interstate Time agency. Their first show there was almost their last. Louise received her usual round of wolf-whistles and the Texans appeared to lap up her corny routines with Lester. But when he came on for his solo spot it was as if they were deaf. Hardly a laugh came and Hope knew he had flopped as a comedian for the first time.

Back in the dressing-room, a confused Lester searched for the reason.

'Everyone else likes my jokes! What's a matter with these people?' he thundered.

'You were going too fast for them,' drawled a tall Texan, who had pushed his way unnoticed into the room. 'Slow up a little and give them a chance to get the joke. Give 'em one at a time.'

'Who the hell was that wise guy?' demanded Hope, after his anonymous adviser had gone.

'Bob O'Donnell,' came the nervous reply.

One thing that Lester had learned was that you always listen to advice – particularly when it comes from the boss. He sought out O'Donnell, who expounded further his theories on timing and appearing relaxed on stage. Hope listened attentively, realizing that he could easily pace his act to incorporate rapid wisecracks and more complicated jokes.

21

The rest of the run at Fort Worth was a huge success. And he began to like the Lone Star State again. When it came time to move on to Dallas, Lester made one more important change: he became Bob Hope.

One can only speculate on how much influence Bob O'Donnell had in that direction. These days Bob is far from serious about the reasons for the third and final change. 'I figured Lester T. Hope still looked a little ginger around the edges,' he quips, 'so I changed it to Bob. I thought that was more chummy and audiences would get to like me, but it took a long time for them to learn how to pronounce that name...'

Hope and Troxell went down well in Dallas, and it gave Bob the confidence to aim high again. His failure on Broadway still rankled and he was determined to get back. So, with Louise in tow, he swapped the warm security of Texas for the cold uncertainty of Brooklyn.

Bob O'Donnell had already helped pave the way for his return by suggesting an interview with the B.F. Keith office in New York City, the biggest booking agents in American vaudeville, with a virtual monopoly on the East Coast. It was a tough meeting, ending in an agreement – not altogether satisfactory to Bob – that the pair should prove themselves at one of the group's lesser known theatres, the Proctor, just off Broadway.

The Proctor had the reputation of being one of the toughest theatres in New York, so a worried Hope scurried around and got a three-day booking across the East River in Brooklyn. It was only worth $24, but Bob believed it would enable him to pre-empt the B.F. Keith try-out with a triumphant hit. Three days later he realized how wrong he had been. It was almost a total disaster. And to make matters worse, a Keith executive turned up to witness his failure.

So it was with a heavy heart and a hint of desperation that he stepped on to the Proctor stage to give his all-important performance. Perhaps, deep down, that was the reason why he introduced a new style to his act – topical satire.

He was following an appearance by the actress Leatrice Joy, whose controversial and often stormy marriage to silent screen star John Gilbert was making front-page news across the nation. Without pausing to say good evening, he pretended to squint through the lights and shouted: 'No lady! I am not John Gilbert.'

The crack brought the house down and Hope never looked back. A few more quips about Miss Joy and Mr Gilbert, a couple of songs, and the evening was his. By the time he had finished his next show, he had a long-term contract with the Keith organization worth $450 a week. Quick to appreciate the impact of his topical jibes, Bob began to broaden his comedy to include a whole range of insult routines. And the Proctor audiences loved it.

'Now that the amateurs are finished ...' became one of his favourite opening lines, as he strutted confidently on stage.

Topicality, though, gave him a whole new set of problems. He now needed a constant supply of good up-to-the-minute material. 'Where the hell am I going to get it from?' he asked himself many times, as he scoured the daily newspapers searching for items that would get him laughs. He found the answer in one Al Boasberg, comedy writer. Boasberg had written material for vaudeville comedy stars. They met one day in the Keith offices and liked each other immediately.

'Can you come up with some topical one-line jokes for me?' asked Bob.

'Sure,' drawled Al. Bob Hope had hired his first gag writer.

It was October 1929, a most fateful month for all concerned.

5

The news of the collapse of Wall Street hit the American people like a sledgehammer. In the Depression that followed millions were thrown out of work, and 'Buddy Can You Spare a Dime?' became the hit song of the era. But for Hope and Troxell there was little sign of the 'impending disaster' everyone was talking about. People still wanted to be entertained, to escape from their misery, and they were prepared to part with what little money they had to do so.

So Bob happily continued to draw his weekly $450 pay cheques for a few months more. Then, with a fierce East Coast winter adding to the gloom, he and Louise caught a train west to the warmth of California. They were booked on a tour of the Keith-Orpheus Time Circuit, which gave them a thorough first look at the West Coast and eventually landed them in Los Angeles. Hope was enthralled and even before reporting to the Hillstreet Theatre – where they were to play – he headed for Hollywood, the purveyor of his childhood dreams.

Hollywood in 1930 was still in its infancy but growing fast. The nation's rapidly increasing appetite for music and laughter, as the slump bit even harder, was seeing to that. The talkies, after a lack-lustre start, were already being hailed as the greatest mass entertainment medium of the century.

Bob's first stop was at the junction of Sunset Boulevard and Vine Street, where there stood one of the original big Hollywood film studios – Famous Players Lasky (later Paramount Pictures). 'So this is where they made those wonderful pieces of

24

fantasy I ogled for so many hours as a kid,' he thought to himself.

Then as he watched the actors and extras hurrying through the famous doors, he turned his mind to the great founding fathers of the movie industry. All, it seemed to him, were foreigners: Louis B. Mayer – a Russian; the four Warner brothers – from Poland; Sam Goldwyn – another Pole; Carl Laemmle – German; Adolph Zukor – a Hungarian; William Fox – also from Hungary; and Marcus Loew – the New York-born son of an Austrian emigré. Those were the men who built Hollywood, those names behind the legendary studios he'd heard so much about – Metro-Goldwyn-Mayer, Universal, the Fox Film Corporation, Paramount and Warner Brothers.

'Maybe, just maybe,' he pondered, 'an Englishman from Eltham could make his mark here too...'

The opening at the Hillstreet went well. The free-and-easy Californians liked Hope's style, and his night was completed by an aftershow phone call from a Los Angeles agent specializing in motion pictures – William Perlberg.

'Al Boasberg suggested I give you a call,' said Perlberg. 'He thinks you're great!'

'Oh really,' chuckled Bob. 'That's just because I'm using his material.'

'Well,' continued Perlberg, 'I haven't seen your act yet, but how'd you like to make a screen test? The studios have been buying a lot of new talent lately...'

Bob hurriedly checked his tour schedule. The next date was in San Diego – over 100 miles away – but not until a few days hence.

'Let's see ... I have a little time between closing here and my next opening. I guess I could work it in,' he said nonchalantly.

'Okay,' said Perlberg, 'report to the Pathe Film Studios the morning after you close at Hillstreet.'

To pass the time, and help calm his nerves, Bob continued his exploration of Hollywood. Over at Universal City – the film company's huge studios – he found they were making a mammoth musical called *The King of Jazz*.

'It's Paul Whiteman's life story,' he was told. 'They've got the whole orchestra here and those young kids, the Rhythm

Boys – you know the new group with that crooner fella Big Crosby...'

'Funny how that name keeps cropping up,' mused Hope. 'Maybe I'll get to meet him one day!'

Bob and Louise celebrated their big day by taking a taxi out to the Pathe Studios in Culver City, a journey of about five miles. Before he even had time to count his change they were hustled into make-up and then on to the studio floor, where Bob was asked to go through his solo routine.

As soon as the test director shouted 'Cut', Louise was ushered on. To the cry of 'Quiet please ... action!' they re-enacted their standard vaudeville performance. Another shout of 'Cut!' and it was all over. 'We'll let you know ...' were the last words Bob heard as they were shown the door.

The San Diego shows went well, but the expected phone call from William Perlberg never came. Their next date was in Salt Lake City, 700 miles away, so Bob decided to break the journey in Los Angeles.

'Do you really want to see it?' asked Perlberg when Hope called him.

'And I knew right then,' admitted Bob many years later, 'that I had laid probably one of the biggest eggs in history. But I still said I wanted to see it.'

Perlberg arranged a viewing at the Pathe studios. 'And I went out there, and I was all alone,' recalls Bob. 'Nobody was there with a contract or anything. It was in projection room eight. I sat there all alone and I came on the screen. And my nose came on about twenty minutes before the rest of my head! I looked at that thing – the same act that I did in vaudeville – and it didn't look too good. And the fella said, "You wanna see it again?" I said, "Oh, thank you, but that's all right." I didn't know how to get out of the studio. I wanted to crawl over the wall. I hated to go through the door. But I got on the train and went to Salt Lake thinking that they didn't understand talent, big talent.'

Bob confesses that the failure left him 'mad at that whole part of the world' for many years and with the view that 'the whole neighbourhood was just for oranges'.

From Salt Lake City the pair went back to New York. More successful vaudeville dates, and a good audition, finally gained them a prize Bob had been longing after for years – a chance to play the Palace Theatre.

The Palace was the flagship of the Keith agency and it ranks alongside the London Palladium as a mecca of vaudeville. At its peak it boasted two shows a day and was making almost a million dollars a year in profits. But by the time Bob and Louise were booked for the revue *Antics of 1931* it was losing about $200,000 annually. However, the Palace was still regarded as the top. 'The high spot of any vaudevillian's career,' as Bob puts it.

Everyone had high hopes for *Antics of 1931*, even though it was up against some tough oppositon: George and Ira Gershwin's *Of Thee I Sing*, which would become the first musical comedy to win a Pulitzer Prize; Fred and Adele Astaire in *The Band Wagon*; Al Jolson in *The Wonder Bar*; and Gertrude Lawrence and Noel Coward in his own *Private Lives*, hailed as the hit of the season. The Saturday night gala opening went reasonably well for all, bar one . . . 'They say that Bob Hope is the sensation of the Midwest,' wrote one critic. 'If that is so, why doesn't he go back there?'

Hope was mortified and, as he said years later, he 'almost quit the Palace right there and then': But he stayed on, and with a little help from some friends – Ken Murray, a veteran vaudeville comedian, and Ted Healey, the man behind the Three Stooges – overcame the first night setback to firmly establish himself and Louise in the show.

During the run of *Antics* Bob acquired one of the first trappings of success – a new Single Six Packard, with a 3.9 litre six-cylinder engine nestling beneath its long blue bonnet. The Packard had been one of America's quality cars since 1899 – 'Ask the man who owns one . . .' ran the advertising slogan – and Hope suddenly found himself in great demand from women. 'I had to push them off the running boards,' he says, 'but never without looking first!'

When *Antics of 1931* closed Bob and Louise pounded the boards of the small vaudeville theatres again until he was offered another shot at Broadway in *Ballyhoo of 1932*. The Keith office, which had him under exclusive contract, offered no objections to a 'temporary leave of absence'. But what about Louise? The deal made no mention of her. After a long talk and some tears, they decided it would be 'best for both' if they parted then.

Hope had Al Jolson's manager, Bill Grady, to thank for his return to Broadway. It was Grady who cajoled the producers of *Ballyhoo* to go and see Hope's Palace show. The result was a salary increase to $600 a week and some unexpected extra hard work. When *Ballyhoo* opened its pre-Broadway warm-up run in Atlantic City, New Jersey, the cast was in disarray. The show was basically a two-act, 26-scene, musical revue and timing was all important; first night nerves resulted in attention being paid to the final 25 scenes, but not the first. As the orchestra began to play the overture for a second time, accompanied by an audience slow-handclap, the backstage discipline dissolved in sheer panic. Fortunately a show backer, standing in the wings, saw Hope strolling by.

'Get out there,' he ordered. 'Do something to keep them quiet until we find out what's wrong.'

Bob's arrival on stage coincided with the orchestra surrendering their unequal battle against the whistling, hooting and clapping coming from the audience.

'Ladies and gentlemen,' shouted the comedian, 'this is the first time I've ever been on before the acrobats...'

The derision turned to laughter. The experienced first-nighters got the joke: acrobats, or other such non-speaking acts, were used to open and close shows to give the audience a chance to either settle down or leave early, thus ensuring a receptive atmosphere for the stars.

Hope's next ploy was to greet an imaginary late-comer in the dress circle. 'That's one of our backers up there,' he informed in a stage-whisper. 'He says he's not nervous, but I notice that he's buckled his safety belt!'

Another five minutes of gags like that and Bob had the restless crowd in the palm of his hand. The producers gave the signal and the show proper began. Afterwards the entire cast congratulated an exhausted Hope on a masterful display of ad-libbing; the relieved backers insisted that he use the same sort of routine to open the show each evening.

Bob's initial reaction was to say 'No!', reasoning that it would expose him to unnecessary dangers. But following a session with writer Al Boasberg he offered an alternative scripted skit with the unlikely title 'The Complaint Department'. The bosses agreed. The routine had Hope sitting in a mock-up of a department store complaint booth. 'I was the only sit-down stand-up comedian in the world,' boasts Bob.

Four or five minutes of banter with the audience would end with him trying to get the orchestra started on the overture. After four abortive attempts, which produced only loud snoring, Hope pulled a pistol from his pocket and fired a deafening shot into the orchestra pit. Again nothing but snoring. Finally, in desperation, he would produce a cash register. The familiar ting, as he depressed the keys, had the desired effect. The theatre would be filled with thunderous music.

When *Ballyhoo of 1932* opened on Broadway even Bob's warm-up couldn't save it; the critics gave it a terrible slating. 'The chief things that *Ballyhoo* lacks are charm, distinction and any kind of theatrical allure,' write a *New York Times* reviewer. The show closed after just four months, but Bob added to his growing reputation rather than damaged it. He returned to the folds of the Keith agency, who put him back on the vaudeville circuit. His first job took him to New York's Capitol Theatre and a date with destiny.

Harry Lillis Crosby was also touring New York in 1932, having first left the band of Paul Whiteman and then his group, the Rhythm Boys, to go solo. His hit record 'I Surrender Dear', a national radio show for Cremo cigars on CBS and a good showing in his first major film – *The Big Broadcast of 1932* – had made him a star. So the Capitol management, looking around for a big name act, hired Crosby and his guitarist Eddie Lang.

Bob couldn't believe his eyes when as was usual with an emcee, he got an advance list of the artists and acts he would be introducing with Bing's name on it. When the crooner, then aged 31, arrived at the theatre Hope was there to offer a warm hand of welcome. It wasn't the first time they had met. Two months before, their paths crossed on 48th Street near the New York Friar's Club, an establishment frequented by actors and entertainers. They had swapped stories about following each other's careers with interest.

Across the road from the Capitol was O'Reilly's Bar, one of the first to offer the legal liquor after the ending of Prohibition a few days earlier, and it was there the pair found they had plenty more in common. Most of O'Reilly's patrons thought that Hope and Crosby were just a couple of solid drinking buddies indulging in plain old bar talk. They were mistaken. What they were in fact witnessing was the birth of a classic partnership.

Bob soon recognized that he and Bing could easily transfer their natural but competitive good humour from the bar to the Capitol stage. So they began to plot in earnest and came up with a couple of routines to supplant Bob's usual semi-straight introductions. Their first featured Hope strolling on stage alone.

'Ah, good evening ladies and gents. I'm afraid we'll have to do without my partner tonight – some cad locked him in the washroom...'

As the laughter died away, Bing would amble on from the other side of the stage holding a brass door-knob attached to a piece of splintered wood.

'Good evening ladies and gentlemen. I feel I must apologize, you'll have to forgive me for working alone tonight – my partner has an upset stomach...'

'Now wait a minute!' Bob would retort. 'I don't have an upset stomach.'

'You will after you swallow this,' Bing would reply, waving the door-knob under Bob's nose.

Between shows, when they weren't in O'Reilly's Bar, the pair were often seen in the nearby Friars Club. 'It had a billiard room,' Bing recalled, 'and of course Bob frequented it because he was a very good billiard player, and he was always looking for clients. Made a very nice living that way. I think he could have become a pool hustler if he hadn't gone into show business.'

Remarks like that were typical of the Hope-Crosby relationship right from the beginning. It came naturally to them and in later years would make both multi-millionaires.

But, in 1932, life was not all Crosby. The Capitol was owned by the Loew's Corporation, which had its own sponsored radio programme – the Capitol Family Hour – hosted by theatre manager Major Edward Bowes. It went out live every Sunday morning and gave Bob an opportunity to break into a new entertainment medium. Bowes was soon to become one of the giants of American show business – a million dollar a year man, according to the trade paper *Variety* – but he got there by exploiting young performers like Hope. The Major insisted that he saw all material prior to transmission and, as producer, would rewrite the script to ensure that he had the best lines. Thus an astounded Hope found himself once more relegated to the role of straight-man.

Bob left the Capitol, and the Keith organisation immediately capitalized on his enhanced reputation by putting him back on the touring vaudeville circuit. He celebrated this, and his thirtieth birthday, by buying a new Pierce-Arrow town car and hiring a chauffeur. It had bigger running boards and therefore room for more girls.

Late in the summer of 1933 Hope ended a long search for an East Coast agent by signing with Louie Shurr – known in the business as 'The Doctor'. Shurr's first task was to negotiate a deal with composer Jerome Kern, who wanted Bob for the juvenile lead in his forthcoming Broadway production *Roberta*. Kern had earmarked him for the part of Huckleberry Haines, a bandleader, after catching one of his Capitol shows. Rehearsals for *Roberta* were held at the New Amsterdam Theatre on 42nd Street (the old Ziegfeld Theatre). Hope arrived brimming with confidence, making a lasting impression on the man who was to play Huckleberry's manager, the dancer and former chorus boy George Murphy.

'He was a very brash, very bright, attractive looking young man with a dynamic personality,' recalls Murphy. 'He really looked like a real sharp vaudevillian.'

Also in the cast were Sidney Greenstreet, later to find fame in *Casablanca* with Humphrey Bogart, Tamara, who would die in a wartime plane crash with the British actor Leslie Howard, and Fred MacMurray, then a saxophonist with the show band the Californian Collegiates.

Roberta opened its pre-New York run in Philadelphia in mid-November looking as though it would never last the course. 'At the end of the first act nothing much had happened,' says Murphy. 'There wasn't much applause: the show was heavy and moved slowly . . .'

The cause, ironically, was Jerome Kern's original score. Although he had written two wonderful songs, 'Smoke Gets in Your Eyes' and 'Yesterday', all the dialogue was adventurously underscored with music. 'And you had to wait for music cues before you spoke,' says Murphy. 'So it gave it kind of a sluggish, unnatural feeling. It sure didn't look good.'

The director thought so too, because by the end of the second act he was on the phone to New York arranging another job. Another director, Hazzard Short, was brought in to save it. His first move was to send for Hope and Murphy.

'If you fellas can think of anything funny to do or say,' he told the pair, 'for goodness' sakes do it ... because there's no comedy in this show whatsoever. So do whatever you like as long as it makes sense.'

Bob took Short at his word. The basic plot revolved around a football player inheriting his aunt's Paris dress shop and being helped out by his best friend, Huckleberry Haines. So when, in one scene, they were discussing fashion trends, he had a joke ready:

Long dresses don't bother me – I've got a good memory ...

He also helped improve the introduction to the show's hit song, 'Smoke Gets in Your Eyes', which was sung by leading lady Tamara. Between her line, 'There's an old Russian proverb – "when your heart's on fire, smoke gets in your eyes" ', Hope interjected with the gag: 'We have a proverb over here in America too – "Love is like hash ... you have to have confidence in it to enjoy it." '

Bob's suggestions, although meeting with the approval of audiences, failed to please everyone. Jerome Kern's show associate, the successful lyricist Otto Harbach, resented his interference and on more than one occasion tried to block his ideas. Fortunately for Hope, Kern chose to back him and not Harbach.

Roberta arrived on Broadway before the end of November, but to rather mediocre reviews. It wavered around uncertainly until Christmas before catching on and ending up as the hit of the 1933–34 season. The show was to run until July 1934, a total of 255 performances. It made Bob a Broadway star. According to George Murphy, later to become a US senator in California, the reward was wholly justified. 'I've always said that Bob Hope had as much to do with *Roberta* being a hit as 'Smoke Gets in Your Eyes'. He made the difference between a hit and a flop.'

Murphy and Hope became close friends during the early problems of the show, and it was George who was responsible for radically changing Bob's lifestyle on two fronts: he introduced him to a girl called Dolores Reade and showed him a bespoke tailor on 5th Avenue. The latter was necessary, George felt, because Ohio did not produce the best clothes in the world. 'I said to Bob, "You won't do very well on the New York stage with those Cleveland clothes you have on." So I took him off and introduced him to a tailor I knew. I believe he still goes there!' Admirers of Hope confirm that he became markedly better dressed during the run of the play.

His new elegant style may have helped when George furtively arranged a blind date with night-club singer Dolores Reade. She had been gaining prominence with bandleader George Olsen. Murphy persuaded Hope to visit the Vogue Club on 57th Street to hear his latest singing 'discovery'. When they walked in Dolores was mid-way through 'Did You Ever See a Dream Walking?'. George Murphy says he did – Hope trying to get to the table nearest to the tiny stage. As her act closed, to rapturous applause, George beckoned Miss Reade across to where they were sitting.

'And he introduced me to Dolores,' recalls Bob, 'because he was wild about her. I'd heard her sing, and in those days I was kind of on the loose and just up for grabs – whoever got the lucky ticket. I met her and changed all my thinking . . .'

Bob swears that his first words after the introduction were: 'Can I take you home?' Dolores can't remember. But she does recall that at first sight she thought him 'good looking' and 'almost handsome'. The short journey to her West Side apartment was long enough for Bob to discover that Dolores was of Irish-Italian descent, single and with no steady boyfriend. He also had enough time to inform her of his current status on Broadway. As he demurely escorted her to the front door, a couple of matinee tickets changed hands and she promised to see the show the following day.

But the expected backstage visit after the matinee never came. Bob was in a foul mood all evening. Later, fortified by a few drinks, the unhappy comedian went to the Vogue Club to find out what had gone wrong.

'I felt too embarrassed to come and see you,' explained a surprised Dolores. 'I had no idea you had such a major part. I thought you were only in the chorus!'

Bob's disappointment was dispelled and the romance was on. 'She was very smart,' says Bob. 'I went with her for quite a while. And then she went to Florida with her mother, which didn't help my case! You know, when I look back I know it was all a plot ... I kept calling her and begging her to come back...'

Dolores did return, but before they could get any further, news came from Cleveland that Avis Hope was desperately ill. Bob rushed home to discover that she had cancer and only had months to live. Bob was heartbroken and his sadness was tinged with bitterness. He felt cheated – at the very moment he was finding happiness and professional acclaim, his greatest supporter during the long hard years was to be taken from him without fully enjoying the fruits of her labours.

There was little time for self-pity, though, when he arrived back in New York. *Roberta* was in full swing and Dolores was on the warpath. She had read a newspaper report that he was planning to marry a chorus girl – an old flame – and was hopping mad. Bob convinced her the story was false by whisking her off to the lakeside town of Erie, Pennsylvania. There, on 19 February 1934, in a tiny Catholic church Dolores Reade became Mrs Bob Hope. She was 29.

The honeymoon was practically nonexistent because Bob had commitments on Broadway, but the celebrations arranged by the *Roberta* cast helped get the marriage off to a glorious start.

Avis Hope eventually died and a dejected Bob once more headed west. As he stood in the comfortable Yorkshire Road house on Cleveland Heights, which he had bought his parents four years previously, he wondered if he had done enough. His head told him he couldn't really have done more; his heart, though, was not appeased.

Roberta had only a few more months to run, but Bob's continued presence in it was just starting to pay dividends. He was booked as a guest on the top radio show of the day – the Fleischman Hour – hosted by Bing Crosby's great rival, the crooner Rudy Vallee. The programme, broadcast nationally on Thursday nights, had a massive audience of 18 million. Hope's debut performance made a tremendous impact – with the show's sound engineers. They discovered, as it went out, that he was nervously booting the microphone after each joke. Forty-four years later, Rudy Vallee could hardly recall Bob's initial contribution to his show. 'None of the comedians we had on made much impression,' he said sourly.

Bob is more humorous. 'I used to get the money, and run around the corner and count it,' he says, 'like I was stealing it! I didn't believe you could get that kind of money in radio and with my act I think it was mostly a theft or some sort of larceny.'

The success of *Roberta* also opened up another door for Bob, one that had been slammed in his face four years before – the movies. Educational Films, a New York-based outfit specialising in two-reeler shorts, contacted Louis Shurr to see if Bob was available for six pictures at $2,500 a throw. He would film by day on Long Island and be finished in time to appear nightly on Broadway. Each movie would take just three days to make. The prospect of earning $15,000 in a little under three weeks made Bob's blood pressure soar. He told Shurr to accept.

Ironically, within hours of the Educational offer, the 'Doc' was presenting his client with another – this time from Hollywood. Paramount Pictures wanted Bob to co-star with Ginger Rogers and Jack Oakie in *Sitting Pretty* on a guaranteed four-week contract of $8,000. He told Louie to turn it down.

Hope began his motion picture career in a small, low-budget movie studio in Astoria, Long Island. His script required him to romp with Leah Ray in a comedy called *Going Spanish* under the watchful eye of Al Christie, who was notching up his 25th year as a film director. Bob's big moment came when he was asked to give an impression of a man who had swallowed some Mexican jumping beans and leap around the set 'like a drunken kangaroo'.

Going Spanish premiered at the Rialto in Manhattan and Hope was amongst the audience to watch his 20 minutes of glory. 'I wanted to run, not walk, to the nearest fire exit,' he admitted later. His dissatisfaction resulted in an early termination of his first film contract. As he left the cinema he ran into Walter Winchell, formerly an advertisizing salesman with

Vaudeville News, but then one of the top columnists in New York. Winchell asked him what he thought of the debut. 'When they catch John Dillinger [then America's public enemy number one],' said Hope, 'they're going to make him sit through it twice!' Winchell repeated the remark in his column the next day. Educational read it, were not amused and promptly dropped his option.

Fortunately for Bob, not everyone shared his view of *Going Spanish*. The East Coast arm of the giant Warner Brothers concern stepped in to sign him to a six-picture deal. Once again they were 20-minute two-reelers, but this time the first of them gave the aspiring star an opportunity to sing on celluloid.

Paree, Paree, directed by Roy Mack, was the film version of Cole Porter's 1929 Broadway musical *Fifty Million Frenchmen*, which starred William Glaxton. Bob's co-star was Dorothy Stone. It was to her that he sang Porter's ballad 'You Do Something To Me':

> You do something to me,
> Something that simply mystifies me.
> Tell me, why should it be
> You have the pow'r to hypnotize me?
> Let me live 'neath your spell,
> Do do that voodoo that you do so well,
> For you do something to me
> That nobody else could do.

The Hope career was now developing apace. His weekly earnings were fast approaching $5,000 and he had a hatful of offers to consider when *Roberta* finished. But Bob was never too busy to help those who needed it, particularly if it was a charitable cause. 'Even at that time,' says Bob's Broadway co-star Fred MacMurray, 'he would appear at any benefit, any place. He did them constantly.'

MacMurray himself benefited from Hope's generosity on one important occasion and, by Fred's own admission, it 'helped' him become a movie star. The young sax player (Bob's understudy in *Roberta*) who had played the vaudeville circuits with the California Collegiates without making much impact, was being given the chance to make a screen test for

Paramount. They wanted him to do a top hat and cane number; he had the tuxedo he wore in the show, but no hat or cane. 'So I went into Bob's dressing room,' says Fred, 'and I said, "Bob ... I've got the chance to do a movie test." And he said, "No kidding!" He was surprised. I said, "Well ... I've got to have a top hat – can I try yours?" He said "Sure ... try it on." Luckily we both had big heads, so he lent it to me.'

Says Bob: 'I thought they would just push him around. But they made a test of him and signed him. From the first picture on he was a featured player and then a star – he never stopped! I wish he'd bring the hat back ...'

In July 1934 *Roberta* closed after a run of nine months. The Hopes decided to cement their relationship further by appearing on stage together, so they hit the vaudeville trail again. Dolores enchanted audiences with standards like 'Blue Moon' and Bob amused them with his quick-fire comedy routine. 'We had a lot of fun,' says Bob.

Two months later Louie Shurr brought them back to New York for Bob to begin rehearsing the Broadway musical comedy *Say When*. Bob was typecast as one of two zany vaude-villians who fall in love with a couple of high society girls. It opened at the Imperial Theatre in November 1934 to luke-warm reviews, but Bob was singled out for praise. 'They have written enough gags, most of which are neatly phrased to put Mr Hope in pretty good form ...' said the *New York Times*.

Say When failed after only four months and Bob 'rescued Dolores from the kitchen' to rejoin him as a touring double-act. This time they were on the road for two years. But it was not a period in the wilderness: Hope returned to Warner Brothers in Brooklyn to complete his six-picture deal.

He also had another shot at Hollywood, after much pleading by Shurr, but his test for Fox Films was 'unsatisfactory'. However, RKO saw the audition and offered a part in *Radio City Revels*, starring Jack Haley. 'Thanks, but no thanks,' said a still piqued Hope. 'Hollywood is hicksville.'

RKO had shown interest in Bob as a film property because of his continuing flirtation with radio. He had made a number of appearances on the company's own RKO Theatre of the Air and was being billed on Bromo Seltzer's 'Intimate Hour' as 'America's Headache'. Bromo teamed Hope with Honey Chile

Wilder, who came from Macon, Georgia and had a natural sense of humour and stunning looks. 'America's Headache' became Bromo's when the show failed to capture the ratings and it was soon cancelled. Bob was disappointed – 'Those were the days when I was learning' – but not overly concerned; he and Dolores were earning plenty on the Loew Circuit.

Broadway beckoned again early in 1936 when Lee Shubert was recasting his 1934 production of the *Ziegfeld Follies* at the Winter Garden. Fanny Brice was the star with Bob, Eve Arden and Josephine Baker in supporting roles. Vincente Minnelli designed a glittering array of costumes and scenery, and Vernon Duke produced a redoubtable score for Ira Gershwin's romantic lyrics. Bob was fortunate to be given one of the hit songs of the show, 'I Can't Get Started With You', with which he wooed the sultry Eve Arden. The *Follies* also gave him an opportunity to return to radio in the Atlantic Oil Show. 'America's Refined Comedian' was his billing this time.

The autumn of 1936 saw Hope leaving the *Follies* to join Ethel Merman and Jimmy 'Snozzle' Durante in Cole Porter's *Red, Hot and Blue!* at the Alvin Theatre on 52nd Street. He was given the part of Merman's attorney after William Gaxton, a regular star of Porter productions, pulled out during rehearsals, protesting that Miss Merman had 'too substantial a role'. Cole remembered Bob's film version of 'You Do Something To Me' and told stage director Howard Lindsay to 'get him'.

Rows were a feature of *Red, Hot and Blue!* By the time it premiered on 6 November, with 'America's Sweetheart' Mary Pickford and Merle Oberon amongst the first-nighters, Porter had intervened to sort out a billing squabble between Merman and Durante. Neither would agree to the other's name going top, so Cole ingeniously solved the problem by criss-crossing both names above the title. He then decreed that the position be changed round every two weeks to 'ensure absolute fairness'. Bob, who didn't join the argument, got third billing, also above the title.

Red, Hot and Blue! was by no means Cole Porter's greatest work, but it did produce one standard, 'It's De-Lovely', which Bob sang as a duet with Ethel Merman. Cole even joined in the escalating Hope-Crosby banter by giving Merman the following verse:

Oh, charming sir, the way you sing
Would break the heart of Missus Crosby's Bing,
For the tone of your tra la la
Has that certain je ne sais quoi.

'It's De-Lovely', which remains a part of Bob's repertoire to this day, gave him his first commercial disc when the show duet was issued as a 78 on the Liberty label, backed with a Merman solo 'Down in the depths'.

Spring 1937 brought Bob mixed blessings. His father died at the age of 66, never having really recovered from the death of his beloved Avis, and Bob sadly ended his 15-year association with vaudeville and Broadway.

The break was made inevitable by the makers of Woodbury Soap, who persuaded Bob to sign an exclusive 26-week radio contract. The Woodbury Soap Show, broadcast nationally from NBC's New York studios, first hit the airwaves in May. 'America's Cleanest Comedian' they called Hope

Crosby had other ways of describing him: 'Shovel Head', 'Scoop Nose' or just plain 'Dad' were some of the endearments he threw Bob's way from his Kraft Music Hall radio studio in California. The Woodbury host retaliated with 'Mattress Hip', 'Blubber', 'Lard' and other such insinuations about Crosby's weight problems. The cleverly contrived stage feud had taken to the air.

The Woodbury show, unlike the earlier Bromo Seltzer programmes – 'When the sponsor took most of the product ...' quips Bob – caught on and started to build a faithful following. He was now one of the hottest properties on the East Coast, but before the series was half over, Louie Shurr was on the phone telling Dolores to start packing. Hollywood was making noises again. They wanted Bob in the movies.

6

On a warm and sunny afternoon in September 1937 Bob and Dolores Hope arrived in Pasadena, California. Bob was under a seven-year contract to Paramount Pictures, but he may well have pondered the wisdom of his decision to give the Dream Factory another try. The Paramount deal called for three films a year at a starting price of $20,000 a film. So far so good. But the contract had options – all held by the studio. 'That meant that at any time during the seven years they could deposit you on Melrose Avenue with the rest of the trash,' Hope joked later.

The remarkable change in Hollywood's attitude towards Bob stemmed from a visit by Paramount film director Mitchell Leisen to the *Ziegfeld Follies*, where he saw a young man singing 'I Can't Get Started With You'. When he was casting *The Big Broadcast of 1938*, and Jack Benny refused the juvenile lead, Leisen remembered Hope's song and persuaded his bosses to sign him.

Not being first choice for the part of radio announcer Buzz Fielding didn't bother Bob at all – because he wasn't aware of it at the time – and he tackled the challenge with his customary enthusiasm. Too much enthusiasm, as it turned out. On the first day of shooting Mitchell Leisen took Bob to a nearby cafe for 'a cup of coffee and a few words of advice'.

'I know you've been on the stage a long time,' the director told him, 'but I just want to explain something about pictures. Everything you do in pictures you do with your eyes.'

Back on the set Bob took Mitch at his word and acted his

eyes out. Says Bob: 'The first thing we did in the *Big Broadcast* was the song 'Thanks for the Memory'. I walked right to the bar where we sang it. And if you ever see that picture, check my eyes because I was so soulful. I'm rubbing my eyeballs all over the screen. Nobody else notices it but me – I really am flipping my eyeballs up and down something awful!'

Hope's 'Thanks for the Memory' duet with Shirley Ross was the highspot of the picture and established him as a name to be reckoned with. It also won the Best Song Oscar of 1938 for its composers Ralph Rainger and Leo Robin, and became Bob's first hit record. He acknowledged the fact by adopting it as his signature tune.

Bob won another important battle during the making of *The Big Broadcast* – he saved his nose from the make-up men. For his first scene he was sent to Wally Westmore, one of a family of experts who dominated the film make-up business. 'We gotta do something about that nose,' exclaimed Wally as he set about lightening one bit and darkening another. Hope soon tired of the lengthy alterations, which by Westmore's expressions he guessed weren't working anyway, and cried 'Enough! Forget it! It stays the way it is. Like me, like my nose!'

Those first few days at Paramount were tremendously exciting for Bob. He had joined an illustrious band and loved evey minute of it. The lad from Eltham was rubbing shoulders with some of the all-time Hollywood greats: Jack Benny, George Burns, Gary Cooper, Bing Crosby, Fred MacMurray, Ray Milland, Anthony Quinn, George Raft, Randolph Scott (all were under contract to Paramount at the time), and Marlene Dietrich, Beatrice Lille, Carole Lombard, Ida Lupino, Martha Raye and Mae West.

One of Bob's happiest memories of the *Big Broadcast*, apart from the money, was working with the comic genius W.C. Fields. Bill, who was getting $50,000 for his cameo role, gave the young comedian a lot of laughs.

On one memorable day Fields, who had a habit of repeating himself, was in the middle of an amazing portrayal of a drunken captain on the bridge of a ship. 'Cut!' screamed the director, Leisen. 'Mr Fields, that's the same scene you did yesterday!'

'Not at all, my good man,' came the reply. 'Yesterday I did

the scene with a bottle of gin. Today I am doing it with a bottle of scotch!'

The Big Broadcast also reunited Bob with Honey Chile Wilder and Dorothy Lamour. He had worked with Honey Chile during the ill-fated Bromo series, but Dorothy was an old acquaintance from his Broadway days. He first saw her singing in One Fifth Avenue, a nightspot he used to frequent. Later they met formally when she moved to the Navarre Club on Central Park South and became firm friends.

As expected, when *The Big Broadcast of 1938* hit the screens, it was 'Thanks for the Memory' that carried off the laurels. 'What a delivery, what a song, what an audience reception,' wrote Damon Runyon after seeing a special preview.

Runyon's glowing tribute convinced Paramount's head of production that he should pick up Bob's option for at least one more film. The man who seven years previously had said 'I don't care for Hollywood' was back to stay.

California was not all movies, though; Bob still had two months to run on his Woodbury contract. The company had readily agreed to his hosting the show from NBC's West Coast studios via a transcontinental hook up. But they had forgotten to make one vital arrangement. Forty-eight hours before the inaugural broadcast Hope discovered, to his horror, that there was not to be a live audience.

'I've got to have an audience or I'm dead,' a worried comedian told his new producer.

'No deal! It's too late,' said the producer. 'You'll just have to bounce your jokes off the listeners at home.'

Bob was terrified at the thought of playing to an empty studio, although he only had about five minutes to do. So he decided to hijack an audience. Ventriloquist Edgar Bergen and his blockheaded dummy Charlie McCarthy were the biggest things in radio. Hope had met Bergen a year before when he was originally cast in the *Ziegfeld Follies,* only to be dropped prior to the Broadway opening. Now the double-act preceded Woodbury in the adjoining NBC studio – in front of a huge audience. With Bergen's connivance and the assistance of an unsuspecting studio attendant, Bob rearranged a system of guide ropes so that the exiting crowd found themselves entering the Hope studio. The crafty manoeuvre worked like a dream and the East Coast announcer's 'And now from Holly-wood ... Bob Hope' cue was greeted with rapturous applause. Bob got his laughs and everyone was happy.

The public had still not had a chance to see Paramount's latest signing (*The Big Broadcast* was not generally released until 18 February 1938) when Bob was back before the cameras to make Adolph Zukor's *College Swing* in the winter of 1937. Initially Hope was to appear only fleetingly, with just a few lines to say. Luckily the producer, Lewis Gensler, had been one of those responsible for the *Ballyhoo of 1932* and allowed his part to be padded out.

College Swing, a low-budget Paramount 'B' movie, starred George Burns and Gracie Allen. Bob's augmented role gave him fourth billing, after Martha Raye, ahead of Betty Grable. It was an undistinguished film. 'We all put on make-up, that's all I remember,' said George Burns in later years. But a Hope-Raye comedy duet, 'How'dja Like to Love Me?' became a hit.

With two pictures safely in the can (*College Swing* would not be premiered until ten weeks after *The Big Broadcast*) Bob turned his attentions to finding a permanent Californian base. 'Living out of a suitcase is no longer for me,' said Dolores as they celebrated Christmas and New Year in their hotel. Spring 1938 saw Bob standing in a North Hollywood walnut grove on the edge of the San Fernando Valley. 'There are three acres of prime land here,' said the real estate salesman. 'Toluca Lake is just a stone's throw away and the Lakeside Golf Club is just around the corner.' Bob bought the land for $6,000. The builders quickly moved in and before the year was out the Hopes moved into their new home. (A few years later Bob bought an adjoining three-acre plot for ten times his initial outlay.)

The early months of 1938 also saw Hope with a new radio sponsor, Lucky Strike cigarettes. Woodbury declined to renew his contract, so he became a regular on Dick Powell's 'Your Hollywood Parade': The producers gave him a seven-minute solo slot and Bob opted to go for something fresh – a mono-logue with topical jokes. Al Boasberg was replaced by a new gag writer, Wilkie Mahoney, and Bob resolved to stop 'dab-bling around' with radio and get his act together. 'He used to rehearse a whole week for those seven minutes,' recalls Dolores with a chuckle, 'but it was worth it.' Mahoney and Hope peppered his monologues with topical jibes about the biggest movie stars of the era; poked fun at the politicians in Washington and highlighted the amusing side of the day's current issues. The audience took to it and Bob became the redeeming feature of an otherwise mediocre series.

Paramount further boosted his confidence by activating another option and reteaming him with Martha Raye and Betty Grable in the romantic farce *Give Me a Sailor*. They also revealed that *College Swing* would be released in Britain under the title *Swing, Teacher, Swing*. But before joining the screen navy, Bob had a filmic golf date to keep with Harry Lillis Crosby. Film producer Herb Polesie, fresh from completing *Doctor Rhythm* with Bing, had been asked by the Professional Golfers' Association to make a two-reeler short of the second annual Crosby golf tournament at Rancho Sante Fe near San Diego. The two-day pro-am event – with prize money of $2,000 – was not overstocked with stars, so Herb rang Bob and suggested he help out. As the crooner sang 'Tomorrow's My Lucky Day', the comedian clowned. An important landmark in the history of the cinema was reached – Hope and Crosby had appeared on film together for the first time.

Give Me a Sailor, yet another Paramount 'B' production, gave Bob little more than a chance to romp with Raye and Grable and a $20,000 fee. He decided to exercise some options of his own and offer himself to other studios. Louie Shurr was not trampled in the rush. The best he could do was a co-starring role in a planned Universal picture, *Bedtime Story*, with Fredric March and Loretta Young, but at half the Paramount money. Bob never got a chance to refuse: Loretta, who had co-star approval rights, vetoed him and chose David Niven instead.

Meanwhile, back at Paramount, the bosses were evaluating the success of 'Thanks for the memory'. 'Let's give this guy Hope another go,' they decided. 'We've got a property called *Up Pops The Devil*. Why not change the title to *Thanks for the Memory* and reunite him with Shirley Ross?'

As the Paramount screen-writers worked on *Thanks for the Memory*, Bob concentrated on resurrecting his ailing radio career. The poorly-received 'Your Hollywood Parade' had been finally struck out by Lucky Strike, but Hope had gained enough fame to convince advertising agents Lord and Thomas that he was the ideal replacement for the veteran radio act Amos 'n' Andy. The sponsor, Pepsodent Toothpaste, agreed and Bob Hope had his own radio show. He could hardly contain his excitement and wanted to start right away on what he saw as 'a whole new concept in radio entertainment'. But that would have to wait – he was needed on the set of *Thanks for the Memory*.

Paramount had budgeted $200,000 for the film, again putting him in the 'B' class, and he was to play a struggling novelist married to a successful model, Shirley Ross. Even with the help of Hedda Hopper and Eddie 'Rochester' Anderson (Jack Benny's sidekick) the only lasting moments were the reprise of 'Thanks for the Memory', and the Frank Loesser-Hoagy Carmichael composition 'Two Sleepy People'. Bob and Shirley had another hit song, but the movie failed to impress.

Hope was determined not to let the same thing happen to his new radio programme. 'A staff of writers is what I need,' he decided, 'but not old-timers who are writing most of the other shows. I want fresh young talent – newcomers!' Most of that first gag-writing team were found on the doorstep in Hollywood, but there was one pair in particular Bob wanted from back East: Melville Shavelson and Hilt Josefsberg. He had already tried to hire them once before, for the Woodbury series. But a vital meeting in the Manhattan Hampshire House ended in deadlock when they asked for $100 each. 'That's a little rich for my blood!' Hope told Mel. Times soon change, though, and just such a high price was paid to lure them the 3,000 miles to sunny California. There they joined the growing band the media would later dub 'Hope's Army'.

To get the best out of his young team, Bob introduced a unique pre-show joke-auditioning routine: each writer was told to come up with a complete half-hour script; then, with Hope officiating, all would gather in one room to take turns reading their contributions out loud.

Says Shavelson: 'If you could make the fellas whose jobs depended on their not laughing, laugh, then Bob would check off the joke and that went into the air show. That's when I developed my first ulcer!'

In addition to is jokes Bob also had to find a signature tune to open the show every week. The advertising agency suggested taking the score of Ira Gershwin's 'Wintergreen for President', from the 1931 Broadway musical *Of Thee I Sing,* and putting it to 'Hope is Here for Pepsodent...'. But the comedian baulked at the cost – $250 each time it was used. 'I think I know a cheaper number,' he told them mysteriously. When the 'Bob Hope Pepsodent Show' first appeared on 27 September 1938, the Skinnay Ennis band launched into 'Thanks for the Memory'.

Adding to the problems of the Hope writers was the three-hour time difference between Los Angeles and New York. As a national programme, the 'Pepsodent' had to be aired in prime-time on both coasts. Recording, either on disc or tape, was not yet commonplace and so they had to go through it twice; the first for the East Coast, the second for the westerners. That, of course, gave the star a chance to re-evaluate his material and analyse the reactions of the first studio audience. It was also not unusual for him to phone friends in New York to ask how the programme had sounded. 'Very often,' recalls Mel Shavelson, 'he would have us rewrite the show in the three hours between broadcasts. It was tough!'

Even with such dedication to detail the new Pepsodent Show was in no way an ovenight success. And by the end of the second week, before the sponsor came looking for him, Bob was searching for even more talent. He found it in the form of two 24-year olds from Chicago, Melvin Frank and Norman Panama. They had arrived in hollywood a year previously to write gags for another top comedian, Milton Berle, only to fall on hard times. They were now busy collecting rejection slips from a host of great performers: W.C. Fields, Eddie Cantor, Al Jolson, Jack Benny and Fred Allen. However, enough of their material was getting through to interest Bob. All he wanted to know was whether they could sustain a whole half-hour.

Says Frank: 'So we sat up all night and we wrote 47 single-spaced pages of jokes. Every Hope-type joke that we could think of!'

Within 24 hours the pair were on their way to keep an appointment at Paramount, where Hope was making yet another 'B' picture. *Never Say Die,* with Martha Raye and Andy Devine. It was a meeting Mel Frank has never forgotten: 'It was the first time either of us had been inside a major studio.

And there was this incredibly handsome guy, in make-up, sitting in a little cubby hole. He just looked up at us and said, 'I've been enjoying you guys all night!' Well, at that time, all he had to do was look and ... wham ... we melted. If he wanted to, at that moment, he could – for $12 – have signed us for life...'

Bob did sign them, but not for $12. They got a hundred a week – although, unlike Shavelson and Josefberg, that bought both of them.

Panama and Frank's first assignment was to write a guest spot for the incomparable Groucho Marx or rather, as Hope put it, 'just supply the straight lines; he'll fill in the jokes, because he's a very funny man'. The new team were horrifed: 'A hell of a way to start out as comedy writers, not writing any jokes!'

They found Groucho sitting on his living-room floor playing a guitar. He didn't say a word as the youngsters stood uneasily before him. He just kept playing. After a few minutes he stopped, looked up at them and snapped: 'Who are you?'

'Panama and Frank,' replied the pair proudly in unison.

'What's that?' retorted the comic.

'Hope writers...'

'Got any ideas?' he asked, rooting them to the spot with a long stare.

At that point Frank decided to throw caution to the wind and ignore the instructions they had been given. Remembering an old play he and Norman had written in Chicago entitled *Utopia Incorporated,* he took a deep breath and blurted out a crafty pitch. 'No! But Bob has an idea. He thinks it may be funny. It's a Depression story about people who go broke and move to a farm in New Jersey and raise rabbits. It might be funny if you come onto the show and try to sell Bob an interest in your rabbit farm.'

Mel stood back and awaited the Marx reaction, trembling slightly. 'That sounds interesting,' said Groucho as he reached for a typewriter. 'Sit down.'

Three hours later the duo left the house clutching three pages of dialogue. 'Mind you,' admits Mel, 'some of those jokes were his, and they were good ones, but some of them were ours and they were also good ones.'

When they arrived back at the NBC studios Hope wanted to know what ideas they had come up with. Mel used the same technique again: 'We didn't get an idea, but Groucho has one he thinks might be funny. He wants to come on and try to sell you an interest in his rabbit farm...'

'What's that?' enquired the mystified comedian.

Panama stepped forward with the script in his hand: 'Well here's what we did...'

'Hey! This is kinda good,' exclaimed a highly delighted Bob. 'It could work.'

On the night the rabbit sketch was a huge success. But Marx still managed to steal the show with a typical closing ad-libbed Grouchoism. 'I'd like to sell you an old suit of clothes,' he told Bob, 'but I see you've already got one...'

From then on Hope adopted the Panama-Frank style of guest spots. Prior to that the major guest star had rambled on throughout the show without any fixed format. In future each visitor would have a tightly-shaped sketch full of running gags. It was a major improvement.

The next change was the introduction of a special Sunday night preview at the NBC studios. An audience would be brought in just to hear two hours of material that was being considered for use; the lines that got the biggest laughs stayed for the Tuesday transmissions and the rest went.

'You could never get into our preview,' recalls Bob with a chuckle. 'Everybody wanted to be there because they didn't know what was going to happen and it was a lot of fun.'

Another innovation was brought about by writer Mel Shavelson – he stopped Bob dressing up for his show. 'Because his training had been in Vaudeville, a visual medium,' explains Mel, 'he went on in full costume to try to get extra laughs. And evey time we did a sketch he changed costume...' Shavelson noticed that the ploy had the opposite effect, 'It just lay there because the audience knew that nobody at home was going to see it,' and advised Bob to drop it. The ever-alert comedian needed no second bidding.

Gradually the Pepsodent Show evolved into a recognizable format: Bob's fast controversial monologue, with an average of seven jokes a minute, was followed by the guest star and then there was a major sketch to finish with. Says Bob: 'We finally hit a format and after about six weeks we went right to the top, and stayed there for many years.'

As Christmas 1938 approached Bob realized he needed more help to run his affairs properly. he had already hired a Californian lawyer, Martin Gang, and a business manager to handle the radio show administration, James Saphire. But with $60,000 in the bank, he was about to take the advice of Fred MacMurray and move into the property world, buying up huge tracts of unsold Californian land. So he sent for his elder brother Jack.

Jack Hope drove to Los Angeles straightaway. He arrived on the outskirts at dawn, only to remember that he had forgotten to ask where Bob would be. 'So I did the only thing I could,' said Jack. 'I drove to Paramount studios and waited.' It was to be many hours before the brothers finally got together. Bob was not filming that morning, but the security guard – confronted with a blue-eyed blond not looking a bit like a dark-haired brown-eyed Hope – was not prepared to put out a panic call. 'You could be a fan claiming to be his brother,' he told an exhausted Jack. Paramount had one very red-faced gateman when Bob eventually roared up to the studio entrance, to warmly embrace the brother he hadn't seen for years. Jack Hope stayed in California and was part of the Hope organization until the day he died.

1939 started badly for Bob. Paramount picked up the sixth option of his contract, which still had five years to run, but gave him his fifth 'B' picture in a row, *Some Like It Hot*. The film's only saving grace, so far as Hope is concerned, was Shirley Ross and orchestra leader Gene Krupa. 'It was the rock-bottom point in my movie career,' he was to admit in later years. 'After that one, there was no place to go but up!'

In 1959 Billy Wilder made an immensely successful film of the same name, but with a different plot, starring Marilyn Monroe, Tony Curtis and Jack Lemmon. To avoid confusion Hope's Paramount picture was retitled *Rhythm Romance*.

The nightmares of his latest movie were soon erased by the rising fortunes of the Pepsodent Show. Judy Garland joined him as the resident singer, and was to stay for two years (later Doris Day and Frances Langford did two year stints too).

Then there was his radio double-act with Bing Crosby,

which really took off at that time. The feud became so big it was a major talking point in homes and bars across the nation. 'There wasn't anything real,' said Bing afterwards. 'No basis for it. It's just that we'd needle one another and kid one another on our own programmes. And I'd appear on his programme and he on mine.'

Says Bob about those days: 'Yeah, we used to kid. He used to talk about my nose and I used to say he was a nice fat little singer and talk about his money. It was a thing we needed for subjects and it was a very successful kind of friendly feud.'

The radio broadcasts of early 1939 established a pattern to the Hope-Crosby relationship that Hollywood would soon be seeking: Bing was the archetypal city-slicker and Bob the brash country bumpkin, who was always being used, but somehow managed to come out all right in the end.

Watching the legend grow from the sidelines was Hope's writer, Mel Frank. 'I think they complemented each other in an unconscious way,' he says. 'I think each man really had what the other wanted. Hope would have liked to have been able to open his mouth and sing like Bing. And Bing, more than anything else in the world, wanted to be glib, articulate, funny, witty – all the things which came naturally to Hope.'

According to Bing's Kraft Music Hall writer, Carroll Carroll, the radio feud was heightened by the fact that each artist kept his script to himself. 'Bob would take his script,' recalls Carroll, 'which we had read though only for time, and go off and do a little doodling on it. And when they finally came to do it, there were a lot of things in there that Bing wasn't looking for. But there were also a lot of things in Bing's script that Bob wasn't looking for!'

Another frequent guest on the Pepsodent Show was George Burns. 'Radio was very easy,' says George, 'although you thought at the time it was very hard. But when you look back now, you did nothing! You held a piece of paper and you read the lines. And the way to become a star was to be able to ad-lib without rattling your paper... Everybody would write down their ad-libs and we wouldn't tell one another. So we were all great ad-libbers, because we all had writers!'

But radio, with its insatiable appetite for material, was a demanding medium for writers. Hope's eleven-strong team found themselves having to produce around 150 jokes a week each just to fill the three-minute monologue and four-minute guest spot.

'That was our whole life,' said Mel Frank. 'That's all we were concerned with – going home and writing that row of jokes that came out of that man's mouth.'

Bob's hectic lifestyle did not help much either. If he was not filming at Paramount, then he would be out performing at one of the many charity functions held in Hollywood each night. 'Which meant that we the writers had to meet him sometimes at two o'clock in the morning, in a state of utter exhaustion,' said Mel. 'We had to sit around and read our jokes to him, and try to be funny, after 14 or 15 hours of writing!

'But I must say there was an incredible feeling of compassion among the writers. Even though you had sweated and worked as hard as you could to get a joke on a certain subject, if one of the other writers came up with a joke that was better you laughed – even though it meant that your joke wouldn't be in the show.'

Hope was, and still is, a hard taskmaster; however, he has always been a tremendously loyal one, although on occasions his efforts to protect have backfired. Once he called a long-suffering writer at home in the wee hours to sort out a problem with a joke. The worn-out scribe, though, was already fast asleep. So his wife answered the phone.

'Is Norman there? This is Bob.'

Glancing at her snoring husband, the wife decided that she'd had enough of being disturbed at night. 'No, Mr Hope,' she lied, 'I thought he was with you.'

'Oh yes!' he replied, without a moment's hesitation. 'I can just see him coming through the door now . . .'

The emergence of the Pepsodent Show did not go unnoticed in the inner sanctums at Paramount. Studio president Adolph Zukor sent for his head of production and indicated that Hope should be upgraded to 'A' class pictures. So Bob spent the summer filming *The Cat and the Canary* with Paulette Goddard.

It was a happy experience; the first time the bosses had produced a film tailor-written for him, a spoof of the traditional mystery-melodramas of the day, and it showed in his performance. Bob has always regarded *The Cat and the Canary* as a turning point in his movie career, and so did the critics. When it was launched in November of the same year they praised both the film and him. 'Mr Hope,' wrote one reviewer, 'is a pillar of strength in holding the film to its particular mood of satirical melodrama.'

Bob was also pleased to be working with Paulette Goddard, the wife of his great boyhood idol Charlie Chaplin. And it was the clown-genius, whom he had never met, who heralded the way the picture would be received. After watching some early rushes with Paulette, Chaplin told Hope that he thought the film would be fine. 'You are one of the best timers of comedy I've ever seen,' Chaplin said to his astonished fan.

Filming on *The Cat and the Canary* was finished in the late summer and Bob rushed home to begin planning a family. The Hopes had been trying to start one ever since their marriage, but the doctors had told them that Dolores could not have children. She favoured adoption, only to meet strong resistance from Bob. Now, though, he felt the time was right.

George Burns and Gracie Allen – who were amongst the few to know of the Hopes' predicament – recommended they try the Cradle, an adoption agency in Evanston on the outskirts of Chicago. Bob got in touch and, after the usual preliminary investigations had been made, he and Dolores had an interview. They returned to North Hollywood to await the outcome anxiously. In September 1939 the formalities were at last complete and the couple headed excitedly for Chicago once more. This time they returned with an eight-week-old baby girl, whom they christened Linda.

Their joy that autumn was increased by the news that Bob's 'Pepsodent Show' was rapidly nearing the top of the ratings. *Radio Daily*, then the top industry journal, highlighted Hope's own popularity by ranking him fourth after Jack Benny, Fred Allen and Edgar Bergen in a poll of radio comedians.

The only sour note of the period was struck by Mel Frank and Norman Panama, who suddenly announced that they were quitting the writing team after a year to further their careers elsewhere. 'Hope offered us a lot more money, but we had another offer for a *lot* more money. And so that was the end of us, until we resumed our association two years later as writers, directors and producers of six Hope films,' said Mel.

Worries about replacing the highly talented team were soon thrust aside, though, by a call from Paramount Pictures. They urgently required Bob to hit the road.

7

As Britain and her allies were plunged into war on 1 September 1939, Paramount was experiencing problems of a very different kind. Staff screen-writers Frank Butler and Don Hartman had to come up with a finale for a lucrative series of frothy South Sea Island films which had been cashing in on the cinema-going public's desire to escape from the harsh realities of life in the Depression. They had found a previously shelved story – a mediocre tropical island tale called *Beach of Dreams* – and cleverly burlesqued it, retitling their work *Road to Mandalay*.

Unfortunately nobody seemed willing to star in it. Hot properties Jack Oakie and Fred MacMurray had been approached. Both firmly refused. Then Bing Crosby, already a major box office attraction, was asked to team up with Burns and Allen. But while Crosby readily agreed, Burns and Allen announced that they weren't available.

The company executives were in a spin. To take advantage of the current vogue they had to get something out fast. Someone, and nobody is really sure who, came up with the bright idea of pairing Crosby with his comic antagonist of the airwaves, Bob Hope. Bill LeBaron, the Paramount production chief, had been thinking along the same lines for some time and jumped at the suggestion.

LeBaron also sent for a lithe dark-haired beauty, the former Miss New Orleans, Dorothy Lamour. She had become a leading Paramount star as a result of her parts in the South Sea Island pictures. She, LeBaron reasoned, would supply the elements of glamour and sex the partnership needed.

Lyricist Johnny Burke and composer James V. Monaco were hired to originate the musical content, the destination was changed to Singapore (to avoid confusion with Al Jolson's hit song 'Mandalay'); Victor Schertzinger became director, and filming began in November 1939.

During the following two decades Bob, Dorothy and Bing were to travel seven filmic roads: to Singapore, Zanzibar, Morocco, Utopia, Bali, Rio and Hong Kong. They were to create a whole new style of cinema and smash long-standing box office records around the globe.

'It was fun from the very first day,' says Dorothy Lamour. 'We were all exuberant about the picture; never dreaming that it would end in one of the greatest series ever to hit the motion picture industry.'

Bob arrived on the Paramount lot hot-foot from New York, where he had docked in the *Queen Mary* following a first trip home to Britain. His return after 31 years had created quite a stir – the conservative British were not used to his glib American patter. 'The machine-gun comic is here,' reported one newspaper.

Says Bob: 'English comedians had mostly character; they were character comedians and there were very few gag-comedians who worked real fast, until the war. Then along came Tommy Trinder, and guys like that, who picked up the style.'

During the 1939 visit Hope sought out his long-lost relatives. By then they had moved to Hitchin in Hertfordshire. 'We had a great ball in the pub down in Hitchin,' said Bob, 'and I invited all the relatives – of course I'd never seen 'em before. I had just come from the Paramount Theatre in New York, and I got up and started talking about them (the relations). But my grand-father James got up – he was 96 – and said, 'Look, you don't know these people. Let me introduce them.' And he introduced everybody to me, and told a couple of jokes and did a little dance. So you can tell where my ham comes from!'

As the *Queen Mary* drew away from Southampton Pier two days before the war started, Bob's white-haired old grand-father led the goodbyes. 'See you on my 100th birthday...' he shouted hopefully. It was a date Bob tried hard to keep.

For Dorothy Lamour, the first morning's shooting on *Road to Singapore* was anything but indicative of the accord that was to follow. She had learned her script as written – just one line for that particular scene. But Bob and Bing had thrown theirs to the gag writers for some additional jokes. When the cameras rolled, with Dotty positioned between the two, she had the shock of her life. Their rapid exchange bore little relation to the dialogue she had read and they left her speechless. After a while, she could stand it no longer.

'Wait a minute! I can't get my line in!' she screeched angrily, stamping her foot, oblivious of the whirring cameras.

'Cut!' bawled an exasperated Schertzinger, as the entire set broke up in helpless laughter.

Dorothy had learned the hard way how the trio was to function – *she* would follow the original screenplay while *they* used their radio writers to score points off each other.

Joining the three-some on that epoch-making film was an aspiring youngster by the name of Anthony Quinn. There was little sign then of his Oscar-winning acting talent and he had been making ends meet by hiring himself out to private film-land parties for two bucks a night, 'doing imitations of Bing Crosby, Louis Armstrong and Maurice Chevalier'.

'I was very happy. I was one of the few young actors to be allied with Bing and Bob in those *Road* pictures. I became like a good-luck charm around the studio, because all the pictures that I was in at the time were making enormous money, and of course, it was all due to Bing and Bob,' says Quinn.

Road to Singapore was premiered at the Paramount Theatre in New York on 13 April 1940. When it was generally released nine days later the public flocked to the cinemas. This was something fresh, this was the tonic they needed. Early returns from the box offices convinced the studio moguls that their brain-child should grow. But it would be almost a year before Butler and Hartman could come up with an acceptable scenario, and Parmount wanted to reunite Bob with Mrs Charles Chaplin.

The Cat and the Canary was making money, so it made good commercial sense to try Hope and Goddard again. This time, however, their producer Arthur Hornblow Junior dredged up a remake of the 1922 remake of a 1915 silent movie, *The Ghost Breakers*. The latest version had Bob as a radio commentator farcically involved with a murder, A Cuban castle full of ghosts and falling in love with Paulette. George Marshall, who went on to direct six more Hope movies, worked long and hard to reconjure the success of the earlier film. When the result hit the screens in June, it did so to full houses and fairly good reviews.

But they were vastly overshadowed by the news from Europe. France had capitulated to Germany; an armada of small ships was plucking an army from the beaches of Dunkirk; the Nazi stain now covered a continent. Britain stood alone. Soon the war would affect America. Already her young men were facing a peace-time call-up, and Franklin Delano Roosevelt was seeking re-election for an unprecedented third term as President of the United States.

The suffering of his homeland concerned Bob greatly and he scanned every available newspaper for the latest reports. But the war could only occupy his mind for moments at a time. 1940 was turning out to be a busy year. His weekly Pepsodent show had now reached Number Two in the ratings to Jack Benny's Jello Show and he had just been voted the nation's top comedian, edging Benny into second place.

The Academy of Motion Picture Arts and Sciences were acknowledging his impact on the movie scene by asking him to officiate at its 12th annual Oscar-giving dinner at the Los Angeles Biltmore Hotel. 'It was a sort of little society thing then,' recalls Bob, 'and people used to dress up, go down there, and sort of mix with one another. It was a lot of fun, but nothing fancy like today. It wasn't even broadcast on radio in those days.'

Bob was also well occupied on the family front. July would herald Linda's first birthday and that meant a return trip to the Cradle in Evanston, because he and Dolores had already decided that her present should be a baby brother. The Hopes called their son Tony.

December saw Bob celebrating his 20th anniversary as an American citizen (he had been naturalized along with his parents and brothers on 20 December 1920) and the start of another *Road*.

Road to Zanzibar was adapted from a Don Hartman story

called *Find Colonel Fawcett* and featured Hope as Hubert 'Fearless' Frazier, a sideshow artist in darkest Africa. It followed the principal format that was to shape the series: a thinly disguised plot augmented with a host of zany adventures involving Hope and Crosby in seemingly impossible situations. They beat the bad guys – usually utilizing the famous pat-a-cake, pat-a-cake routine which made its debut in *Singapore* – and vied with one another for the attentions of Lamour.

Zanzibar also firmly set the seal on the comic character Bob had been gradually building over the years; from now on he would portray himself as the egotistic, exitable, fumbling, cowardly, romantic who inevitably loses the girl – particularly if the suave, cool Bing was around. He became the butt of the biggest jokes and the world loved him for it. His *Road* persona was to dominate his film, radio, stage and (in later years) television performances.

A major talking point on the *Zanzibar* set that winter was the Hope-Crosby ad-libbing. The duo were again tossing their lines to the gag-writers for more point-scoring asides. This upset the originators Butler and Hartman, who 'fought like hell against changing a word', said Bing.

'The stories were nice.' Bing continued, 'but they weren't really anything. We didn't pay any attention to them and the two writers would come on the set and see us doing a scene that they had no recollection of writing. They'd make a mild objection, but we'd say "It's funny, it plays funny – what do you care?" So they finally got inured to it and said "Go ahead".'

But not before a crisis point was reached. Says Hope: 'We were very popular on radio – we had the two top shows in the country – and people wanted to see us doing that sort of thing, because they understood our humour. One time, Don Hartman walked on the set and I yelled "If you hear one of your lines, yell Bingo!"; he got so mad, he went up to the front office and yelled.'

One of Dorothy Lamour's fondest memories of *Road to Zanzibar* came during the filming of an intended silent safari scene. 'There wasn't supposed to be one line of dialogue,' she recalls, 'but they set up the microphones to get the atmosphere. Now, there were something like seven takes of that particular scene – and for each take there weren't ever less than five pages of dialogue taken down by the script girl. That's the way it was, the whole way through; you never knew what they were going to say. You had the feeling that maybe they stayed home the night before and read their scripts to see who could out-do the other.'

Says Bob: 'They weren't really happy until they saw the results in the box office. They thought we were messing their scripts up, but after the box office results came in, they were very happy to be associated, like everybody else!'

Road to Zanzibar, released in the spring of 1941, proved to be an even bigger hit than the first. The critics liked it too. 'Mostly nonsense, but it is nonsense of the most delightful sort,' trumpeted the *New York Herald Tribune.*

Within days of finishing *Zanzibar* Bob was back on the Paramount lot with Dorothy Lamour starting work on *Caught in the Draft,* a topical farce that had him playing a movie star who is conscripted into the army. In summer 1941 the film was released in beleaguered Britain; Londoners braved the Luftwaffe blitz to see round-the-clock performances, and in the Midlands a bomb-wrecked Coventry Cathedral was turned into an open-air cinema so that the city's homeless could watch Bob Hope's latest comedy. 'It felt good to be able to help the morale of my native country,' said Bob in later years.

Hope was to go before the cameras twice more that year, in *Nothing But the Truth,* with Paulette Goddard and Edward Arnold, and *Louisiana Purchase,* with Frankie Albertson. In the meantime, he had to hit the road with his radio show.

8

Bob Hope believed that taking the Pepsodent Show to the airmen at March Field army air base, 70 miles east of Hollywood, would be just a one-off broadcast. But the reaction he got that day convinced him he was wrong. In fact he went on entertaining troops for another 35 years.

Never before had he experienced such atmosphere, such enthusiastic laughter and applause, from a radio audience. Before the week was out, a new Hope broadcasting schedule had been hastily drawn up and the Pepsodent Show took on a distinct military flavour. Army, Navy, Marine and Air Force bases would now be his studios, and the GIs his audiences, so much so that between that first May concert and June 1948, only two Pepsodents came from a non-military location. (Both originated from the NBC's Hollywood studios, because Hope was confined to the city for medical treatment.)

The armed services shows had a dramatic effect on the audience at home and were instrumental in pushing his programme to the peak of the ratings. Later the *Motion Picture Daily* named him the top radio star of 1941, with Crosby and Jack Benny trailing behind. It was Bob's second honour of the year: the Academy of Motion Picture Arts and Sciences had already recognized more than 200 benefit performances, and over $100,000 raised for charity, by giving him a special plaque for 'services as a humanitarian'.

But there was a growing unease in the United States. Hitler's invasion of Russia had spurred those who advocated an ending of the State of Neutrality, and the Roosevelt Administration was under tremendous pressure. Bob saw this at firsthand when he attended the American Convention of Great War Veterans, at Milwaukee in Wisconsin, with Navy Secretary Colonel Knox and heard the veterans urge the repeal of the Neutrality Acts. Hope's English roots made him an obvious supporter of such action.

The argument became academic, however, at dawn on 7 December 1941, when Japan's attack on Pearl Harbor thrust America into conflict. While the nation was still reeling from this blow, Bob was putting the finishing touches to his latest movie, *My Favourite Blonde*. He was given the lead role after Paramount decreed that Bob Hope should be 'transformed into a major *solo* movie star' to complement his team success in the *Road* films.

The new film reunited him with his former radio writers Panama and Frank, on whose original story it was based. Panama and Frank had called their story *Snowball in Hell,* but the studio bosses thought it too rude and ordered a change. Says Frank: 'Our basis idea was to do a comedy version of a theme that had been used in a very serious picture called *The 39 Steps* by Alfred Hitchcock (made in 1935 with Robert Donat and Madeleine Carroll).'

Miss Carroll was one of Hollywood's hottest properties. Paramount capitalized on the connection by signing her. Bob's other co-star, with whom he sang 'Thanks for the Memory', as a duet, was Percy, a trained penguin.

Another feature of *Blonde* was a surprise guest appearance by Bing Crosby. He was unbilled and made cinema history by becoming the first major film star to undertake a walk-on cameo part.

'We were in need of a truck driver to say a few lines,' says Bob. 'And I said to Buddy de Silva – who was head of production at the time – "Why not Crosby?" He said: "Oh, he wouldn't do that?" I said, "Wait and see!". So I said to Bing, "Come on over and put a leather jacket on . . ." He came over that afternoon!'

Bing's scene was brief but effective: Bob, playing a small-time vaudevillian, asked a man leaning against a truck the way to a picnic ground; having told him, the driver asked for a match . . . only then did the camera show it was Crosby. As he walked away Bob did a double-take, stopped dead and muttered to himself: 'No, it couldn't be!'

My Favourite Blonde, with its clever screenplay by *Road* writers Hartman and Butler, began something else – a series of its own (Bob made two more *My Favourites*) and a string of films with him as the romantic lead. 'Hope at that point was catapulted,' says Melvin Frank. 'And I believe that we (Panama and Frank) were responsible for coming up with a piece of property which made him into something that he hadn't been before.'

His new sex-symbol status gave Bob additional material for his self-abasing style of comedy. It also allowed him to develop a most effective feature of his career – he would use each medium to promote his other activities. When on stage he joked about his radio shows and movies; when broadcasting he gagged about his latest pictures.

Madeleine Carroll and I are making a picture called My Favourite Blonde. *She's a spy and she keeps chasing me. That's right! Madeleine Carroll chasing me – and you think Walt Disney makes fantasy pictures . . .*

They gave Madeleine the choice of three leading men, and she chose me! Boy, did the others get sore – in fact, Donald Duck, Dumbo and I still aren't on speaking terms . . .

The following year, 1942, was the time Americans learned to do without many items. There were fewer rubber tyres, fewer clothes and cigarettes, less petrol, and even less Bing Crosby (his hour-long Kraft variety show was cut by half). But at least there was more Bob Hope. Apart from his regular Pepsodent Show, and the three films he would make, he willingly became the most prolific performer on a new Armed Forces Radio series launched that February – *Command Performance.* Broadcast on short wave to American troops everywhere, it quickly established itself as a major part of the wartime morale-boosting effort. All Hollywood stars gave freely of their time and talent, but none more so than Hope. Later he extended his AFR commitments by appearing on *Male Call* and *GI Journal,* two other hit shows of the war years.

In June the boys were back at Paramount with Dorothy to frolic along the *Road to Morocco.* It was almost their last. New director Dave Butler got carried away with a scene which called for Bob and Bing to be chased through the casbah by Arabian horsemen. Says Bob: 'We were running down an alley and he sent those horses coming down full speed right behind us. And if we hadn't found a doorway we would have both been trampled to death! That was how careless they were – Bing and I were one and two in the box office at that time.'

Anthony Quinn again led the baddies in *Morocco*. It was his third film with Hope, but the real villain of the piece turned out to be a camel. The intrepid duo were supposed to take a ride on it. But before they could mount, the beast – a 'kangaroo' Bob called it seconds earlier – ad-libbed a stream of spittle right in the comedian's eyes. As Bing gleefully shouted, 'Good girl! Good girl!' and the crew broke up in laughter, Bob staggered backwards out of camera shot. Butler thought the scene so good he included it in the finished picture, spit and all.

The same animal got a further laugh, with the help of the special effects department, when it delivered the line: 'This is the screwiest picture I was ever in.'

Special effects worked hard during *Morocco*, and not only with the camels. Another scene called for the curled toes on Bob's Arabian slippers to straighten after a long and passionate kiss from Dorothy. That prompted the obvious Crosby crack: 'Now kiss him on the nose and see if you can straighten *that* out!'

Morocco, like all the *Road* pictures, was heavily costumed; which was fine by Hope and Lamour, but not always with Crosby. 'Bing hated dressing up,' remembers Edith Head, Paramount's Ocar-winning costume designer. 'Bing said, "Oh! Do I have to wear this stuff . . . the jewelled kaftans and turbans?" But Bob was enthusiastic. He'd put on a turban and be amused by it.' According to Edith, who had already fitted him in a dozen films and would work with him on 24 more, Bob was a natural costume man. '. . . he had what you call "no figure problems",' she says. 'Sometimes I have actresses and actors who are a bit squarish, or shortish, or dumpish; all he figure faults. But Bob had what you call the "average perfect male figure". He could be very elegant.'

Despite Crosby's loathing of flashy costumes, he was often unable to resist competing with Hope in the dress stakes. 'He would say, "Hey! You gave him a better necktie!" Or Bob would say, "What's he got that I haven't got?",' says Edith.

'This at least made costuming a little more exciting. One time, when we were doing a thing where both Bing and Bob were wearing kilts, the question arose as to which of them had the better legs. You know, they stood in the dressing room in front of those enormous mirrors ... can you imagine? Bob Hope and Bing Crosby showing off their legs, and saying: "Wow! There's a fine pair!"'

As soon as filming on *Road to Morocco* finished, Bob crossed to another Paramount sound stage where George Marshall was shooting *Star Spangled Rhythm* – a morale-boosting musical extravaganza for the men at war. Including Hope, there were forty-three stars; among them Gary Cooper, Bing, Paulette Goddard, Susan Hayward, Betty Hutton, Alan Ladd, Veronica Lake, Dorothy Lamour, Fred MacMurray, Mary Martin, Dick Powell and – making one of his rare on-screen appearances – an epic film-maker Cecil B. de Mille.

By now Bob had concluded that, although his movie career was progressing nicely, his talents weren't being sufficiently rewarded by Paramount at fifty or sixty thousand dollars a picture. A tour in Chicago – during which he was mobbed by 'the biggest crowds I'd ever seen' – convinced *him* of the fact, but not the bosses at Paramount. They firmly refused him more money.

Ironically, it was Gary Cooper's part in *Star Spangled Rhythm* that gave Hope the leverage he needed. 'Coop' was under exclusive contract to Sam Goldwyn, but Goldwyn had 'loaned' him to his rivals for that picture. Bob's agent tackled Paramount about this and demanded a reciprocal deal with Goldwyn, who had already indicated that he would like to produce a film with Hope as the star. Paramount could hardly refuse.

And so, after four years and 16 pictures at Paramount, Bob 'crossed the street' to the smaller Goldwyn Studios to make *They Got Me Covered* with Mary Martin and Otto Preminger. Just for luck he took Dorothy Lamour along too. His fee for the film, a musical spy farce released by RKO Pictures, was a cool $100,000.

While at the Goldwyn lot Bob was also able to help Danny Kaye, then a hopeful young comedian trying to break into films. Kaye had shot a test for Sam which, says Danny, 'both he and I hated'. Bob got hold of his new *Road* director Dave Butler and persuaded him to make another test with Danny. This time both Goldwyn and Kaye liked it, and a star was born. 'I can never thank Bob enough for that,' admits Danny, 'although he keeps asking me to . . .'

Celebrations for Christmas 1942 were interrupted on 23 December when the Hopes' phone rang. It was George Murphy, now head of the Hollywood Victory Committee and responsible for organizing entertainment for the troops. (During World War II the committee arranged over 86,000 variety shows around the world.) He had a problem. The Secretary of the Air Force, Stuart Symington, had called to say that a group of airmen were snowbound in Alaska. They were going 'crazy – and the air force had a 'morale problem'. Some sort of Christmas show had to be put on for them.

Bob heard him out before telling him: 'You're out of your cotton-picking mind. You know what we're doing don't you? We're trimming the Christmas tree!' But he had not said no, so Murphy asked to speak to Dolores and then explained the predicament to her. 'There was silence for a moment,' says George, 'and then she said, "Well . . . could I go with him?" I said, "Anything you want. You are doing him favour; of course you can go."'

The next day Bob and Dolores gave the children their presents, kissed them goodbye and caught a plane to Great Falls in Montana. There they met up with Secretary Symington and the three of them flew on up to Alaska. It was a rough flight and Bob now admits that all he needed to have turned back was a message from Bing saying: Get out of there you silly fellow; get home by the fireplace, have a drink and warm your toes!'

During the following 48 hours Bob and Dolores cheered up the dispirited airmen with seven two-hour shows. As they boarded the plane for home, Bob left them laughing with the Hope battle cry.

Be happy, you guys. Be proud! You know what you are – you're God's frozen people . . .

There was hardly time to thaw out in the Californian winter sunshine before Bob was back on the air advising his listeners to use Pepsodent, 'while your teeth are still underpups, so they won't grow up to be Golden Boys'.

The new year brought bad news: his sister-in-law, Mrs Marine Townes, filed a $2,300 law suit claiming back wages. In an action which shocked everyone, including Bob, she alleged that she had answered his mountainous fan mail and acted as his secretary for only $12.50 a week. Mrs Townes thought she should have been paid $50 a week for the two years she had been working for him. But Bob quickly intervened and the matter was dropped.

By the spring of 1943 Hollywood was committed to a whole new genre of films – the war movies. Until Pearl Harbor the studios had been forbidden by the Neutrality Acts to touch upon the Nazi threat; Germany was the most lucrative outlet for American films in Europe and the politicians sought to protect it. However, the pendulum had swung the other way. As the nation's men went off to war, the film-makers immortalized every victory and act of heroism on celluloid. Cary Grant was given *Destination Tokyo*, Flynn fought *Operation Burma* single-handedly, Robert Taylor was told to die heroically in *Bataan*, Bogart was in *Action in the North Atlantic* and Bob Hope played a gigolo in *Let's Face It*.

The film, a comedy based on the Cole Porter Broadway hit which starred Danny Kaye, marked his return to Paramount, and teamed him again with Eve Arden and Betty Hutton. But there was little chance to see the finished film because it was time to hit the road to Europe.

9

The Drive for Victory had started when Bob Hope arrived in London on 25 June 1943. The Afrika Korps had been defeated, the Germans had been driven from Russia and the Allies were bombing German cities.

'Feeling more like a prisoner being marched off to detention' than a $5,000-a-week entertainer, he was escorted by American army officers to the side entrance of his hotel – 'the one nearest the "American Quarter" of Grosvenor Square,' reported the security conscious British press (it was Claridge's).

The next day, accompanied by Frances Langford, Tony Romano and Jack Pepper, he held a news conference to announce a ten-week morale-boosting tour of Britain, North Africa and the Mediterranean that would begin on 29 June. Then it was back to the hotel for a weekend sifting through the mountain of gags supplied by his writers and a glance at the review of *They Got Me Covered*, which had just opened at the Regal and London Pavilion cinemas.

The Times had this to say:

> For one so circumscribed Mr Hope has a rare air of spontaneity and his personality survives the tricks of script and direction with which it is beset ... Mr Hope is a genuine droll and his goings-on in this film, which has Miss Dorothy Lamour to decorate it, are extremely funny.

Shortly after the tour began in the English provinces, Bob's

99-year old grandfather James fell ill at his home in Hitchin. In his delirium the old man kept calling for his grandson. Bob, who was on his way to a show at Burton-upon-Trent in Staffordshire, dashed to his bedside.

'He clasped his grandfather by the hand,' said Bob's aunt, Lucy Symons. 'And said, "Come on Grandpa – I'm going to take you on stage with me..." Mr Hope nodded his head. I believe he understood who was standing there at his bed.'

James Hope died two days later.

The three-month tour was gruelling: more than 200 shows in all, including 70 during an action-packed 21-day tour through recently liberated Africa and Sicily. Tunis, Bizerta, Tripoli, Bone, Catania and Palermo – all fell before the Hope onslaught. They travelled in everything from fully-armed Flying Fortresses (B–23s) to rickety unarmed air transports. On the ground they fared little better: many hundreds of painful miles were spent bouncing along pot-holed roads in open jeeps, leaving few able to sit with comfort.

But it was in Sicily that the realities of troop entertaining were really brought home to the group. Halfway through a show at Messina for 19,000 soldiers the Germans hit back with a series of surprise air raids. As the bombs rained down, Bob joined the rest of the company in running for the nearest cover. He chose the deepest ditch he could find, but his headlong dive gave him a badly wrenched knee, and he needed a cane for the rest of the trip.

An inveterate collector of bric-à-brac, Bob picked up some war trophies to take home: the German version of America's Purple Heart medal, a vicious-looking Nazi general's dagger and one of Benito Mussolini's famous 'Mother Medals' – presented to some super-productive Fascist parent. He also carried signed photographs of him posing with American generals Dwight 'Ike' Eisenhower, George 'Blood and Guts' Patton and J.H. 'Jimmy' Doolittle.

The troupe returned to London in time for a late August show at the Odeon cinema in Leicester Square for 5,000 Allied servicemen. Bob danced with Hal Le Roy and raised the roof with a string of gags about Winston Churchill, whom he had met under unusual circumstances earlier in the visit. Five American senators, on a fact-finding tour of Britain had been invited to 10 Downing Street to meet Churchill. One of them, 'Happy' Chandler, thought it would be 'fun' to take Bob along. So when the group lined up to be officially presented, they had mysteriously gained an extra member. United States Ambassador Winant effected the introductions individually. But when he reached the end of the line and spotted Hope, his face numbed with shock; the Prime Minister too looked taken aback – with a 'I know that nose from somewhere' glint in his eyes. However, as Bob himself was later to report, before anything could be said he grabbed the half-outstretched hand and warmly shook it: 'Pleased to meet you, Mr Churchill.' The American Ambassador was not amused, but no one bothered to ask Churchill what he thought about it all.

The comedian was also unwittingly involved in another incident which somewhat dented the 'special relationship'. A few days before he was due to end the tour he got a call for help from friend and fellow actor Burgess Meredith. Burgess, then a first lieutenant attached to the US Office of War Information, was producing a semi-humorous educational short for showing to GIs in America called *Welcome to Britain*. He wanted Bob to make a guest appearance as a helpful pedestrian who explains the British currency system to a private (played by Meredith) who is having difficulty paying his taxi fare.

The British director, Anthony Asquith, chose Dean's Yard in Westminster as the location for the scene and Hope duly presented himself there on 31 August. His presence drew huge crowds, requiring a squad of local police to control them, and he gave them a performance to remember. In fact he threw in so many gags that Asquith was forced to plead with the onlookers: 'Keep the laughs down!' The proceedings were abruptly halted, however, by an angry Dean of Westminster. No one had sought permission to use his private enclave and he was furious. The unit was asked politely but firmly to leave the exalted shadows of Westminster Abbey, and *Welcome to Britain* had to be completed in Kensington Gardens.

Back in North Hollywood, Bob sat down to reflect upon his first taste of war and, in 1944, produced a book of his reminiscences called *I Never Left Home*. In it he wrote eloquently about the realities of the conflict:

I came back to find people exulting over the thousand plane raids over Germany ... and saying how wonderful they are. Those people never watched the face of a pilot as he read a bulletin board and saw his buddy marked up as missing. Those thousand plane raids are wonderful only because of the courage and spirit of the men who make them possible.

We at home would understand all this better if every one of us could go through a few hospital wards, stop at a few emergency dressing stations, pray for our own courage in operating rooms as we watched twelve and eighteen teams of steel-fingered surgeons perform miracles of science on men who had performed miracles of courage.

The early months of 1944 were almost all Crosby. With Bing, Bob pounded California, as part of the campaign to raise cash for the fighting, selling war bonds. They played knock-about golf in Los Angeles, sang and danced at the air bases, and even clowned with Vice President Wallace at the popular Hollywood Canteen – where servicemen on leave could get free food served by their favourite stage or screen stars and have pin-ups such as Rita Hayworth ask for a dance. But it was not all charity work. Bing had another cameo role in Bob's new film *The Princess and the Pirate*, which saw the comedian once again on loan to Sam Goldwyn. This time Hope was cast as a very un-Flynnish swashbuckling English eighteenth-century failed actor sailing to America in search of better parts.

At the end of the picture, which also starred Virginia Mayo, Walter Brennan and Victor McLaglen, Der Bingle (an ordinary sailor) grabs the Princess Margaret (Mayo) from a surprised Sylvester the Great (Hope) and engages her in a passionate embrace.

'Stick around son,' says Bing, pausing to be recognized. 'Something older may show up for you.'

'How do you like that?' demands Hope of the cinema audience. 'I knock my brains out for nine reels, and a bit player from Paramount comes over and gets the girl. This is the last picture I do for Goldwyn!'

It was.

For Bob Hope, and many other Hollywood stars, 1944 was

to prove a watershed in relations with the powerful film studios. In the good old days, when a star had a dispute with a company, he or she could walk out in the knowledge that half a dozen other studios would be only too glad to offer another contract. By the early forties this was no longer the case. The top producers got together and agreed that a ban by one studio meant blacking by the lot. This allowed them to introduce a highly successful suspension system. Now, however, many stars were rebelling against what they saw as a restrictive practice. Some openly defied efforts to make them toe the line.

Ann Sheridan walked out in dispute over her $450-a-week salary and then walked back with $750 a week and almost $15,000 in back pay. Carole Lombard refused to co-star with James Cagney and was suspended (although she later made it up). And then Olivia de Havilland blew the issue wide open by taking her studio to court for trying to extend her contract even though she had been suspended. She won her case, with the judge warning that the studio suspension system was in danger of being stretched to a point where actors were subject 'even to life bondage'.

Bob was still smarting from his unsuccessful attempt to get more money out of Paramount. He felt his $10,000-a-week earnings from radio and movies were insufficient. So he decided to set-up his own production company, Hope Enterprises Inc., to 'take a bigger slice of the action from the filmmakers'. Unfortunately his Paramount bosses reacted badly. The ensuing row soon got out of hand. 'If you insist, we'll have to suspend you,' the studio head informed Bob darkly.

'Too late,' retorted the comedian. 'I am suspending Paramount.'

So began a split that would take many months of stubborn negotiations to heal.

But all this paled into insignificance when the long-awaited news came from across the Atlantic. Bob – like the rest of the West Coast – eagerly listened to the details: 4,000 ships, backed by 11,000 planes, had poured a liberating force of American, British and Canadian troops onto the beaches of Normandy.

The continuing dispute with Paramount put Bob in an unusually tetchy mood that summer. So he was in just the right frame of mind to deal with a growing tendency for officers and their wives to occupy the front rows during his armed forces shows.

'These shows are for the men,' he told one nonplussed commandant after refusing to start a show until all those above the rank of sergeant were moved to the rear.

At another, when the wife of an army officer made a disparaging remark about his performance, he snapped back: 'Madam, how did you get in here? I thought this show was for the armed forces.'

Even without the demands from films Bob was plenty busy. Apart from the troop shows, he went to work with a vengeance on his Pepsodent programme and even became a syndicated newspaper columnist, churning out six articles a week.

The coming of autumn mellowed the Hope-Paramount feud and a compromise was at last reached. Bob was allowed to form his Enterprises, which would make a certain number of films in partnership with the studio. On other pictures, for a period of seven years, he would operate as a contract player. Hope now had the financial freedom he wanted and Paramount had the exclusivity it desired. 'It was a good feeling,' commented a much relieved Hope.

The episode cost Hope a number of films. Paramount made amends, however, by welcoming him back into the fold in grand style: another *Road*.

The *Road to Utopia* went into production shortly after President Roosevelt secured an astounding fourth four-year term in the White House. It was the first *Road* to be made without founder-writers Hartman and Butler. This time the screenplay was written by Hope's former radio writers, Panama and Frank. Their only brief was that the picture should be set in Alaska during the Gold Rush era; but they had a filmfull of ideas. All they had to do was sell them to the big three.

'In those days,' explains Mel, 'they were enormous stars; it's impossible to imagine the prestige of those three people. You really had to have their permission, even though they were under contract and technically could be forced to do what you wanted. First we had to sit down with Mr Crosby and tell him the story. And it sounded like it was going to be a Bing Crosby picture! Then we had to tell Bob the story, so that it sounded attractive from his point of view. Then, of course, we told it to Dorothy Lamour.'

All three bought the Panama-Frank scenario without reservation. This script contained just the right *Road* ingredients – lots of impossible situations and amazing escapes; although some of the schemes turned out to be a little too hair-raising. One piece of action called for the pair to share the limelight with an ugly extra – a fully-grown grisly bear.

'In the scene,' says Bob, 'Bing and I had to be hiding under a carpet, when this bear – now let off its chain – walked in looking for us. We had been told that after the director said 'Cut!' we weren't to move until its trainer had the bear back on the chain and into the cage. We didn't realize how important that was until after the scene. During it the bear walked over this lump – which consisted of Crosby and myself – and growled. 'Grrr...' Believe me Crosby and I had a laundry problem right there! After the fellow said 'Cut!' and the trainer had said 'Okay, I've got him back in the cage', Crosby got up and said, 'Well, that's all with this thing! To hell with that!' – and a nurse carried me out...'

They had been lucky: the next day the bear mauled its trainer, tearing his arm off.

On another occasion Panama and Frank wrote the boys into the frozen wastes of Alaska. Hope still shivers at the thought of it. 'We were walking along an ice glacier,' he recalls, 'and if we'd have slipped off we'd have fallen fifty or sixty feet.'

Worse was to come, though. 'Bing and I were climbing up the side of this mountain,' says Bob, 'and he was on the bottom. The rope broke and I fell back onto him! In those days, we were numbers one and two at the box office. Paramount didn't care – I guess it was another way of dropping your option!'

Notwithstanding the perils of the screenplay, Bob found the free-and-easy atmosphere of the whole *Road* series most attractive. 'We were doing so many things. I was doing radio, had conferences with my writers in the dressing-room – or with my tax man. And Bing would go over to the driving-range or somewhere, so when everything was ready to shoot a scene, there would be a shout "OK! FIND THEM!" It used to take half an hour to find us...'

Wardrobe also found their continual absences difficult. 'One Sunday Bing and I were playing golf,' says Bob, 'and we were on the fourth tee. And I said, "Look who's coming!" It was the producer with the wardrobe man, holding two suits in the air. They fitted us on the fourth tee, they stuck pins in us and everything!'

Says Mel Frank: 'They were like children acting out their fantasies. They were essentially anti-authoritarian. They behaved in a way a lot of us who have routine jobs would like to behave; they went to exotic places; they were with beautiful women; they hit terrible people; they did all those wonderful carefree things that society won't let us do.'

Melvin Frank was responsible for a *Utopia* line which became a movie classic. And it has haunted him ever since. Bing and Bob were in a Klondike bar, posing as a pair of ruthless killers. 'Act tough!' Bing continually reminded his partner.

'What'll you have?' asked the head heavy.

'Couple of fingers of rotgut,' growled Crosby.

'I'll take a lemonade,' squeaked a falsetto Hope, before responding to Bing's kick with a menacing: 'In a dirty glass!'

For years – almost until after he had made *A Touch of Class* with Glenda Jackson to become an Oscar-winning producer-director – Mel was dubbed by the press as 'the man who wrote, "I'll take a lemonade – in a dirty glass!"'

The final scene in *Road to Utopia* was memorable too. For once Hope won Lamour and married her, because Crosby was thought to be lost on an ice floe. Decades later, however, he turned up. They introduced him to their son – standing there in short trousers was ... Bing. 'How we ever got that past the censors in those days, I'll never know,' chuckles Bob.

Before *Utopia* was released, in June 1945, Bob was busy dashing between Paramount and the 20th Century Fox studios making two short films for the War Activities Committee and the United States Treasury Department. Fox's *All Star Bond Rally* put him with Bing, Frank Sinatra, Betty Grable, Harpo Marx and Harry James. Bing joined him again for the *Hollywood Victory Caravan* with Humphry Bogart, Betty Hutton, Alan Ladd and Barbara Stanwyck.

It was while commuting between the sets that Bob learned the great news: GERMANY SURRENDERS! The date was 7

May and right away he started planning his next invasion of Britain and Europe. But this time he would play Germany.

The voyage in the *Queen Mary* was smooth enough, and his fellow passengers enjoyed two rousing 'victory shows', but Bob found himself on the Scottish Clyde instead of Southampton Water. He described the rest of the trip as a series of 'hitch-hikes'.

'First of all we hitched a ride to Prestwick in an army car,' he told reporters in London. 'Then the boys at the airport said, "What about a show?" We gave them the show and stepped into a C–47, and just after midnight we were in London. Tomorrow I'm going to see my people in Hitchin. On Wednesday we leave for Paris, and an eight-week tour of France and Germany. We should be there now – I guess we're absent without leave?'

But he was to be absent for a while longer. Before crossing the Channel he took in a Sid Field show at the Prince of Wales Theatre, and entertained 10,000 men and women at the Royal Albert hall.

The Albert Hall concert almost turned into a riot. It was 4 July, American Independence Day, and an hour and a half before showtime the building was encircled by two queues – each ten deep. Annual ticket holders were thrust aside as ratings and privates clambered into their reserved boxes. When the doors were finally bolted shut another thousand were locked outside.

The roar of the crowd, when Hope first appeared, forced him to his knees, salaaming before the packed tiers of audience. 'I want to tell you seriously,' he began, 'how it thrills me to be here. We get a big kick out of coming to these out-of-the-way places.'

Within minutes of his act starting, though, he was facing opposition from the sound system. In the middle of a torrent of jokes the microphone went dead, reducing the punch-lines to a whisper. 'Keep the microphone alive!' he yelled. 'Pay the bill, someone!' He battled with it all night, until finally the mouthpiece suddenly dropped three feet and Bob again went on his knees – this time to finish a yarn. 'I don't know what they did with the microphone,' he said afterwards. 'But I guess I'll have to carry it around with me as a new gag!'

The tour of France and Germany was another triumph; although in Paris he admitted that he found some audiences restless and preoccupied. 'I think that it is the uncertainties of the future which is taking their minds off the show,' he said.

In Germany there was just time to collect his final souvenir of the war – the key to Adolph Hitler's bedroom in the Berlin Chancellery. Then he was off, to answer an urgent call from Washington. The new President, Harry S. Truman, wanted Bob Hope to perform in the White House.

10

If there is one thing that has always fascinated Bob Hope more than comedy, and women, it is politics and politicians. Therefore it was with some joy that he greeted the suggestion that he should perform for his president. Even during the dark days of his rise to fame, he had found that the biggest laughs came when he poked fun at the elected leaders. Roosevelt, who had died in April 1945, had been the butt of many a Hope crack, and his successor Harry Truman was to be no exception. And Truman found the prospect inviting. Forty of Truman's closest friends joined him for Hope's debut at the White House and none were disappointed. Least of all the comedian. 'It was just great,' he told newsmen afterwards.

Later, in 1948, Bob further cemented his relationship with Truman by firing off a one-word telegram – 'UNPACK' – when the incumbent upset all the predictions by beating Governor Thomas Dewey to gain a second term in office.

Bob's White House show gave him a golden opportunity to break in a new stage act. For he had decided that, when radio and filming commitments allowed, he would start taking paid theatre dates again. His reasoning was simple – there was gold in them thar returning servicemen. The shows were a tremendous success: as Bob had astutely forecast the dischargees who had heard him on radio overseas flocked to see him. Some of his biggest triumphs were at the New York Paramount Theatre in Times Square, the scene of Bing Crosby's first major stage record-breaking season in the early thirties. Bob emulated his achievements, but not without a little skulduggery.

The Paramount was a veritable gold-mine. It churned out entertainment 18 hours a day, every day, combining the latest movies with the best in live stage performers. Bob found himslf doing six shows a day, between the films, plus an extra late performance on Saturday. He was playing to a full house each time and the records tumbled.

That was not enough, however. Some people were staying to sit through him twice and, as there were always long queues outside, it meant another paying customer could be lost. Manager Bob Weitman had ways of dealing with that problem: he would announce that Bob was handing out autographed pictures at the stage door and then the mighty Whirlitzer would burst into life with 'The Star-Spangled Banner'. That got them on their feet.

Another record fell when Hope and Weitman conspired to scissor the films. By taking ten to twelve minutes out they were able to squeeze in an extra stage show every day. 'I knew what they were doing,' said Paramount founder Adolph Zukor in 1973, 'but I didn't really care; just so long as they didn't ruin the movie, and it was good for business.'

1946 was to turn out a bumper year for Hope fans; he signed a new ten-year contract with Pepsodent – 'The World's Longest', said the publicity blurb – for $5,000 a half-hour show; and there were three more films to be made at Paramount.

The first saw him back in the swashbuckling business in the costume farce *Monsieur Beaucaire*, a remake of the 1924 silent starring his childhood hero Rudolph Valentino. By July he had finished his part in a star-studded tribute to the Variety Clubs of America, who had been caring for millions of underprivileged children since 1928, entitled *Variety Girl*.

Then came *My Favourite Brunette*, the first Hope Enterprises-Paramount co-production under his new deal and his 20th major film. Dorothy Lamour was the colour in the title and Bob played a whacky murderer condemned to die in the San Quentin gas chamber. Peter Lorre and Lon Chaney added the necessary menace.

Bob was delighted to be his own boss at last. 'When you're under contract to a certain studio you are obligated to do certain stories, whether you like it or not,' he said. 'Of course they will fix it for you, but it is not the way to make pictures today.'

But he soon found out what it cost to be an independent producer. He had to pay $25,000 for the traditional Crosby twenty-second cameo.

However, Bob did have more control over the Panama and Frank script, and it was Bing who was thwarted for a change. He played the eager executioner, who is told by the warden at the last minute that the gassing is off.

'Off?' enquired a disgusted Crosby.

'Yes!' confirmed the warden, while the reprieved Hope murmured: 'Well, he'll take any kind of part!'

Dorothy Lamour's fondest memory of *My Favourite Brunette* involves a love scene and a piece of bubble gum. 'He used to chew gum between takes to moisturize his vocal chords,' explains Dorothy. 'So I started chewing gum too. Then we were told we had to do this love scene. I had to kiss him... That day I decided that I was going to chew bubble gum. So I bought some and I had it chewed to just the right consistency. And after I had kissed him, I blew a great big bubble, and broke it right on his nose! You've never seen such an expression on anybody's face!'

1946 ended in a flurry of activity for Hope. In early October he rushed to San Francisco for the first peace-time convention held by America's three million Legionaires to receive an award for 'Entertaining 12,000,000 servicemen throughout the world'.

Then he and Dolores took off for Chicago, and another assignation with the Cradle adoption agency. Before the war Bob had promised that they could 'take on board another child' once the hostilities were over. The agency had a lively eight-week-old girl in need of a good home, but there was a snag. 'There's a boy too,' the Hopes were told. 'Which one do you want?' Dolores could not make up her mind. 'So I fooled her,' says Bob. 'I signed the papers for both...' A few days later, Linda and Tony Hope had a sister, Honora, plus an unexpected three-month-old brother, Kelly.

1947 brought a revolution to Hollywood; one that would eventually transform the movie capital and strike fear into the hearts of film company executives everywhere – television came to the West Coast. Bob Hope was earmarked for a leading role.

Astute investment brains at Paramount had bought an experimental television station and now they were ready to go public, with commercials. The first show, sponsored by Lincoln cars, featured many of the studio's big stars. Melville Shavelson wrote it and Bob emceed. But it was a traumatic debut. The comedian made a basic error, similar to his early radio mistake of adopting his vaudeville dressing-up routine; this time he took his radio habits to television.

Says Shavelson: 'He went on with the big cameras and the monitors, and no laughs! And he said, "What's wrong with the jokes?" I said, "There can't be anything wrong Bob – these are the same jokes you've been using for years!" He said, "Well what's happening then?" I said, "The audience is watching you on the monitors and you're holding a script in your hand." So he did visual radio and sightless television for a while!'

Brushing aside Bob's 'Well, it works on radio!' protestations, Shavelson recommended that he threw the sheef of jokes away. 'So he did it,' says Mel. 'Nobody could remember a line and it was the biggest clambake of all time . . .'

This is Bob 'First Commercial Television Broadcast' Hope telling you gals who have tuned me in – and I wanna make this emphatic – if my face isn't handsome and debonaire, it isn't me – it's the static . . .

Here it is, 1947, and we're holding the first commercial television broadcast in the West. 'Commercial' what a lovely word! Up 'til tonight, I looked on television as something I might dabble in for a night or so . . . a week . . . maybe a month. But now it's gone commercial – meet the Yearling . . .

Everybody wants me to go on television. I know they do. Anytime I hear somebody discuss my radio programme, they always say – 'I never could see that guy . . .'

After the show Hope turned to his writer and delivered his verdict: 'This will never catch on! What actor is going to give up his golf to study a script?'

Says Mel: 'Then along came Milton Berle and the golf was over for a lot of people!'

Shortly after the television launch, Shavelson found the answer to Hope's script learning problems – the new stars of the 'tube' would use cue cards. 'Now you can do it,' Mel goaded the comedian, 'because they've invented the idiot card and you should feel very honoured – they've named it after you!'

Bob was quick to try the latest aid and, being far-sighted, found them a great help. In fact he relied heavily on them for the rest of his career; not even bothering to switch to the tele-prompter when it was brought in and even utilizing them for the last-minute topical material in his stage act. For a long time his addiction was not common knowledge, which often surprised other artists working with him.

Broadway and screen star Mary Martin still laughs about her introduction to the Hope 'idiot boards'. It happened on the occasion of *Life* magazine's 25th anniversary. Both had featured on the front cover many times, but had never worked together, so the publishers teamed them for a television special during which they would sing a *Life* version of 'Thanks for the Memory'.

'They gave us these things to learn,' remembers Mary. 'The new lyrics for 'Thanks for the Memory'. And I took mine back home and memorized them like mad, because I'd always done that.'

When Mary and Bob started studio rehearsals, though, it slowly dawned on her that maybe he had not done the same. 'He was singing every word perfectly,' she says. 'Finally I saw that he really was not looking right at me – he was looking a little past me. And there they were! Down on the floor; everywhere you looked! He can read a cue card like you have never seen; he can read it in braille – way off.'

Mary was furious. 'I thought you knew every word!' she thundered.

'But I do,' replied Bob unconvincingly.

'Well, what are you doing behind my back?' she retorted.

'Oh, those people...' blustered Hope. But it was too late, the game was up.

Over the years there have been times when Bob's cue cards have rebounded on him. The British comedian Tommy Trinder once used them as the basis for a practical joke. He was compering Val Parnell's *Sunday Night at the London Palladium* television show and Hope was the guest star.

'All his cue cards were in the front row of the stalls,' says Trinder. 'So when I came on to do the camera rehearsal I said, "Ladies and gentlemen, I want to introduce to you a man with a great sense of humour – should have a great sense of humour, he was born in England! He comes from America – a man called Bob Hope. Now you're going to love him because this is the kind of thing he does..."'

Tommy then proceeded to read what was on the boards in front of him and did the whole of Bob's act.

'By the time I came off,' says the comedian, 'Bob was almost in tears! He said, "Oh no! You're not going to do that tonight? That's all I've got!" Well he treated me like royalty until I had finished introducing him, when the actual television show came. When he arrived on stage he looked as though he could have kissed me.'

It would be some years before Bob established himself as a television performer. 1947 was to be another year of the movies and one that would see Hope nearing his peak as a film actor.

Road to Rio, the fifth in the series, went into production soon after the inaugural television show. When details of the picture were announced, it was revealed that Hope, Crosby and Paramount each owned a third of the rights. The deal set Bob and Bing back almost a million dollars each, but they more than doubled their money when the box office receipts were finally counted.

Rio also had a new director, Norman McLeod, with fresh ideas about handling the two stars. He proudly told the world that he would be departing from tradition by 'checking' the pair's tendency to 'introduce gags about themselves and Hollywood'. McLeod's avowed aims came to nought, however, and he even goaded the pair into producing special scenes for the studio heads to find when they viewed the rushes each morning.

'They had no idea what was coming,' said Bing. 'We'd put in something very dirty and they'd come rushing out of the projection room, and send us over notes which we'd ignore. We'd let them believe that we were going to use the scenes and were going to fight for them! Then they began to realize it was all just a gag.'

During *Rio* the Hope and Crosby off-screen antics caused

Avis Hope and her six sons in 1908, shortly after arriving in Cleveland, Ohio. Leslie, aged five, is standing in the centre

10-year-old Leslie Hope posing at Luna Park, Cleveland

Leslie and his first vaudeville dancing partner, 19-year-old Mildred Rosequist

On stage with Louise Troxell in 1929

Singing with the Vanderbilt Trio in the 1930s

Enjoying the spotlight on Broadway

After their marriage Bob and Dolores toured as a vaudeville double-act for two years

With Fanny Brice as 'Baby Snooks' in the *Ziegfeld Follies* (1936)

Bob with Honey Chile Wilder, his partner on the Bromo Seltzer 'Intimate Hour' (1936)

Jimmy Durante, Ethel Merman and Bob on Broadway in Cole Porter's *Red, Hot and Blue!* (1939)

On the air for NBC

Rehearsing for radio with Doris Day, one of Bob's regulars on the
Pepsodent Show

The 'machine-gun comedian' and his wife arriving in London for their first visit to England

Bob visited his 99-year-old grandfather, James Hope, shortly before he died

almost as much mirth as their on-camera patter. They couldn't even get from their dressing-rooms to the set first thing in the morning without clowning. In those days Paramount supplied their stars with bicycles for transport around the lot. Bob and Bing used them to good effect – to see who could arrive on the set last.

Says Bing's stand-in, Jimmy Cottrell: 'Bing's dressing-room was close to Stage Five and Bob's was down an alley nearby. Neither would set-off first; they always wanted the other to get there before. Bing would get his bicycle and start out, but he'd turn left and go clear round, and return the back way to watch for Hope. Then Hope, having seen Bing, would start off, figuring, "Well, Crosby's there." He'd walk into the studio and say, "Where's the Groaner? Where's Fatso?" But Bing was still back in his dressing-room!'

When filming on *Road to Rio* finished at the end of April, Bob was able to roast Bing with a fresh news item from Tokyo – American troops based in the Far East had voted Bob Hope their favourite radio star, in preference to Bing Crosby.

April was also the month when the American radio networks got tough with their stars. It had been common practice for comedians like Bob to poke fun at their bosses. But, on 20 April NBC decided the joke had gone far enough. When New York-based Fred Allen gagged about a mythical NBC vice-president, he was taken off the air for 35 seconds. Two days later Hope and fellow comic Red Skelton suffered the same indignity. Skelton was silenced for about 12 seconds after telling his straight man: 'Be careful, we might ad-lib something that will hurt the dignity of some NBC vice-president! Did you hear them cut Fred Allen off last Sunday?'

Half an hour later Hope's plugs were pulled when he referred to Fred Allen as a comedian who 'can be faded anytime'. Network officials refused to comment on the incidents beyond issuing a brief statement that the censored material was 'objectionable to NBC'.

Years later Bob again fell foul of the hierarchy (though this time it was his sponsors) when he ignored a stipulation that he should appear on a rival Frank Sinatra show. The angry sponsor fired him immediately, but Bob had the last laugh – he found a new backer the very next day.

The summer of 1947 saw Bob and Dolores taking a rare holiday in South America. He had already completed his second picture of the year – *Where There's Life*, with William Bendix – and was in need of a rest. Unfortunately it did him more harm than good. He returned to Chicago with bad sunburn and a high fever, and had to be treated with penicillin. He was still suffering when shooting began on *The Paleface* in the autumn. To make matters worse he developed a raging toothache (he was playing a dentist in the film) and had to rush off for a wisdom tooth to be extracted, and then some gunpowder exploded, burning his right arm.

Paleface co-starred the Howard Hughes discovery Jane Russell, who had replaced original choice Ginger Rogers after a disagreement over money. The film marked a high spot in Bob's film career. When it was released a year later it stormed the country, grossing more than five million dollars and putting him firmly at the top of the box-office popularity charts.

Part of the reason for the film's great success was the song 'Buttons and Bows', written by a couple of British ex-patriates, Jay Livingstone and Ray Evans. It won the Oscar for the best movie song of 1948 and joined 'Thanks for the Memory' in Hope's permanent repertoire. But although it was penned especially for him, his was not the version that climbed the hit-parade first. Frustrated by Paramount's delay in releasing *Paleface*, Livingstone and Evans offered the song to Dinah Shore. She liked it and managed to record it minutes before a national musicians' strike began. Her release was an immediate smash, leaving Bob high and dry. He eventually got a version out on Capitol Records, made in the lounge of the company's building with backing music recorded across the border in Mexico.

When *The Paleface* finally made the screens it was generally favourably reviewed, but *The Times* paid him this double-edge compliment:

Mr Hope riots through the coloured West in the dangerous company of Miss Jane Russell ... Mr Hope is not one of those comedians who can rise above their material by the sheer force of genius and personality. No man is more perfect in his timing, more assured in his technique, more certain to squeeze the last virtue from a line, but he remains in the last analysis at the mercy of the 'gags' and situations with which he is supplied.

Bob's final engagement of 1947 returned him to London and a date with King George VI. He had been chosen to compere a special stage show, following the Royal Command film performance at the Leicester Square Odeon on 25 November. The occasion was to be enhanced by the marriage of Philip Mountbatten, the Duke of Edinburgh, to Princess Elizabeth, heir to the throne.

After a rough crossing in the *Queen Mary*, Bob and Dolores joined a group of stars at the Savoy Hotel. Loretta Young, who starred with Cary Grant and David Niven in the royal premiere film *The Bishop's Wife*, was there; so too were Rex Harrison, Lilli Palmer, Alexis Smith, Burgess Meredith and Robert Montgomery.

Bob ignored the pre-wedding celebrations to catch his Pepsodent Show on short wave radio. The incomparable Eddie Cantor was spelling for him and he was naturally concerned to hear how it went. 'Not bad, not bad,' murmured the comedian as he headed for bed at 3.00 a.m.

The next morning, 20 November, Bob was amongst an excited group on the terrace of Crockford's Club, overlooking the Mall, to watch the royal wedding procession. With him were three of his writers, who worked in the club manager's office while their boss dashed between them and the crowned heads of Europe parading towards Westminster Abbey. For a change Bob was bereft of wisecracks: 'Wonderful, wonderful,' he kept saying. 'Magnificent!'

Five days later he was on stage at the Odeon with co-host Peter Ustinov introducing a 45-minute array of entertainers: Cary Grant, Loretta Young, David Niven, Gene Kelly, Joan Fontaine and Robert Montgomery. Everything went smoothly until it was time for the King and Queen to leave. Earlier Bob had presented the sovereign with a book of 400 autographed portraits of Hollywood stars – the film industry's wedding gift to Princess Elizabeth. But now it was missing.

'We can't go without that,' said the Queen.

'They've probably put it in the safe and lost the key,' quipped the King to Bob.

Finally the book was found in the manager's office and the royal party paused to leaf through it. 'Where's Bing Crosby's portrait?' asked the King and Queen in unison.

'Here it is,' replied Hope, hurriedly flicking through the pages, 'and he's signed it with his middle name – three crosses . . .'

Before flying off to Hamburg for an American Forces concert, Bob stayed on in London to broadcast his Pepsodent show from the Prince of Wales Theatre in the Haymarket. Two thousand fans – including revellers from night clubs and shirt-sleeved night-workers – crammed into the theatre, and stayed up until 3.30 a.m. to hear the programme go out live to Hollywood. The audience was overflowing onto the stage as compere Leslie Mitchell introduced Bob and Britain's Sid Field. When the red light blinked on, Hope was first away with the obligatory tooth-paste commercial:

Everyone from Washington to the White Cliffs of Dover uses it . .

Then it was joke time:

English people do not tighten their belts – they ate them long ago . . .

From where I sat, the wedding procession looked like six white mice pulling a golden snuff box . . .

Another couple of Pepsodent commercials from Hollywood and it was into a double-act with Sid Field, ending with a topical telephone routine: Sid informs Bob that Buckingham Palace is on the line with one last command from the King.

'What is it?' enquires the comic eagerly.

'Get out within 24 hours!' quips Field.

And he did. But a year later he was back, for his first Royal Command Performance at the London Palladium with George VI in the royal box.

Bob returned briefly to Hollywood, where he put the finishing touches to *Sorrowful Jones* with Lucille Ball. 'A competition between two hams,' remarked screen-writer Mel Shavelson. The film was a remake of Damon Runyon's *Little Miss Marker*, which starred Gary Cooper and Shirley Temple, and gave Hope his first semi-serious role. It was not well received by the British critics. 'There is an air of expectancy about a Bob Hope film,' commented the London *Evening Standard*. 'The customers sit poised on the edge of their plush seats waiting and wanting, oh wanting so much to laugh ... But after that first hilarious greeting of that pointed nose and familiar face it should slowly dawn upon even his most ardent disciples that in *Sorrowful Jones* Mr Hope isn't saying anything very funny or doing anything funny ...'

Christmas 1948 came during the height of the Berlin airlift and with east-west relations at their lowest ebb, United States Air Secretary Stuart Symington once again asked Bob to spend the festive season in Europe. Hope flew first to Berlin, where he and his troupe put on a number of shows for the GIs involved in the airlift; then it was on to other key points in the operation, before completing his tour at the US Air Force base at Burton-wood in Lancashire. He had begun an annual event that would continue for the next 24 years.

Coincidently, because the decision had already been made, as Bob was opening up a whole new aspect to his career, he was ending another. After seven years on the military road he was retiring from the bases to take his radio show back into the studios of NBC. He was also about to replace the toothpaste with some nice new soap.

11

Bob Hope had been selling Pepsodent – or 'rack shellac' as Crosby called it – for a decade. But by the time his eleventh radio season rolled around, he was looking for a new patron. He found one in the form of the giant Lever Brothers concern and was back in the business of plugging soap.

His new clean image did nothing for the ratings, though. They were now falling steadily and even the most comprehensive of shake-ups, a number of sackings and the introduction of singer Doris Day, failed to stop the slide. The golden age of radio was going; soon it would be gone altogether; the American public were not only turning off their radios, they were turning on their newly-acquired television sets. Bob got turned on too and began to court the new medium seriously.

Almost three years after the experimental Paramount show, he reappeared on the small screen, doing an eight-minute monologue on talent spotter Ed Sullivan's *Toast of the Town* programme. A few months later he was talking to NBC Television about having his own networked show. Frigidaire had agreed to sponsor him in a musical spectacular co-starring Douglas Fairbanks Junior, Dinah Shore and Beatrice Lillie. If that was successful, there would be four more. His fee for the first show was a staggering $40,000, the highest figure paid to any single performer at that time.

Bob Hope's *Star Spangled Revue* was broadcast from New York on Easter Sunday, 9 April 1950. He appeared in top hat and full morning suit, and twirling a cane:

Well, they finally got me . . . the last time I was in New York I was at the Paramount Theatre with Jane Russell. Now here I am working for Frigidaire – a fella can get pneumonia this way . . .

The real reason I'm wearing this little outfit is the fact that a lot of performers die on television – if that happens to me I want to be prepared for it . . .

The opening special was not widely acclaimed, but Frigidaire thought enough of it to bring him back on Mother's Day, this time teamed with Frank Sinatra and Peggy Lee:

I'm very happy to be here once again on television. This is my second show for the Frigidaire people – I'm surprised too . . .

I want to thank the thousands of people who wrote letters about the first show – also the three who mailed them . . .

It's amazing how many people see you on TV. I did my first television show a month ago and the next day five million television sets were sold – the people who couldn't sell theirs threw them away . . .

Bob's monologue technique on those early shows, though far from perfect, was good enough to keep both sponsors and network interested; thus allowing him the breathing space he needed to master the medium.

'I wasn't too successful at first,' says Bob. 'I was going too fast for the audience at home. I got too far ahead of them. I just had to learn to slow down and project my personality more.'

According to Hope, one of the main reasons why he was able to get the feel of television audiences quickly enough to survive was his long experience as a vaudeville performer. 'When you get in front of a camera, there's an imaginary audience there and you time it that way . . . And that's a technique that a lot of people miss. When you do comedy in front of a camera you have had this background, this experience to understand just how an audience will react.'

Today Bob Hope is one of the most successful performers on television anywhere in the world. But his longevity has been built on a decision he took back in the early fifties: 'Never allow yourself to become overexposed on TV.' Right from the start he refused to do a weekly show, preferring instead to do around eight 'specials' a year backed up by a regular spattering of guest spots on other stars' shows. The formula still works.

But in 1950 television had not yet taken its vice-like grip on the world of entertainment. Stars were still created and maintained by the movie studios. And Bob was the industry's top money-maker, with an established legend like Clark Gable only managing to make tenth place in the list.

Paramount, who had been concerned about Hope's television excursions, put him back to work with Lucille Ball in *Fancy Pants*, a remake of the 1935 Charles Laughton comedy classic *Ruggles of Red Gap*. For Bob it turned out to be a painful experience. While filming a scene sitting astride a saddle, strapped to a wooden barrel, attached to a mechanical rocking 'horse', which Lucille was supposedly using to teach him to ride, the 'beast' malfunctioned, throwing him to the hard studio floor. The fall knocked him senseless and a worried studio doctor ordered him to be rushed to the nearby Hollywood Presbyterian Hospital, where doctors hurriedly carried out tests and took extensive X-rays. 'Nothing worse than a badly bruised back,' they informed director George Marshall later. 'But we'd like to keep him in for two or three days.'

Although genuinely shaken by the mishap, the next day Bob managed a rueful wisecrack for inquisitive newsmen: 'I'm sticking strictly to drawing-room dramas in future,' he quipped. 'And I'm wiring Noel Coward to start writing for me...'

When Bob returned to work on *Fancy Pants* he thought it would be safer to swap the riding lessons for a spot of 'hoofing'. It was certainly less dangerous, though not the cake-walk he expected. One complicated scene called for an imitation of Fred Astaire in full flow; however, Bob just could not get the steps right. So it was a relieved director who spied Astaire – making another film on an adjacent sound-stage – watching with amusement from the sidelines. The nimble 'King of the Hoofers' was quickly pressed into rehearsal service. Astaire spent an energetic hour schooling Hope in the finer arts of his technique, but left him protesting plaintively: 'I still can't do it the way Fred does!'

Fancy Pants was generally well received by the critics. Even the astringent *Times*, which had taken to castigating Bob for relying too heavily on gags, saw merit in it. Its correspondent wrote:

Mr Bob Hope succeeds in at least giving the illusion of

escape from the formula, the elaborate 'gags', which so often imprison him. He is always a comedian who depends on timing, on the mechanics rather than the humanities of his craft. But here, as a kind of Ruggles of Red Gap, a gentleman's gentleman, he expands into something like a character.

The reviews were reflected in the box-office returns. In Britain the film jumped into eighth place in the *Motion Picture Herald* top money-making list and helped persuade 4,500 cinema exhibitors to vote Bob the country's 'greatest screen favourite'. Abbott and Costello came second, Anna Neagle third and Jean Simmons fourth.

By the winter of 1950 the United States was again at war: President Truman had earlier committed American troops to help South Korea against Chinese-backed aggression from the North. General Douglas MacArthur, Officer Commanding all UN forces in Korea, requested Christmas entertainment for his men. Bob was among the first to heed the call.

He had just finished making a troublesome picture called *The Lemon Drop Kid*, with Marilyn Maxwell and Lloyd Nolan. It was based on yet another Damon Runyon story, musically backed by the Oscar-winning songwriting partnership of Jay Livingston and Ray Evans. But Bob was not happy with the result and, after a special Hollywood preview, persuaded Paramount to undertake $300,000 worth of retakes, and to give humorist Frank Tashlin a chance to make his debut as a film director.

Amongst the reshot scenes was a musical number called 'Silver Bells'. Livingston and Evans had resisted the idea of doing a Christmas song. 'Crosby, it seemed to us,' says Evans, 'had cornered the market with "White Christmas".' But they had produced one nevertheless.

The first film version of the song had failed to impress, but Tashlin's rechoreographed treatment spawned a massive hit; though not immediately for Hope. As with 'Buttons and Bows' another artist got there first – this time the Old Groaner captured the honours and the bulk of the record sales. 'Just my luck,' moaned Bob.

Bob returned from his 1950–51 Christmas tour of Korea and

the Pacific to begin work on *My Favourite Spy* with Hedy Lemarr. Before it was completed, it was revealed that his services in the military field had gained him a rather special title: the United States Reserve Officers' Association named him as the first civilian honorary chairman of America's National Defence Week and dubbed him 'the GI in greasepaint'.

His tenure as leader of the event would be served overseas, though – thanks to a chance meeting on the Paramount lot with an accentric English vicar. The Reverend James Butterworth was in Hollywood trying to raise funds for a young peoples' club he ran at the Elephant and Castle in London. While he was visiting Paramount Bob heard the English accent and wandered over to talk about the land of his birth.

'I had no idea who he was,' said Butterworth afterwards, 'and we just talked about home. He asked me what I was doing in America and I told him about the club, and the shortage of money to keep it going.'

Hope was immediately taken with the diminutive but determined Yorkshireman and somewhat amazed that for once he had met someone who did not recognize him as a film star. Later he took 'Jimmy' home to Toluca Lake. Hope questioned him further about the Camberwell Youth Centre and heard how it had been blitzed during the war. 'We had some tea and I guess I lost my head, and said I'd do a benefit,' says Bob.

Butterworth returned to Bermondsey believing Bob's promise was 'just Hollywood talk'. But he was soon jolted by the news that the comedian was to donate the proceeds of a two-week Prince of Wales season to the club – as much as £20,000. Initially Hope had wanted the gift to remain a secret. Even after the story leaked out he denied it at first. When reporters tackled him about it in Hollywood he told them he was 'very angry' that his gesture had hit the headlines. 'I never intended that my offer should reach the newspapers,' he said. 'I'm afraid it will give people the wrong impression. They'll think I'm doing it just for the publicity.'

The Hope arrival in Britain on the evening of 19 April 1951 had all the ballyhoo of a Hollywood road show. Four limousines conveyed his retinue of sixteen people, 100 pieces of baggage and a set of golf clubs from Southampton to London's Savoy Hotel. With him, when he checked in at 2.30 a.m. were four gag writers, two radio technicians, a producer, a secretary, a radio station executive, a sponsor, two agents, a honeymoon couple and his co-star from *The Lemon Drop Kid*, the singer Marilyn Maxwell.

During an impromptu press conference held in the hotel lobby he revealed that he would be fitting in three shows in Manchester, Blackpool and Dudley before opening his first West End variety season. 'When I got boned-up on English personalities and the English scene I'll sit down with my gag writers, and work out a complete new routine,' he said.

His premiere at the Prince of Wales Theatre was a smash. A packed audience of first-nighters saw an hour and twenty minutes of comedy from him alone; then there was the glossy Miss Maxwell; the late Sid Field's stooge – Jerry Desmonde; a juggler; a troupe of tumblers; some comic trick-cyclists and Peg-Leg Bates, the renowned one-legged negro tap-dancing vaudevillian.

Said *The Times* on the morning of 24 April:

Mr Bob Hope, who began a two weeks' season at the Prince of Wales Theatre last night, is exceptionally well-endowed as a comedian. His careless assurance, his serious face, his far-away look dispersed now and then by an engaging smile, his square jaw and sharply serpentine nose – all these predispose one to laugh, and the timing with which he brings each of these assets into play is admirable.

The *Daily Express*, under the headline 'World's No 1 Mechanical Wit', enthused: 'The genial, burly American comic, with the huge head and battleship jaw, unpacks his gags with the silken speed of a master-salesman with sure-fire samples...'

Reviews like those ensured that the engagement was a sell-out. They also helped attract a royal visitor; two nights after the debut, Princess Margaret arrived with a group and walked to her stalls seat almost unrecognized. She laughed and clapped as Bob joked about everything from sex to Californian smog:

I never give women a second thought – my first thought covers everything...

My father told me all about the birds and bees. The liar – I went steady with a woodpecker till I was twenty-one . . .

What's a shilling? A pound with taxes taken out . . .

My aunt came out to California for asthma – in three days she had it . . .

A few days after the two-week triumph Hope paid his first visit to the object of his charity, Clubland, in south-east London. The entire neighbourhood took to the streets to welcome him, causing a traffic jam along the already congested Walworth Road. Amongst the many happy faces that day was a 14-year-old tearaway who would eventually find international fame as a film actor, Michael Caine.

'I was one of the two hundred newly reformed delinquents,' says Michael, 'who were being pushed around by the Reverend. You could almost say Bob paid for part of my training as an actor because I was an amateur actor in the club's drama classes. Bob was really great to us kids. You can always send money – but to actually leave the West End and come right down to the Walworth Road, which isn't the Beverly Hills of London, takes a really charming man.'

Young Michael had been one of the few fortunate enough to meet Bob before the visit. As chairman of the drama class, he had to get up on stage at the Prince of Wales and make a special speech thanking the comedian for his generosity.

'So naturally, as it was a show business thing,' says Caine. 'I was the kind of show business representative. The only thing I really remember about the night is suffering from abject fear of actually getting up and saying things that I had thought up; because all I'd been used to was saying other people's lines. I remember being quite funny . . . considering!'

Bob could do no wrong during his introductory tour of the Camberwell club. The walls were plastered with hand-painted posters, proclaiming: BOB'S YOUR HOPE! or BOB'S YOUR UNCLE! And the comedian obliged with a knockabout show with Marilyn Maxwell and Jerry Desmonde.

Before leaving he gave a semi-serious talk about the value of such clubs: 'They really keep you out of bad company,' he told the youngsters. 'If I'd had a place like this to go when I was a kid I might never have run into Crosby . . .'

Bob continued supporting the Clubland cause for a number

of years, again using West End variety shows to raise the money. Eventually enough cash had been garnered to rebuild the bomb-damaged site. He was invited back to unveil a plaque commemorating his valuable role. He heard a near-to-tears Reverend Butterworth pay this tribute: 'This would have been a junk yard or a ruin, but for you. And you've really come home. To stand here and know that a life's work would have faded – but for you – makes one feel very humble, Mr Hope.'

The early and mid-fifties were halcyon years for Bob Hope's British fans. He took the country by storm. Not only did he tame the Prince of Wales Theatre, but there were highly successful provincial tours and a series of sell-out concerts at the London Palladium. To handle the vast amount of work, and to anglicize his act, he built up a British staff. Albert Knight – 'Burlington Bertie' Bob nicknamed him – became his booking agent (show business mogul Lew Grade was also handling his affairs) and spent many long nights getting things right.

Says Knight: 'He would sit up in bed, in his pyjamas, going through his material book and dot off the gags he thought might go. Then he would say to me, "Here is the stuff we should try and do." And we would get the typist down, put her in another room and we'd talk about what time the next performance was or low long he wanted. All of a sudden the typist would laugh out loud. So, he'd shout: "Stop! What did you laugh at? Keep it in! Keep it in!"'

As his conquest of Britain continued, Bob's American-based material wore thin, so he hired a couple of young British writers, Bob Monkhouse and Denis Goodwin. They had made a name for themselves writing for comedians like Jack Buchanan, Ted Ray and Arthur Askey in the radio shows *Calling All Forces* and *The Forces Show*. Buchanan, a close friend of Bob's, recommended them. All they had to do was supply the right kind of material.

Said Goodwin before he died: 'We didn't believe it and it worried us because this was the zenith of comedy at that time. We spent two nights writing this stuff. But we had great difficulty in getting to see Bob Hope because he always seemed to have other appointments.'

When the pair were eventually ushered before the presence, they were greeted with: 'Been working all night, huh?'

'We've been working for *two* nights,' retorted a slightly impatient Denis Goodwin, 'and we've been waiting to see you for two days!'

The comedian quickly ran through their material, until he got to a section of jokes about Danny Kaye – who had become the king of the Palladium and the darling of Britain – 'Do you mind if I use these second house?' he asked.

I wanna tell you it's great to be in London. Danny Kaye nearly refused me a re-entry permit – but I made it . . .

He loves it here in London you know. He always get the best of everything – he even has monogramed fog . . .

He visits me when he comes to America. You should see his dressing-room here – two mirrors and a throne . . .

'And I thought, my God!' said Goodwin. 'We've got applause with Bob Hope.' So started a long association which developed into the team becoming his official European writers. Bob Monkhouse acquired the Hope nickname of 'Topper'. Says Monkhouse: 'If someone did a gag, he'd turn to me and say, "Can you top it?" I did . . . because when Hope asked you to top something, you topped it!'

Hope's constant thirst for perfection and last-second topical material dragged the boys to Germany, and almost on to the stage with him. 'He'd be standing in the wings waiting to go on,' recalls Bob Monkhouse, 'and he would say, "Give me a line on German streets because they have funny names." Denis would say, "Well you could do it with a cab-driver and ask him to take you to Ha Ho Ah Strasse, which is right around the corner from the Ha Ho Ah Keller – and by the time you finish telling him it's too late to get there . . ." And I would say, "Or by the time you finish telling him you can't afford to get there . . ." Bob would say, "That's it! That's the topper!" And he'd walk out, do five minutes and then put the gag in correctly placed. No cue cards there. Just an uncanny sense.'

There were times, though, when Bob gave the impression that other things were more important than the never-ending search for fresh jokes. Once he phoned Denis Goodwin in London and asked him to fly immediately to Berlin to prepare a special radio show monologue.

'When I got there,' said Denis, 'he was far more interested in showing me this beautiful house that belonged to some

German general, that he was living in, than the monologue. It was quite refreshing; he was just like a teenager. He said, "Look at this! It looks just like a Christmas postcard, doesn't it?" And I knew we didn't have much time, so I said, "Do you want to have a look at the monologue, Bob?" He said, "Yeah, that's funny; yeah, I like that; like that..." And he did it, and it went very well!'

But not all Bob's continental dates went so well. In August 1952 he agreed to give a midnight show for a small audience of 900 – paying £10 a head for dinner, champagne and him – at the exclusive Sporting Club de Monte Carlo, on the shores of the Mediterranean. Countless diamonds sparkled on some of the most elegant necks in Europe; Paris gowns revealed golden tans acquired on the best beaches in Europe; the balmy air was filled with the scent of expensive European perfume. And that was all.

For when Bob opened his act with the usual gags, the few Americans sprinkled amongst the audience laughed. The rest sat in stony silence. 'My French is tres mauvais,' he apologized. Then, looking out to sea, he shouted: 'Keep the motor running in that launch – for a quick getaway...'

Still nothing. And then came the final indignity – trains screeching along the tracks behind the club. 'It's the first time I've had to compete with engine drivers,' cracked the comedian ruefully.

After almost an hour's unequal struggle Hope gave up the fight and retired. Only to be the congratulated by the manager. 'Our audiences are cold, but you are the most successful star we've had at the Sporting Club,' he said.

'Who are the others?' asked the comedian, as he headed for the airport and the safety of London.

Unresponsive audiences were never a problem at the Palladium. In that same year Bob easily broke all existing box-office records. This so pleased impresarios Val Parnell and Lew Grade that they decided to have some fun with their star on his last night of the season.

The comedian used a number of unknown stooges during his act, who would walk on with various props on a cue for him. The first time he gave the signal, Val Parnell ambled on in place of the regular assistant. 'That baffled him,' remembers

Palladium stage door-keeper, George Cooper. 'That threw him off a bit! Then a bit later he asked for a trolley to be wheeled on. And Lew Grade wheeled it on from the other side of the stage...'

Bob quickly recovered and tried to turn the tables: 'Is that all you can do – push a trolley?' he goaded Grade.

'Oh no,' came the reply, 'I can dance.'

'Well dance then,' countered the comedian.

With that the orchestra struck up a Charleston and the portly Lew brought the house down with an agile array of steps. Bob had no idea at that time that his agent was a former Charleston dancing champion.

Bob's extensive touring of Britain and Europe during the fifties placed a strain on his already grossly overloaded work schedule. He became a regular commuter back and forth across the Atlantic long before David Frost made it fashionable. There were Californian radio and television commitments to keep, awards to accept, charity functions to attend, Hollywood films to make, and a wife and four children to remind who was boss. 'I was away so much,' said Bob, 'that one morning at breakfast my son Tony came up with "Good morning Bob Hope." Can you imagine that? Having to do a benefit in your own home...'

But at the end of the day, there was always one sure way of shaking off the pressures of show business – go chase a golf ball somewhere.

12

A cheerful mood of optimism was in the air as the Hope limousine purred westwards out of London towards the Principality of Wales. The news that his entry for the 1951 British Amateur Golf Championship had been accepted had delighted Bob almost as much as his first hole-in-one. Every club golfer likes a crack at the big one. And he was no exception.

His arrival at the Royal Porthcawl course in Glamorgan caused a sensation. Police struggled with two thousand fans as they stampeded the famous links just to catch a glimpse of him. He was hard to miss – decked out in a blue and red shirt, yellow jersey, grey trousers, tartan socks, and with a garish tartan tam-o-shanter perched jauntily upon his head.

This was the second time an American entertainer had stolen the limelight at the ancient event. Crosby had created a similar stir the year before, when he competed at St Andrews in Scotland. But his joy was short-lived – he went out after only 16 holes. The memory stirred Bob to remark: 'Don't tell Crosby about this. He'll be green with envy when I get through the first round . . .'

It was not to be. Even though the crowd rooted for him all the way, Bob's joke turned sour on the 17th green when Chris Fox – a tall, bespectacled and modest 41-year-old Yorkshireman – beat him two and one after a three-hour marathon match. Consoled in defeat by Marilyn Maxwell, Bob was forced to admit that his golf that day had not matched his colourful costume, nor his four handicap. Local statisticians calculated, rather unkindly, that his score for the round would have been a 91, compared with the course par of 74.

But Bob managed to live up to his image of the happy-go-lucky gagster. Much of his humour was directed at a slightly bemused pipe-smoking opponent. 'What are you smoking in that pipe, brother?' he queried after one near-perfect drive. And, 'What will Crosby say when he hears that The Man With The Pipe has beaten me?'

Bob took no chances. Anticipating a long-range riposte from the crooner, he dashed off a telegram to Hollywood: '*You lost three and two stop I was only beaten two and one stop How about that stop Regards Hope stop*'

The following day, British newspapers gave great coverage to Bob's Porthcawl antics and accused him of demeaning the championship's stature. They were most annoyed about him posing for photographers in a bobby's helmet after the game and by a joke he made on the first tee. 'I'm here to put some comic relief into this serious game,' he had quipped.

One of Britain's best loved actors stepped into the affray with an 'Unfair to Bob Hope' letter to the *Daily Express*:

Bob Hope played very bad golf indeed in the first round of our Amateur Championship. As a result of this he was soundly defeated by an opponent who played a great deal better. So far so good (and incidentally the last person to complain would be Bob Hope).

But why the sniping? Why the sneers? Almost without exception our national Press has seen fit to have a field day at the loser's expense.

Bob Hope, as I can testify, has consistently scored in the low seventies on his home course – Lakeside, California – and consequently was well qualified to enter himself for the British Amateur Championship.

I know him well enough to state that he entered the competition as a private sportsman with a great love of the game and of England, and not, as many newspapers have suggested, as a professional entertainer in search of publicity.

If I may coin an American phrase: 'Just how unsporting can sportswriters get?'

The letter was signed 'David Niven, Pinewood Studios'.

While Hope pursued golfing and stage glory in Britain, Paramount was trying to come up with a new *Road* for him to travel. It was proving difficult and there would be time for *The Paleface* to become a proud parent. *Son of Paleface* went into production early in 1952, with Bob once again lasciviously chasing Jane Russell, aided this time by Roy Rogers and Trigger. Although the film was originally intended simply to cash in on the success of its predecessor, it transpired as an hilarious spoof of westerns in general. Bob played the son of the zany dentist character he created four years previously, a callow Harvard graduate called Junior.

Jane Russell was well pleased to be making her second Hope picture. Her initial casting in the first was, she considers, very fortunate and largely due to Bob. Having made an impact in *The Outlaw* Howard Hughes' notorious sex-western featuring her as the girlfriend of Billy the Kid, she was summoned for an urgent audition at Paramount.

Recalls Jane: 'I wasn't dressed properly to go for an interview about a motion picture; I had jeans on and was scruffy. But I went down there. And Bob came in. He said, "I guess she'll do. I think she'll do? Yes! Turn around. Yes! I guess she'll do?" From that moment on we just got along beautifully; it was rather marvellous because we're both Geminis and we have a similar sense of humour.'

Jane's untidiness was caused by a simple case of oversleeping – a fault which was to provide them with another moment to remember. It came during a record-breaking *Paleface* promotional season at the New York Paramount, just as Miss Russell thought she had solved the tardiness problem.

'I stayed in an hotel right across the street from the theatre,' she explains, 'because I couldn't be bothered trying to find a cab. I wanted to sleep as long as possible and if I ran to bed after the last show – we were doing something like eight shows a day – I could get my nine hours sleep a night. I always slept in a long flannel nightgown. And I would throw my fur coat over it, run across the street, and then zip into my beads (stage costume) when I got over there, getting on stage just as Bob was announcing me.'

But like all well-laid plans, it had to go wrong once.

Says Jane: 'One day I came tearing across – I had overslept – and there he was announcing me! And I was still in my flannel nightgown! So I ran to the side-wings and threw the fur coat open wide so he could see, and whispered, "I'll be with you in a minute..." Then I went running back to the dressing-room and got into the beads!'

Hope carried on gagging until Jane finished dressing and then calmly introduced her as if nothing was amiss. 'Nothing throws him,' she says. 'He can absolutely handle anything.'

The second *Paleface* also featured another major star – Bing was again present for his customary walk-on part; although this time it was more of a drive-off scene. Right at the start of the film the Groaner was seen driving home from the studio. 'What's this?' said Hope. 'This is an old character actor on the Paramount lot whom we try to keep working. He's supporting a large family, but I guarantee this fellow won't be in the picture tonight!'

By the time *Son of Paleface* was in the can Paramount had come up with a script and a destination for the sixth *Road* picture. Dotty and the boys were off to Bali, and for the first time in glorious Technicolor too. The news sent them scrambling for the atlas. Having discovered that it was just the merest of dots on the map – in Indonesia – Bob and Bing settled down to bargain a sizable financial deal for themselves. Again they each took a third of the profits and bore two-thirds of the costs, but achieved a major breakthrough in wresting the copyright from Paramount.

When shooting started in May it was patently obvious that the five-year lay-off had in no way dampened their youthful exuberance; if anything it had been heightened. They turned the film into an even greater vehicle for their personal insult routine. Typical samples of the sort of Hope-Crosby nonsense that went on: when Bing was about to croon, Bob made an aside to the audience, 'He's gonna sing now folks – now's the time to go out and get the popcorn!'

And when Crosby said, 'I've got a dame lined up for you!' Hope retorted, 'A dame! What's wrong with her?'

Later Bob alluded further to his envy of Bing's singing by calling him a 'collapsible Como'. But the Groaner got his revenge in the end – by walking off with not only Dorothy

Lamour, but guest star Jane Russell too.

Frustrated at losing Lamour, Bob conjured up Jane by blowing a chanter over a woven basket (a trick he had used successfully before). But when she materialized, she plumped for Crosby instead. 'What are you going to do with two girls?' whined Hope.

'That's my problem,' came the airy reply as the crooner wandered off arm-in-arm.

'This picture isn't over yet,' pleaded Hope as he struggled to keep THE END from appearing on the screen. 'Call the producer . . . call the writers . . .'

The *Road to Bali*, described at its premiere as 'a pantomime for grown-ups', was an expensive film, making extensive use of trick photography and big-name guest artists. Along with Jane Russell were Humphrey Bogart, Dean Martin, Jerry Lewis and Bing's younger brother Bob.

Bogart had come fresh from winning the Academy Award for best actor in *The African Queen* and they jumped on the bandwagon by recreating his famous hauling a boat through a swamp scene. He also offered Bob a chance to show his envy of Bing's getting a best actor Oscar for his portrayal of the priest, Father O'Malley, in the 1945 movie *Going My Way*. During a mirage scene Bogey forgets his Oscar and Crosby picks it up. 'Give me that!' snaps Hope, snatching it away from him. 'You've already got one!'

Not all the fun and games were on screen, though. Both the crooner and the comedian celebrated birthdays while making *Bali*. When Bing notched up 51 years, protesting that he was 'really only 48', Bob and Dorothy presented him with a cake, and only one candle. 'To save your embarrassment,' read the inscription.

Bob's 49 years, 'I really am', were marked by an old-fashioned rocking chair from Bing and Dotty and a specially printed gag edition of the show business bible *Variety*. 'CROSBY BREAKS IN NEW BOY' screamed the mock headline. '*Entertainment King auditions new stooge replacement*,' said a sub-heading. And underneath was a large picture of Crosby with Jerry Lewis.

Another event occurred during *Bali*: American television conducted its first coast-to-coast fund-raising 'marathon' (a type of show now known as telethons). Bob was chosen to host the gruelling thirteen-and-a-half hour affair. He persuaded Bing to take a weekend off from golf to fly with him to New York. It was the Groaner's television debut and he helped Bob exhort viewers to phone in and pledge money towards a $750,000 fund to be used for sending athletes to the 1952 Helsinki Olympics. The show was a huge success, but over-ran and the pair had to bear two-thirds of the cost of a missed day's filming.

August and September were hectic months for Bob. He just had time to accept the Al Jolson Medal for entertaining the American armed forces (Jolson had died in October 1950 after returning from entertaining in Korea and the award was struck in his honour) before he was attending the Republican and Democratic political conventions. He had recently swapped Lever Brothers soaps for Chesterfield cigarettes and his new sponsors wanted a series of five-minute commentaries from each event. It was not Bob's usual style of radio, but he did it anyway. Then he was off back to Europe; there were stage shows to do on the continent and in Britain, and he had a very special golfing date with Bing Crosby at Maidenhead in England.

The Duke of Edinburgh had enlisted their help to raise money for his National Playing Fields Association. They were to play a charity golf match at the Temple course against Welsh crooner Donald Peers and comedian Ted Ray. Bob arrived in time to give some more aid to the Clubland centre at Camberwell. Then, clubs at the ready, he joined Bing at the course.

The match itself, played on a Sunday, was a near riot. Thousands of non-golfing spectators turned up and created havoc all over the course. The Duke's Association benefited greatly, but the occasion did little to further the cause of golf. Even the usually placid Bing was shocked. 'It was quite an experience,' he said. 'They'd never tried this sort of event in England before and they had no conception of what kind of gallery it would attract.' As the fans jostled for the best view of their idols the four-some fought its way to the first tee, only to be confronted by a solid wall of people stretching right across the fairway.

'We're going to drive-off down that way,' yelled an unusually subdued Hope.

'We don't care, go ahead,' shouted a host of voices.

Said Ted Ray: 'The first part of Temple is downhill. It was like looking down a black keyhole! Eighty per cent of those people had never seen a golf course before; they didn't realize that a golf-ball leaves a club at about 180 miles an hour – or in my case 110 – and can cause an awful lot of damage.'

Worse was to come. The marshalls let the crowd get completely out of hand; children were building sand-castles in the bunkers and women with stiletto heels strolled casually over the greens. Although concerned, Bob tried hard to keep up a steady flow of gags to ease the tension. 'By that time,' said Ted Ray, 'Bing was pale with fear.'

Soon, what they all feared finally happened: Hope badly sliced a ball and it flew straight at a press photographer, smashing the lens of his expensive camera. As the group filed from the tee, the photographer grabbed Ted Ray by the arm and demanded to know what he was going to do about it. 'Don't ask me,' joked Ted, 'ask Mr Hope – he has got more money than I have!'

At the next hole Ted got another funny line in when, as he was about to drive, he warned one woman in the pressing crowd: 'Excuse me, madam, would you mind either standing back or closing your mouth – I've lost four balls already . . .'

He was not the only one. Balls were vanishing like magic into souvenir hunters' pockets almost before they were struck. Finally, at the tenth green, the quartet was forced to abandon any hopes of playing a full round. A car was brought up and took them on a mad dash for the 18th tee to try and get ahead of the teeming fans.

It was a classic scene that might have come from any *Road* film: a big black limousine, with Bob and Bing bouncing around in the back seat and Ray and Peers clinging to the running boards outside, careering perilously across the countryside.

They reached the tee ahead of the madding crowd and drove-off hurriedly. Ted and Donald won the match, if it could be termed such, by one hole – the last. Bob blamed himself for 'pulling a seven-iron shot when we were still in with a chance'.

Bob later sent Ted Ray a telegram, which read: '*Bing and I challenge you and Donald to a return game in Hollywood stop With just a few of your relatives present this time stop All the best stop Bob stop.'*

After the shambles at Maidenhead, Bob had less than 24 hours to get an act together for a big charity show on 21 September 1952 at the Stoll Theatre, in London's Kingsway, in aid of the Clubland settlement and the Midwife Teachers' Training College. Jack Buchanan was compering the first half, he the second. And he had a special surprise for everyone – Bing had agreed to make his long-awaited British stage debut. Once again there was a touch of chaos about the proceedings. Newspapers got wind of the event and the theatre was seething with scribes and photographers. The Groaner took refuge in a nearby hostelry.

As the late Denis Goodwin saw it: 'During the interval I went backstage with a couple of extra lines and Bob told me, "Bing is in the pub over the road! I'm going to go and get him out of there."'

Also on the bill was Donald Peers. 'I was on fairly early in the first half,' he recalled, 'and I nipped round to the back of the stalls afterwards. Bob Hope came on and did some gags – talking about "Dad" Crosby – and suddenly the spotlight moved from Hope and there was Bing, with his pipe, leaning against the scenery. The applause was something like you'd never heard. It was just fantastic.'

By 1953 Bob was wearing a new hat, that of President of the American Guild of Variety Artists. The role gave him a busy twelve months: a New York Friars Club dinner for Paramount founder Adolph Zukor to mark the 50th anniversary of motion pictures; a charity baseball game in aid of the Damon Runyan Cancer Fund with Jack Benny, George Burns and Groucho Marx; and a charity golf tournament in New York with the Duke of Windsor.

He thought his appointment was the highest honour the profession could pay him – until Charles Brackett stepped forward to present him with a special Oscar at the 1952 Academy of Motion Picture Arts and Sciences awards dinner in Hollywood. *'For enormous contributions to the laughter of the world and your services to the film industry,'* read the inscription. It was quite a night. 'I just don't believe it,' mumbled the comedian.

There was hardly time that year even to sign a new long-term radio contract for $2 million with the giant General Foods concern for six shows a week. 'The biggest single season deal in radio history,' proclaimed the publicity handout. The Bob Hope Jell-O Show, as they called it, broke with tradition and took the comedian into America's kitchens for the first time. He moved from the evening 'living-room' slot to woo housewives for 15 minutes every weekday morning at 9.30. His sixth programme of the week would be a half-hour night-time variety show. Daytime radio, Hope-style, was voted a hit. The show biz daily *Variety* reviewed his first week:

It may well set the pattern for a complete reshuffle in network radio programming, in that a number of other name personalities may follow Hope into the after-breakfast hours if he can draw a rating ... the Tuesday stanza gave indication that the show is Hope at his oldtime radio best – and that's good.

Daily radio bit deep into his time, and so did his first full-length 60-minute colour television show, but Paramount was a relentless employer. The company's other big comedy team, Jerry Lewis and Dean Martin, were making *Scared Stiff* – yet another remake of his 1940 film *The Ghost Breakers* – and Bob had a unbilled walk-on part. Then they wanted him to exercise his manly talents as an ageing chorus boy in the farcical melodrama, *Here Come The Girls*, with Bing's renowned singing partner, Rosemary Clooney.

Says Rosie: 'Oh yes! One of the world's worst pictures! Here come the girls – there went the girls ... it was a very fast, nothing at all film. But it was funny, because Bob was doing about twelve other things at the same time. It seemed to me that he would show up for about an hour a day and we would shoot around him the rest of the time.'

Bob's amorous antics in *Here Come The Girls* endeared him to few bar Paramount – who saw him as the Great Lover.

13

The philandering adventures of the legendary eighteenth-century Venetian scoundrel and imposter Casanova de Seingalt have always fascinated Hollywood. The Great Lover, as the Dream Factory so astutely named him, is a screen character of endless potential.

So when Paramount suggested the costume farce, *Casanova's Big Night*, Bob was quietly confident of getting an immortal role. After all, had he not been the lead in *The Great Lover*, in 1949, and romantically pursued Rhonda Fleming? The fact that he had only played a Boy Scout leader hardly mattered at all, surely?

The studio bosses told him not to worry – this time he would get to pose as the famed knave, a neat twist they thought, and the up-and-coming Vincent Price would have a small part ... as the errant Lover.

Casanova's Big Night was memorable only for its all-star cast – Joan Fontaine, Basil Rathbone, John Carradine, Lon Chaney and a young Raymond Burr – Bob in drag as a Venetian dowager, and a surprise double-ending. Just as an axe was descending upon Hope's neck, the action was halted. 'That is how Paramount planned to end the picture,' intoned an announcer. 'Now an alternative ending written, directed and produced by Bob 'Orson Welles' Hope.' The comic was then pictured escaping execution; killing his enemies three at a time; then, encircled by swordsmen, he ducked – going free as they pierced one another. 'There, wasn't that better?' he asked the audience.

They obviously thought so; the film took more than $3,000,000 at the box-office.

There was fighting off-screen during the picture too. Bob had recently signed a lengthy contract with NBC for a series of television specials. Paramount objected, arguing that he was 'selling out to the enemy'. Hollywood still believed that television would kill the cinema, just as movies had seen the end of vaudeville. Hope would not accept such a premise. He calculated that both could survive side-by-side and eventually complement each other. And he told the studio as much. Bob proved how strong his convictions were at the next opportunity, when he agreed to forgo his salary for *The Seven Little Foys* and just take a percentage of the profits, albeit a sizable one.

The project was a brain-child of two former Hope radio show writers, Mel Shavelson and Jack Rose, who had hit upon the idea of doing a film biography of the entertainer Eddie Foy. He was a vaudevillian who had put his seven children to work after his wife died and made them into the most famous family act in the old-time theatre. Rose and Shavelson had a first-class screenplay, but no finance. Hope liked what he read, waived his fee and sold the whole package to Paramount as a joint venture.

It was a milestone in his career. For the first time he played a real-life character and, although there was plenty of comedy, he was making his debut as a dramatic actor. The film was his fiftieth since *Going Spanish* 20 years before. The one-liners he had survived on for so long were to go in favour of long sections of dramatic speech. Bob worked hard on *The Seven Little Foys*. In an effort to capture the real Eddie Foy, he read every piece of historical material he could find, watched the vaudevillian's silent movies and sought out the family for help. When the result reached the screen, the critics adjudged him to have succeeded. Said *The Times*:

> The children, whose accompaniment of their gifted father on the stage was, apparently, reluctant, are a novel kind of foil for Mr Bob Hope, who gives a delightful performance as the implacable Foy. Fortunately for the film the Foys do not

seem to have had much to do with the world outside the theatre. This makes for an unusual singleness of purpose in this kind of story.

The New York *Daily News* was even more euphoric:

> Bob Hope doesn't have to take any more insults from Bing Crosby about his acting. Hope can now hold up his head with Hollywood's dramatic thespians as, for the first time in his career, Hope isn't playing Hope on the screen. He is acting and doing a commendable job.

Working almost as hard as Bob on the picture was celebrated guest star James Cagney. He recreated his 1942 Oscar-winning portrayal of song-and-dance supremo George M. Cohen from the film *Yankee Doodle Dandy*. Cagney insisted on doing it for nothing: 'As a way of paying back all the food and kindness I had from the Foys as a young actor.'

Hope and Cagney spent days in the rehearsal hall perfecting a 'simple little dance number' tossed into the script by Mel Shavelson. The hard-nosed Foy and equally tough Cohen had been rivals, and the 'little' dance arose out of a challenge issued during a Friars Club banquet. Their efforts produced a show-stopper, the highlight of the movie and a magical piece of cinema that is now regarded as a classic.

Pausing only long enough to give Maurice Chevalier his first chance on American television, Bob packed his bags and caught a plane. He had an appointment with Queen Elizabeth II at the Palladium in London.

The 1954 Royal Variety Show boasted one of its biggest star casts ever. Over thirty American and British entertainers lined up to greet the Queen on 1 November, including Noel Coward, Howard Keel, Frankie Lane, Guy Mitchell, Moira Lister, Norman Wisdom, Peter Sellers, Jack Buchanan, Donald Wolfit, Jack Hawkins, and of course Bob Hope.

'It's the greatest vaudeville theatre in the world,' said Bob. 'Palladium audiences are just sensational. And Queen Elizabeth, well...'

Twenty-four hours after the Command Performance Bob flew to Paris to entertain American soldiers and landed right in the arms of the law. He had forgotten his passport in the rush and the French authorities took a dim view, even threatening to lock him up at one point. As usual he talked his way out of trouble. Two days later he was made an honorary citizen of Paris by the President of the Municipal Council.

'This is a wonderful country,' he quipped, 'they give you the choice of going to jail or becoming a citizen of Paris . . .'

During his 48 hours in France Bob gave four shows: first he performed at La Rochelle on the Bay of Biscay, then he drove the 150 miles to Chateauroux for the second show of the evening; a plane took him back to Paris, where the next day he was at the Olympia Theatre before going on stage at the Hotel Continental to help the US Marines celebrate their 179th birthday.

His European sojourn was tough on his writers. At one time three of them were holed up in a London hotel room for three days and nights churning out new jokes one after another. 'Gee,' said Hope when he finally made an appearance, 'I've been very inconsiderate of you people. You boys probably haven't seen anything of London! Don't go away . . .'

With that he disappeared downstairs to his room, leaving the trio speculating on what fantastic treat he had in store for them. A few minutes later 40 postcards of famous London scenes arrived at their door. Everyone laughed, but the gagmen not so heartily as Bob.

The comedian's next overseas tour, during Christmas of the same year, took him up to the icy wastes of the Arctic Circle and Thule Air Base in Greenland, a remote installation perched on the edge of the icecap overlooking Baffin Bay, and home for the airmen who form part of North America's outer air defence network. They almost felt outnumbered by Bob, his twenty-strong troupe of entertainers, the US Air Force Secretary Harold Talbott and what seemed like the whole NBC television division.

The Thule trip was a new departure for Hope; the tour would be filmed by television cameras for the first time and the result would be edited into a Bob Hope special. Hedda Hopper, actor William Holden (recent winner of an Academy Award for his performance in the war film *Stalag 17*) and an unknown college beauty queen, Anita Ekberg, helped the experiment succeed. From then on the Christmas tours were recorded and slotted into his television schedule.

This not only gave Bob a ready-made subject for at least one show a year, but the revenue from his sponsors helped off-set the tremendous cost of the annual operation; which, apart from USO contributions and taxpayer-funded transportation, was born by the Hope organization. Later, at the height of the anti-Vietnam war campaign, Bob was accused of 'exploiting conflict' and 'cashing-in on human misery' by using the televised troop shows to fill his own coffers. But all that was a million laughs away from Greenland in the winter of 1954:

I'm very happy to be here at Thule. The temperature is 36 below. We don't know below what – the thermometer just went over the hill . . .

It's really cold here. One guy jumped out of his bunk at six this morning, ran in and turned on the shower – and was stoned to death . . .

It was so cold last night – one GI fell out of bed and broke his pyjamas . . .

Up here, a pin-up calendar isn't a luxury – it's a necessity . . .

Bob returned home to the warmth of California suffering from exhaustion. His 52nd birthday was fast approaching and he seemed to be feeling the pace of more than 30 non-stop years in show business. In February 1955 he informed the world that he would be retiring temporarily from television to devote more time to his family and to making independent films for his own company. 'Because I am tired, run down and I want a rest,' he said.

Bob was echoing warnings from his doctors. For some time they had been warning of the consequences of overwork and for once he paid attention. He left with Dolores on a peaceful cruise in the Pacific. But the lay-off soon bored him. He quickly returned to Hollywood, and the movie studios. 'Fish don't applaud,' he explained blandly.

He went to work on *That Certain Feeling*, a romantic comedy co-starring Eve Marie Saint, George Sanders and singer Pearl Bailey. The film realised an ambition for its directors, Melvin Frank and Norman Panama. A decade earlier they had been upset by the way their screenplay for *Monsieur Beaucaire* was treated. Mel felt it was an 'incredibly good script', but ruined by director George Marshall. 'He went so wild in the last reel,' alleges Frank, 'that he nullified what we had done to establish

Hope as a believable eighteenth-century character.'

Mel was also piqued by a fight with Bob. 'Which he won,' recalls the writer ruefully. It arose during the planning of a suicide scene: Hope's character was supposed to be discussing the merits of various weapons with a friend.

'Why not have me suggest a gun?' said the comedian. 'Then he could ask me, "What's so good about that?" And I could say, "Well, you put it to your head and it goes . . . Bing!"'

'Please don't put a Crosby joke in the first reel of this picture,' implored Frank. 'We're trying to establish you as a barber to the Court of Louis XIV and . . . My God! If you put a Crosby joke in . . . you're just going to ruin it.'

'He put it in,' says Mel, 'and got a big laugh. That made us determined to direct our own pictures, but it took us a few years to get there.'

That Certain Feeling heralded the end of Hope's 17-year association with Paramount that, apart from the one spat about money, had lasted for 40 films. Now he was to make films for whoever wanted him and although this would include Paramount, Metro-Goldwyn-Mayer were first in line. Cary Grant had turned down the latest Katherine Hepburn film, *The Iron Petticoat*, and writer Ben Hecht had ended up on Bob's doorstep. It was a cold war political satire in the *Ninotchka* mould, with Hope playing a captain in the psychological warfare division of the US Army based in Germany. Hepburn was a Russian pilot who crashes in the Western zone and then falls in love with the captain. Betty Box produced, and James Robertson Justice, Robert Helpmann and David Kossoff co-starred.

The plot was tame compared with the financial and production arrangements. MGM distributed it, the tiny independent British Lion helped make it and Harry Saltzman – later to hit the jackpot with the James Bond films – had a hand in funding it. But for all that it was Bob's first major motion picture outside the United States.

His teaming with the formidable Hepburn electrified everyone. None more so than the cast, who expected fireworks. 'The word was,' says David Kossoff, 'that Katherine Hepburn was very difficult; an absolute professional, but very difficult. And everyone was slightly frightened. This wasn't helped by the fact that on the first morning she came on to the set and immediately sat down on the floor, and conducted a question and answer from there. This demoralized everybody and we were expecting ... not trouble, I think that's the wrong word, but we thought things were going to be a little that way. But not for one minute, throughout the film, was there any sign of this. They didn't exactly go out drinking in the evenings; they went off in different directions, but every day their studio behaviour was flawless. It was a great lesson to everybody.'

With so many pre-production problems, the complicated chain of command and the edginess during shooting, it was obvious that something had to give. Hecht started it by taking a $275 back page in the *Hollywood Reporter* to tell Hope and the rest of Hollywood what he thought of the finished product:

My dear partner Bob Hope,
    This is to notify you that I have removed my name as author from our mutilated venture, *The Iron Petticoat*.
    Unfortunately, your other partner, Katherine Hepburn, can't shy out of the fractured picture with me.
    Although her magnificent comic performance has been blow-torched out of the film, there is enough left of the Hepburn footage to identify her for her sharpshooters.
    I am assured by my hopeful predators that *The Iron Petticoat* will go over big with people 'who can't get enough of Bob Hope'.
    Let us hope this swooning contingent is not confined to yourself and your euphoric agent, Louie Shurr.
    Yours anonymously,
    Ben Hecht

Hope was furious and angrily hit back in the same organ, and in a similar sarcastic vein:

My dear ex-partner Ben,
    I am most understanding. The way things are going you simply can't afford to be associated with a hit.
    As for Kate Hepburn, I don't think she was depressed with the preview audience rave about her performance.
    Let's do all our correspondence this way in future ... in print.

Yours,
Bob (Blow-Torch) Hope

The row was the talk of Hollywood. But at the end of the day the people had their say and neither artist was adjudged to have given one of their best performances. Surprisingly, the critics were not too unkind. Commented *The Times*:

Miss Hepburn has not only the problem of coping with the contrasting style of Mr Hope, and preventing the film from turning itself into a tug-of-war with no holds barred, but she is throughout haunted by the haunting shadow of Miss Greta Garbo in *Ninotchka* ... the more the matter is pondered, the better, indeed, does Mr Hope seem to come out of a very ticklish business.

Bob was in hot water again before *Petticoat* was released – this time with a large part of the Canadian nation. In mid-November 1955 he cracked a number of gags about Princess Margaret's recently broken romance with Group Captain Peter Townsend on a television programme.

Next time I'm in London I expect to see the Princess's handkerchiefs hanging out of the Palace windows to dry ...

Townsend should have known better than to try to play the Palace – I never could ...

Coast-to-coast airing of the show in the United States brought little adverse reaction. But when the Canadian Broadcasting Corporation put it out on ten stations in Ontario and Quebec, its headquarters was besieged with angry telephone calls. Then the *Toronto Telegram* condemned the wisecracks as 'in extremely poor taste, off-colour and not very funny'. Hope was stunned by the ferocity of the criticism and issued a hasty apology. 'All my friends in England will know that I meant no offence,' he said. 'Whenever I make a joke about England or any British person I get squawks from everywhere but England itself. I have had the honour of meeting Princess Margaret. On my last broadcast I also made a joke about her – that everyone in England approved of her marriage to Group Captain Townsend and all they were waiting for now was to hear from Danny Kaye! There was no complaint about that.' He went on to explain that the jokes were 'made in the same spirit in which I've wisecracked about President Eisenhower and Sir Winston Churchill'.

A few weeks later Bob was in London making a film for Prince Philip and, in doing so, turned down an invitation to perform at the Windsor Castle staff Christmas party before the Queen and Princess Margaret. 'That shows you how much ill-feeling there is about the incident,' he told reporters.

The film, a £7,000 short for the Duke's National Playing Fields Association, had Bob clad in mock cricket gear – a striped cap and shorts two sizes too small. He was supported by a cast of small boys from a St Pancras youth club and the actor Kenneth More. The Prince opened the feature, striding out towards a cricket pitch, and the comedian closed it. More than £200,000 was raised for the royal charity.

Bob's next British performance came in June of the following year. Old friend Sir Laurence Olivier roped him in for the *Night of 100 Stars* charity show he was organizing at the Palladium. They had known each other since 1938, when Olivier was in Hollywood under contract to Sam Goldwyn, and Bob had agreed to close the show despite the fact that it did not start until midnight and he was due to catch a plane at eight the next morning. It was after two before he finally got on stage, but there was no question of short-changing the packed audience. Bob gave them the works, including a string of Crosby jokes, and even came up with a topical Jack Benny gag:

They asked Jack Benny if he would do something for the Actors' Orphanage – so he shot both his parents and moved in . . .

It's not that he's cheap – he just hates to give away money after he's memorized the serial numbers . . .

'I couldn't believe it,' says Olivier. 'There he was still on the stage at the Palladium at three o'clock in the morning! I had to interrupt him! I said, "Ladies and gentlemen . . . this is too much . . . Bob has got to go now . . . he's got to be on a plane flying to America at eight o'clock. We can accept just so much charity from people; we can't have any more from Bob tonight. I'm very sorry." I then turned to Bob and said, "Will you please get out . . . bless your heart . . . and thank you a million, million times . . ." And he just sort of waved at me, and disappeared.'

As an actor himself Sir Laurence found himself observing Bob's stage presence closely and being intrigued by his deportment. 'It's very attractive, the extreme dignity of his entrances,' he says. 'He's always come on, whenever I've seen him, as if he were a very portly man. Even when he was quite young; he came on as if he was carrying a great weight of almost civic dignity in front of him. It's very amusing.'

Another English actor to notice the Hope entrance was David Kossoff. It was during rehearsals for the comedian's hugely successful Prince of Wales season. 'I watched him walk towards the microphone,' recalls Kossoff, 'and then turn round and pace back into the wings. And he did that about four times, and I sat there with my mouth open. He was doing this slightly swivel-hipped walk he has; it's a kind of cocky walk; which is almost a trade-mark, with the feet slightly splayed-out. It was essential to that man, for some reason of his own, to know how long that walk was to the microphone. And at that time he was the biggest, biggest thing – and there he was rehearsing his walk to the mike! Imagine that . . .'

1956 gave Bob his second screen biographical role, as Mayor James Walker in Paramount's *Beau James*. Walker, a one-time songwriter and occasional entertainer, became New York's most renowned politician and a gay blade in the dizzy 1920s. Once more Hope was given a complex character and a chance to combine comedy with drama. Vera Miles, Alexis Smith and Jimmy Durante assisted him. Portraying Jimmy Walker brought him many plaudits, including this from *The Times*:

The part is played – surprisingly enough – by Mr Bob Hope, and played straight, without any reaching after farce or absurdity. He plays it well, because he understands show-manship and knows that it is a thing of gaiety, effrontery – and panache. One believes in him because one can also believe in his background – New York in the boisterous, bounding 1920s, when people, as Mr Alistair Cooke dryly remarks in his commentary, were at least having fun.

There was more fun later that year – 1957 – when Bob turned ideas man and movie producer, and talked United Artists into releasing a story of his own called *Paris Holiday*. It was made in a rambling chateau at Gambais, near Paris, and co-starred the horse-toothed French comedian Fernandel.

'This film will be a battle of the faces,' declared Hope. 'I'm supposed to have a flexible face, but against this guy I feel like a straight man...'

Bob's story-line had an American entertainer and a Frenchman becoming involved with a bevy of beautiful girls and a spy ring. In retrospect he may have been wiser to have filmed what went on behind the scenes. Fernandel spoke not a word of English, or American, and Hope could only painfully articulate 'Bonjour'. Two days before shooting started the Frenchman flatly refused to appear unless the screenplay was rewritten. 'He wanted a bigger part than he had,' says Bob. 'So I had my gag writers change the script. The way things were, with no one understanding anyone, the guy would have felt we were plotting against him every time we talked in English in front of him.'

Next, Fernandel came up with a demand which really rocked Hope – another $10,000 in addition to the $100,000 he was already getting, and he wanted it in cash. Hope had no option but to dispatch the faithful 'Doc' Shurr to a friendly Swiss bank in Geneva.

Then Anthony Steele, husband of Anita Ekberg – who had a supporting role – contracted scarlet fever. Before he was hospitalized Steele frequently visited the set and the whole unit spent many anxious days searching their bodies for signs of the highly contagious disease.

When *Paris Holiday* was finally wrapped up, Bob needed one – it came in a million dollars over budget to mixed reviews. 'Back to the great days of Keaton and Lloyd,' shrilled the *Daily Telegraph*; 'An unsatisfactory mixture of styles,' moaned *The Times*.

But there was little time for a rest – the road to Moscow was beckoning.

14

The Cold War between the United States and the Soviet Union was still blowing decidedly chilly early in 1958. But there were signs of a distinct thaw – Krushchev and Eisenhower were to meet for summit talks, and the USSR Ministry of Culture had given its approval to a visit by Bob Hope.

'If anybody can thaw out the Cold War by going to Moscow it's Bob Hope,' said Eisenhower's Vice President, Richard Nixon.

'And if I've got any Russian jokes left over, I'll give them to Ike for the summit conference,' quipped Hope.

However, the road to Moscow was by no means easy; it took Hope 21 days and 10,000 miles to get his visa. First he flew to London and waited in vain for days for the piece of official paper which would let him in. Then in desperation he flew to Washington; only to be told it was waiting for him back in London. Madame Tamara Mamedova, the Soviet Embassy's cultural attaché in Washington, explained: 'Mr Hope moves so fast we couldn't catch up with him.'

Formalities were resolved in time for him to arrive in Moscow for his six-day visit on 16 March. His arrival flummoxed the dour Russian reporters. They expected serious answers to their questions.

Do you think your type of humour will go over well in Russia? 'I would like to find one country in the world where I can be a hit! If necessary, I would go to Tibet for that.'

Would you like to meet Mr Krushchev during your visit? 'I would like to explain Bing Crosby to him.'

Does the cold worry you? 'I have been to so many cold places: Iceland, Greenland, Alaska – and Hollywood's Academy Award presentations.'

For the foreign press in Moscow, Bob had some ready-made jibes about the visa delays. 'I can't understand why it took so long,' he said slyly. 'I gave the names of two czars who would guarantee my good behaviour ... Cary Grant got his Soviet visa in five days – they always did favour the peasants here.'

It soon became clear that the Moscovites were not going to provide the best sounding-board for his brand of comedy. But just as he was beginning to get depressed, all was saved by a show at the American Embassy staff club, when he entertained the entire diplomatic corps:

The State Department was glad to let me come here, because I'm co-operative, I'm personable, I'm charming – and I'm expendable.

I had a little trouble getting my visa. I guess they were worried about the capitalistic influence. But I explained our income tax system – and they yelled TOVARICH.

I got a wonderful tribute at the airport; they fired twenty-one shots in the air in my honour – of course, it would have been nicer if they'd waited for the plane to land.

Surprisingly enough, I'm not having any trouble with the language – nobody speaks to me.

You know, the Russian language is very guttural. I cleared my throat in a restaurant today – and a waitress slapped my face.

The Russian trip taught Bob a few lessons about his world of comedy. For instance, being a jokester in the Soviet Union could be a risky occupation. 'They had a guy there who used to rib the Communists a little bit,' he recalls, 'and they put him away for a while. They actually did – to clean him up for a little bit!'

He also found that his countrymen could be sensitive too. 'As soon as you begin to talk about Russia,' he said later, 'people begin to cringe a little. They realize this is a very serious enemy and it is no kidding matter. When you make a gag about it, you can hear the audience start to build up to laugh and then fall away into silence.'

Much of the problem was due to the unsophisticated nature

of American television audiences in the late 1950s. And Bob, who had that year ended his 24-year radio career to concentrate on television, found he had to be very careful.

'When you're on television you're playing to a mass audience,' he said at the time, 'and they don't mind if you kid the White House or you kid the President, but just don't get into any other field. You are really in trouble if you tell a religious or any kind of racial joke; then the hammer will fall on your head.'

Television was the prime mover behind his journey to Moscow. General Motors were prepared to pay $2,250,000 for eight shows a year and Bob realized that to continue commanding that sort of top money, his 'specials' would have to be very special indeed. (Currently a Bob Hope television special costs in the region of $1,000,000 to get on the air.) What could be more special than the first television programme from the Soviet capital?

Says his head writer and producer at the time, Mort Lachman, 'He wanted to be first at everything. We even tried to get into China! If we'd succeeded, Bob Hope would have made China before Nixon. The specials are to Bob's credit and nobody else's; he really tries to make an event out of every show, they're always hooked to something new. And also he makes the subject something he's interested in.'

Since 1958 Hope has been the highest rated television performer in the United States; few of his specials have slipped out of the top ten shows in almost thirty years of continuous exposure, though they have often been belittled by the critics. In 1970, and again in 1971, his Christmas show scored the largest Neilsen rating ever returned for a variety 'one-off'. And his opening programme for the 1972 season achieved a viewing audience second only to the showing of the film *Love Story* the year before. Such success was built upon Bob's early decision to limit his television appearances, apart from guest shots on other stars' shows.

According to leading Hollywood show business columnist, James Bacon, artists like Bob Hope and George Burns have survived the rigours of television for another reason, their vaudeville backgrounds. 'In the old hoofing days of vaudeville,' says Bacon, 'if you didn't come across you were pulled – you might be fired in the matinee and not do the evening show. It was a life or death existence. So these guys are hungry comedians; they're still hungry; not for the money, but hungry for the job – hungry to make good.'

An outstanding feature of any Hope television special is always his guest stars. The list reads like a *Who's Who* of the superstars: Sinatra, Wayne, Benny, Martin, Como, Durante, Marvin, Streisand, Crosby, are some of the names who have graced his studios.

Says Bob: 'We also work very hard on our shows: we try to get very potent guest stars and also we sell 'em. If we didn't sell them, I think the ratings would be down a little bit. But when you go on different talk shows and plug the specials, and time those shows so they hit on the afternoon of the night you're on, you're reminding people who don't buy the newspapers, or can't read 'em, that you're on. It's just a matter of keeping the ratings up. And that's part of the package so far as I'm concerned.'

But it is his keen eye for the topical star, like the topical joke, that really sets him apart from the rest. When Tom Jones was taking America by storm, Hope had him on; when Mark Spitz became the first man to win seven Olympic gold medals, Hope had him on; when Bobby Fischer became world chess champion, Hope had him on; and when Mark Hamill starred in *Star Wars*, Bob booked him. These days he chases names that will attract the younger generation, like Olivia Newton-John, Farrah Fawcett-Majors or Linda Rondstadt. 'We normally booked the show with the youth and the kids in mind,' says Bob's former executive producer and business manager, Elliott Kozak. 'We always liked to have a Donny or Marie Osmond on the show, or a David Cassidy.'

Over the years, Hope has not only used others to boost his ratings, he has used his show to make and even save fellow performers. Comedienne Phyllis Diller, who later made three films with him (*Boy Did I Get A Wrong Number*, 1966, *Eight On The Lamb*, 1967, and *The Private Army of Sgt. O'Farrell*, 1968), was 'discovered' after he saw her flop in a small Washington night club.

'He had purposely come to see me because I was very new in the business and he thought I was interesting,' says Phyllis. 'I was working with two guys and we were bombing terribly on a very small audience. I knew he was there and tried to sneak out... But he hid behind a pillar and caught me leaving; he grabbed me and told me that he thought I was great. You see, he understood that I knew I was being very bad; what he saw was the fact of the matter – I had never given up on the audience. He thought that was wonderful and told me so. I must say that it was truly the turning point because I was terribly insecure as all new comics are.'

Zsa Zsa Gabor also benefited from the Hope treatment on television. In fact she says he 'saved' her after a promising early movie career had been ruined by her having an affair with another man while she was still married to actor George Sanders.

'America became furious about this,' says Zsa Zsa. 'They said I had loose morals and I couldn't get a job anywhere in America. Then Hope said, "Oh! This is ridiculous . . . this girl is funny! I love her sense of humour . . . I'll put her in a show." And he put me in his television special, and ever since I've been on his specials. He actually gave me back my career.'

Many Hope specials are linked to a central theme, such as the funniest extracts from his films, the golden days of vaudeville, or compilations of his overseas tours. Twice he has gathered all his leading ladies together for a nostalgic meander down memory lane. In 1958 and 1969 he revived his 1933 Broadway hit *Roberta* for the small screen.

Modern television is a canned medium; most variety shows these days are wholly or partly video-taped and this makes life difficult for the topical comedian. Most of a show can be pre-recorded in front of a live audience, because their laughter prompts the viewer to laugh, but up-to-the-minute monologues often have to be taped with only a laugh machine for company.

Says former Hope writer and director, Mel Shavelson: 'I think the laugh machine has done more to ruin the level of comedy than anything else because a comedian feels his way in his jokes. You suddenly strike a topic that starts to get laughter and you know you've hit something. But when the laughs are manufactured– you can't fail and you never really know where the audience is. I think the machine is necessary mechanically for the type of show Bob does, because quite often they edit and they need the laughs to smooth it over. But you know very well that sometimes Bob does that monologue with no audience at all, because of time, but the laughs are always there. I do think he would be well advised, and most of the others, to take the risk of failing and connect a little closer with the audience.'

However, there are times when Hope goes the other way: in the autumn of 1977, when Hope was recording his tribute special to the late Bing Crosby, he changed his mind about speaking directly from his home. The director, Howard Koch, President of the Academy of Motion Picture Arts and Sciences, had already arranged for mobile taping facilities to be brought to the house. But only hours before the equipment arrived, Bob asked for a change of venue and did it before an audience at the nearby NBC studios. The rescheduling cost thousands of dollars. 'I thought it would have been more intimate the other way,' says Koch, 'but he's the boss and it turned out well anyway.'

When Bob dropped radio in 1958 he didn't drop films as well. After a couple of guest appearances – in *Showdown at Ulcer Gulch*, a promotional film for the *Saturday Evening Post*, and *Five Pennies*, for Danny Kaye and Mel Shavelson – he joined United Artists to make *Alias Jesse James*. This time he was credited as the executive producer, with brother Jack getting the producer billing.

Alias reunited him with Rhonda Fleming after a gap of ten years. It turned out to be a tough film. Loosely called 'an adult western', it was packed with difficult stunts and as usual Bob insisted on doing as many as possible himself. 'And some were quite dangerous,' Rhonda recalls 'but he wanted it that way because he always liked the camera to come in close enough for the audience to see who it was – that meant he couldn't use stunt men.'

One scene, which when finished would show Bob chasing a careering buckboard for miles, involved a great deal of pounding a treadmill. 'And he really worried us all,' says Rhonda, 'because he would run and run, and run ... until we got the whole scene right. It was quite a complicated scene and so he ran that treadmill for almost a whole day. That was the last bit of the film to be shot and we didn't finish until late that night.'

Two days later Bob collapsed and was rushed to hospital. His seemingly boundless energy had run out at last.

15

For more than thirty-five years Bob Hope has been known in Hollywood as Rapid Robert. The widely-used nickname came early on, but not because of his quicksilver-like brand of humour. It was bestowed instead for his incessant travelling and compulsive work rate.

'The energy of the man is incredible,' says Rhonda Fleming. 'It's beautiful to behold. I wish we could bottle it!'

Even while striving to construct a career on four separate fronts – the stage, radio, films and television – he rushed everywhere doing benefits, playing golf, making personal appearances and giving after-dinner speeches. And with Bob, unlike most entertainers, it is not just a question of doing one thing one day and another the next – he will often undertake the lot all in the same day.

George Burns, no slouch himself at 83, finds it a most incredible trait. 'He can go to four different cities in one day and entertain in each,' said George. 'But he sleeps, you know! He gets on a plane, closes his eyes and goes to sleep. Then he gets up in front of an audience, makes them scream, and goes back on the plane and goes to sleep again.'

That is Bob's energy-giving secret – cat naps. He is renowned throughout show business as the master of the fast forty-winks. Almost all Bob's co-stars have noticed his amazing facility for recharging the batteries. 'He has that facility,' Rosemary Clooney says, 'of going directly to sleep the moment he sets his mind to it. So there's no time wasted. I envy that tremendously.'

Cat naps came in especially handy during Bob's hectic years on the troop-entertaining circuit. One Christmas Day he flew from Bangkok to the island of Diego Garcia in the Indian Ocean to put on a show for the US Navy, and then returned the same day. He flew 6,000 miles.

Columnist James Bacon made the strenuous trip with him. 'After the show we hung around with the guys and had a little reception in the officers' quarters. Then we flew the six-and-a-half hours back to Bangkok that night. Now, we had a bunch of young girls with us – 18- and 19-year-old beauties! They were dead, absolutely dead, when we got back to Bangkok. And I was a little tired myself; it had been a rough day. I was in my room, it was two o'clock in the morning, and I got a call from Hope. He says, "Let's go out and get some Chinese food..." I nearly died,' says Bacon.

So it was a huge surprise to everyone, including Bob himself, when he was hospitalized soon after *Alias Jesse James* early in February 1959. The surprise quickly turned to shock when it transpired that it was not a simple case of nervous exhaustion: his doctors discovered a blood clot behind the left eye and delivered an ultimatum – 'Relax NOW ... or risk losing your sight!' The stunned comedian immediately cancelled a television show he had been working on and pulled out of a score of benefit appearances.

Forbidden to work, read, swim, or even play golf, Bob heeded the warning and retired to lie in the shade at his Palm Springs winter home. It was a bitter blow. For once the wisecracks were muted when he talked about his condition a few days later. 'I was proud of the fact that I hadn't had a sick day in my life until now. They say I worked too hard; long hours built up a pressure in my head. I was in the television studio this week when I felt faint and fell to my knees. I had to be carried to a couch. Imagine ... me – being carried to a couch!' he said.

He only made one attempt to test the seriousness of the diagnosis, by asking if it would be all right to fulfil a benefit engagement in Florida. The doctors forbade it, explaining that flying could inflame the clotted vein more.

In an attempt to dissolve the blood clot, which – despite the rest – had started to cloud the cornea, the doctors tried a course of cortisone, a drug which thins the blood. But the treatment left him so weak that it had to be stopped after only a short time.

Three weeks later he was back at NBC taping the aborted television show. It was a foolish move. Fuzzy vision and dizziness hit him during the final segment, and although he tried to laugh the relapse off as a 'little set-back', he was obviously badly shaken.

The next morning, Monday 2 March 1959, he flew to New York to consult one of the world's leading eye specialists, Doctor Algernon Reese of Columbia University. Doctor Reese conducted his tests at the university's medical centre over a period of four days, during which Bob had 'to face the possibility of being forced to quit show business'. By the end of the week he had the surgeon's verdict: 'Operation unnecessary. Chances of full recovery excellent.'

The 'worst two months of my life' were over. But for the first time in his supercharged life, Hope had to face the fact that the pace had to change down a gear.

'My sight is still only 50 percent normal,' he admitted. 'You get plenty of shocks in show business and I've had my share. But the prospect of losing my sight was the worst yet. I can't describe what I felt like when they said I'd be okay. When it gradually dawned on me that I might lose my eyesight, I had plenty of time to think ... but I'm not thinking of quitting ... I'm not the retiring kind.'

That became apparent a few months later when Bob arrived in Britain to prepare for another Actors' Orphanage charity show at the London Palladium. He joined Michael Redgrave, Peggy Ashcroft, Beatrice Lillie, Paul Robeson and Sir Laurence Olivier for an event which again began at midnight and ended at 3.00 a.m. As the *Manchester Guardian* reported the next day, there was no hint of his recent sickness: 'Bob Hope was pure delight. For half an hour this pouter pigeon of comedians had the audience responding to every subtle movement of his rhythmic self-inflation and deflation.'

The old hustle and bustle was still there: less than seven hours after winding up the Palladium concert, Hope was on a plane bound for Brussels and a golf date with King Baudouin of the Belgians. The King had challenged him to a game when they met on the Paramount lot in 1955. 'I'm taking lots of money with me,' quipped Bob as he boarded the flight. 'They tell me he's pretty hot...'

Two months passed before the signs of overwork returned. In mid-September vision from his left eye was once more blurred and over Christmas he experienced two further dizzy spells while touring army bases in Alaska. By then the doctors had traced the trouble to sporadic high blood pressure aggravated by tension. The 'slow down' edicts were becoming increasingly stern. Hope tried, but as he confessed to friends, 'It's hard for me to slow down.'

Bob finally took life more easily in 1960. Apart from his television commitments, at NBC, he only made one film – *The Facts of Life* – and restricted himself to a short Christmas tour of the Caribbean and Cuba. It was also the year that America's actors and actresses went on strike against the major studios. They were still out in April when the Academy of Motion Picture Arts and Sciences held its 32nd annual Oscar awards. Bob was Master of Ceremonies and made good use of the topical action when he got the event off to a good humoured start:

This is the most glamorous strike meeting in history.

This is the only industry in the world where people refuse to get out of their swimming pools until conditions improve.

The picture of the night was *Ben Hur*, striking gold eleven times – an all-time record. Simone Signoret of France got the best actress vote for her role in the British film *Room at the Top*, but Charlton Heston kept the home flag flying by taking best actor for his powerful performance in *Ben Hur*. Then, just as Hope was lamenting his inability to win one of the prized statuettes, he was honoured with the Jean Hersholt Humanitarian Award for his 'philanthropic services'.

Bob was well rested by the time he reported for work on *The Facts of Life*. It was made at the Desilu Studios, owned by his co-star Lucille Ball. Between them the couple picked up the lion's share of the profits.

Norman Panama and Melvin Frank had originally conceived the idea for Olivia De Havilland and William Holden, but they had turned it down. The plot was a combination of

Noel Coward's *Brief Encounter* and a real life incident that followed a raucous Groucho Marx party. A Hollywood film producer offers a lift home to a drunk young actress, who he has been unsuccessfully flirting with for some time. She gratefully accepts and along the way he persuades her to sleep with him. He stops at the first motel they come to and they prepare for a night of love-making. But by then the actress is rather the worse for wear – 'very damp', is how Mel Frank puts it – and she asks him to get some black coffee. Ten miles later he has the coffee, but the motel owner has extinguished all the outside lights. The frustrated producer is unable to find the place again and returns home to his wife with the coffee. The actress awakes later to an empty room and sends for a taxi to take her back to her husband. The pair never meet again.

Panama and Frank successfully amalgamated the fact with the fiction, but after their first rejection were stumped for the right stars. Then Frank thought of Bob and Lucy. 'The trick to make it work,' he says, 'was to take two people who had been brought up as great clowns – Bob Hope and Lucille Ball – and to put them into a realistic and sensitive situation.'

There were times when the reality of the situation worried Bob. He was concerned that his part was too straight. Matters came to a head when they shot the entering the motel room scene.

Says Frank: 'As Hope and Ball walked into the room I felt it was important that these two sophisticates, who were all ready to have their first assignation, should suddenly take on an extreme naivety; and become very shy and bashful when faced with the actual implements of sexuality – such as beds and a motel room. I thought that was the charm of the scene. And they did it absolutely perfectly; this glib sort of a guy began talking about inconsequential things, 'It's a nice-looking room. I love the curtains ... and the reading lamp's good.' And she says, 'It's just what we needed to talk things over.' Then she sat on the bed and I shouted 'Cut! Perfect!''

Hope, however, was not so ecstatic.

'Can I try that again?' he asked Mel.

'What for?' replied the bemused director. 'It's perfect!'

'Please let me try it again,' begged Bob.

Frank let him do anything he wanted; the couple walked in

as before, but this time the comedian dropped the dialogue and simply reached across the bed and tested the springs. As Mel yelled 'Cut!' the whole set fell about laughing.

'They thought it was hilarious,' Mel recalls. 'There's this guy who is supposed to be naive feeling the bed to see how good it is ... I said, "Is that it?" and Bob said, "Yeah, isn't that great!" I said, "No! It takes away all the ingenuousness, it takes away the innocence.' He said, "But it's funny; it's going to get a laugh." So then I told him that I didn't care because it would be the wrong sort of laugh.'

When the rushes of the scene were previewed by United Artists the next night, both versions were shown. It was Bob's that had everybody in stitches.

'Which one are you going to use?' asked Hope.

'The one where you don't touch the bed,' replied a defiant Frank.

'Well,' says Mel, 'from that point on if anybody went to him with a suggestion he'd say, "Let's not do that! Mr Frank's afraid somebody might think we're doing a comedy here..." But in the end I think he was glad we did it the way we finally did it.'

Not all the critics agreed. *The Times* said:

Had the film been prepared to take itself less seriously ... *The Facts of Life* could have attained a farcical unreality that would have admirably suited its leading players, two excellent comics with a style which blends to perfection ... Mr Hope, in moments of unaccustomed solemnity, looks out of place and even, alas, a trifle dull. Miss Ball could never be dull, but she is equally ill at ease...

In spite of such critiques *The Facts of Life* was widely acclaimed as one of Bob's most successful films and his performance was highly praised. Seventeen years later Mel Frank, who believes Hope to be 'an incredible actor', said: 'Lucille Ball gave a really remarkable comedy performance and I think he stayed right up there with her. But you were always aware of the fact that he was somewhat of a comedian all the way through, rather than a character.'

Bob made one other significant contribution in 1960 – he

advised presidential candidate Richard Nixon to meet his opponent John Kennedy face-to-face in the now historic televised debate. On 4 November J.F.K. became President by a margin of only 118,000 votes. Sixty-eight million votes were cast and many said that the confrontation on the small screen swung things Kennedy's way.

The following year Bob was heavily involved in Britain: first attending a charity premier of *Bachelor in Paradise*, which he made in Hollywood with Lana Turner, and then filming *Road to Hong Kong* with old buddy Bing.

It had been a long time between *Roads* – almost a decade – and big changes were made for the seventh in the series. Frank and Panama became producers, directors, writers and part owners; Paramount was replaced by United Artists; and Dorothy Lamour lost her third spot in the billing.

'I was very upset to lose the leading lady role,' says Dorothy, 'but there wasn't anything I could do about it – Bing didn't want me...'

Bing favoured first Brigitte Bardot and then Gina Lollobrigida for the role, but it eventually went to Britain's Joan Collins. Her delight at getting the part was tinged with regret. 'I felt a little bit sad,' says Joan, 'in the way that the two men were still able to play their roles and the woman wasn't. I took it as a sort of blow against feminism. But in fact they both still looked quite remarkable at the time, while I think that Dorothy didn't look quite up to the same standard. I felt bad at first, but then just took it in my stride.'

Bob also felt disturbed by the change and there was a big row behind the scenes about the decision. Panama and Frank, and United Artists, reasoned that Miss Lamour was no longer the sexy sarong wearing lass of past films and that a younger actress would give the film more appeal. 'Anyway,' they argued, 'Dorothy will still be in the movie making a guest appearance.'

The compromise satisfied Bob, but not Dotty. She turned the offer down after discovering that a song they wanted her to do would be 'ruined' by a comedy sequence. Finally, after Bob intervened, she was persuaded to make a brief appearance as herself.

Hong Kong went before the cameras in the Shepperton

Studios, near Staines in Surrey, on 2 August 1961 and took three months to complete. The extended stay afforded the comedian and the crooner an opportunity to live together for the first time. To begin with, they and their families had booked into separate London hotels. (Bob had brought Dolores, Linda, Tony, Kelly and Norah; Bing had brought Kathryn who was heavily pregnant, and son Harry.) But producer Mel Frank wanted them nearer the action. After weeks of searching he came up with a winner – Cranbourne Court, a luxurious country mansion at Winkfield, near Windsor in Berkshire, with 25 acres of grounds and 22 bedrooms; the Wentworth and Sunningdale golf courses close at hand and Shepperton only minutes away. The house came complete with a classic butler named Pope. The only snag was a rent of £400 a week. Mel offered it to Dolores first. Her enthusiasm was enough to convince the pair that it was worth missing the rest of the round to dash off and give the place the once-over.

'Jeez, it's too big,' exclaimed Bob when he saw the size of the house. 'It's got 22 bedrooms!'

'Why don't we both live in it?' suggested Bing casually. "There are plenty of rooms; it's just like a hotel.'

So the families moved in under one roof. Crosby went in search of a nanny for Harry, while Hope hired a £100-a-week Rolls Royce to ferry them back and forth each day.

The last *Road* was in many ways a complicated film to make. For a start it was being shot in three versions: one with American dialogue for the United States and Canada; another with anglicized lines for the United Kingdom; and a third without songs for the foreign language market. For instance, in the British release Crosby said things like, 'Business first, fun and games later,' while the North American version had him saying, 'Business first, social activities later.'

Then there was the added difficulty of easing Joan Collins into Dotty's place. The girl in the middle was a vital ingredient of a *Road* picture. 'I did feel that the rapport between Bing and me was not there as it had been with Dorothy Lamour,' says Joan. 'But with Bob I just got along tremendously well.'

A feature of *Hong Kong* was the array of guest stars, Frank Sinatra, Dean Martin, David Niven, Zsa Zsa Gabor and Peter Sellers. Sellers spent a day cameoing an Indian doctor and was much impressed with Hope. 'He was a fascinating person to work with,' he said. 'He is so versatile. And very aware of trends in humour, he doesn't just stick to one type.'

Some of the guest spots surprised more than just the cinema audiences. Sinatra and Martin's appearances were something of a shock to Bob and Bing too.

Said Joan Collins: 'Hope and Crosby were arguing over who was going to get me. They were saying, "I'll have her Monday, Thursday and Saturday and you'll have her Tuesday, Wednesday and Friday." And while they were doing this two astronauts came along, and I was hugging and kissing them. The two happened to be Frank Sinatra and Dean Martin, wearing space helmets; and they didn't know who it was until the astronauts took their hats off as we were shooting it. There was great hilarity . . .'

Next Bing joined the revelation stakes, enlisting the help of Zsa Zsa Gabor. 'I was in London making a picture,' says Zsa Zsa, 'and Bing Crosby called, and I nearly fainted. He said, "Let's make a big joke on Bob Hope. We are shooting a scene in which he is supposed to be in a coma. We will dress you up as a nurse and you are going to kiss him on the lips!" It was the first and the last time I ever kissed him . . . and when Hope opened his eyes, and saw who it was, he nearly fainted. He laughed so much and of course for the rest of the day there was no shooting – we played golf.'

For producer Mel Frank one of the biggest headaches was the weather. Too many warm, sunny days meant not enough Hope and Crosby. 'When it got to be about four o'clock in the afternoon,' he says, 'they had a way of looking at each other. Then they'd both indicate that it was a beautiful day outside.'

Bing admitted: 'Sometimes I used to work without make-up, if it was an exterior scene, because if there was any daylight left we wanted to hit a few golf shots. Why, I'd even have my golf clothes on underneath the clothes I was wearing in the picture, so all I had to do was rip off my wardrobe and fly.'

One day the boys left the set in too much of a hurry. They had been shooting a harem scene, during which Bob's toe-nails were painted bright red. When Panama yelled 'Cut!' at five o'clock. Bob scurried off with Bing to Wentworth for nine fast holes – forgetting about his feet.

'Afterwards,' said Bing, 'we sat down to change out of golf shoes and there were two elderly English gentlemen – typical Colonel Blimp types, with the luxuriant moustaches, the tweed coats and the knickers – sitting across from us. I saw one of them's eyes fly to Hope's bare feet. He gave a shocked look, then nudged his partner to look at these red toe-nails.'

Bob was unaware that his feet were being scrutinized, or that the Groaner was pretending he could not believe it either, until one of the members enquired: 'Mr Crosby, is your friend in the ballet?'

'Hope put on his shoes and socks, and rushed out,' said Bing. 'That's the first time I ever saw him stuck without a retort – he was half mad, half embarrassed!'

A few weeks later the script called for the pair to be rocketed to the moon and then be showered with confetti upon their return. 'They threw confetti on us all day,' says Bob, 'and I went back to play at Wentworth again. It was very warm and I decided to take a shower before I went home. I walked in, took off my shorts in front of two Scotsmen – and confetti fell out of my shorts. They looked at me like I hadn't had a bath since New Year. Around Wentworth I was known as the fellow with red toe-nails and confetti in his shorts. I was a rare novelty in those days.'

Road to Hong Kong differed from its predecessors in that the amount of knockabout, or slapstick, comedy was reduced. It was, admitted Hope at the time, just a matter of age. 'I find with the increasing years that you can't do the hokum,' he said, 'it looks a little silly for you to do some of the things that you would do. And Bing and I are conscious of that. Although we're doing our same characters, we're not doing as many physical things. I think the public expects this type of perform-ance because they know you; you're on television; you're in their eye all the time ... they know your age practically and they don't want you acting too silly.'

Bob was fifty-eight and Bing sixty. *Hong Kong* would be the last road the pair would travel together. Notwithstanding the critics, who roundly condemned it as 'one *Road* too many', the film was a box-office smash. The magazine *Films and Filming* rated it as the fifth most successful picture of 1962, and it was also claimed that Bob and Bing would pick up at least

$2,000,000 each from the receipts. So at the age of 22 the highly successful series ground to a halt. Many years later the two principals had a final word about this considerable slice of cinema history.

'I used to love it,' said Bob, 'because I enjoyed working with Bing so much. He was such a pro and it was all great fun. He was what you call a sympathetic comic and straight-man. He had a good sense of comedy, but he also knew more about feeding a line than anybody. I'm the best straight-man for anybody, because I know how I would like to be fed a straight line.'

Bing reciprocated, but felt his partner was the true master of the quick quip. 'I couldn't cope with him,' he said. 'In the *Road* pictures I would break about even, because I'd get the script and study it – and have a few singers or arrows in my bow.'

One of the great legends which sprang up during the series, with the help of the pair, was that Bob and Bing ad-libbed their way around and over all the scripts. Bob's former writers dispute that almost to a man.

'This is no way meant to depreciate their powers of ad-libbing,' said Mel Frank, 'but to my knowledge – and I would look both of them in the eye and say it – there was not one single ad-lib that wasn't written for them. Mind you, they may have called us in, any of us writers, and say we need a little something ... but I can show you the scripts of the ones that we [Panama and Frank] were involved in – and it was all on paper.'

Nevertheless, insists Frank, Hope and Crosby – through the *Road* films – made an immeasurable contribution to celluloid comedy; one that has not yet been sufficiently honoured.

The *Road to Hong Kong* marked the beginning of the end of Hope's glittering screen career. After sixty films since 1938, which included forty-four major features, his two-decade domination of the leading money earners at the cinema box-office was coming to a conclusion. In the following ten years he would make only nine more major movies, including *Critic's Choice* (1963), his fourth with Lucille Ball; *Call Me Bwana* (1963) made in England with Anita Ekberg; *A Global Affair* (1964); *I'll Take Sweden* (1965), with Tuesday Weld; *How to Commit Marriage* (1969) with Jane Wyman and Jackie Gleason;

135

and *Cancel My Reservation* (1972), with Eve Marie Saint.

None of those films recaptured his past glories, and never again would Bob appear on the silver screen with Bing Crosby. But by then he was growing disenchanted with the movie business anyway. He found that independently producing your own pictures meant policing them too, and there were plenty of distributors and cinema managers ready to rob you blind.

'Once,' says Bob, 'we were in Europe and saw queues of people waiting to see one of my pictures; they were right round the block and the manager told us it was that way every night. Now, everyone back home had been telling us that that film was not making any money. So we discovered that they were fiddling the returns. And that was going on all over. It just didn't make it worth our while.'

Hope was not overly concerned about the decline on the film front. He was still the Number One television star and there was something else looming on the horizon that was going to more than amply fill the sixties and early seventies. The powers-that-were in Washington wanted him to go to war again.

16

When President Eisenhower and Secretary of State John Dulles committed United States troops to Vietnam in 1954, to act in an advisory capacity to the Saigon regime of Ngo Dinh Diem, the news barely reached the front pages of America's newspapers. But less than a decade later it was a topic which hardly ever deserted the headlines. Successive American presidents escalated the campaign against the Communists until over 550,000 American troops were fighting a vicious guerrilla war that tore south-east Asia apart. By the time the United States withdrew in 1973, 56,000 Americans lay dead, along with a million North and South Vietnamese. Vietnam had been devastated and America had suffered the gravest defeat in its history at a cost of $150 billion.

Bob's involvement began quietly enough. During Christmas of 1964 he took his annual touring company to Saigon for the first time. The reception he got rekindled his enthusiasm for troop entertainment and persuaded him that he should go back every year from then on.

The following Christmas Hope took a 63-strong company more than 23,000 miles for a 12-day, 19-stop, 24-show hike around Thailand, South Vietnam, the Philippines, the South China Sea and a couple of Pacific Ocean islands. Accompanying him were Les Brown and his Orchestra, singer Jack Jones, actress Carroll Baker, nightclub artist Joey Heatherton, Miss USA, Pepsodent radio favourite Jerry Colonna and a group of chorus girls.

From the first show on Wake Island to the last at Guam, around 70,000 servicemen cheered and shouted as the troupe performed on a variety of make-shift stages on land, sea or jungle. Once Bob found himself trying to be funny atop a mass of 50-gallon drums containing high octane aviation fuel, while within easy range of Viet Cong mortar attacks. Another concert had him cracking gags from the rolling deck of the massive American aircraft-carrier *Ticondoroga* as it patrolled the China Sea.

The highlight of the gruelling trip was a party given by the King and Queen of Thailand at their palace in Bangkok. The King presented Bob with a special gift – a stuffed king cobra, the most poisonous reptile in the world.

By then the Bob Hope Christmas tours were taking six months to arrange and organize. They were no longer a quick jaunt around the military outposts.

Each summer representatives of the US Joint Chiefs of Staff met with those of the United Service Organization to plan the forthcoming winter's entertainment. By mid-autumn Bob was told what his itinerary would be and was able to despatch a sound engineer and a television production assistant to recce the ten or eleven bases on the list. It was their job to check each location for stage, lighting and sound facilities; plan camera positions for the television filming; make sure important items like dressing-rooms and toilets would be available; and gather intelligence about the units and their commanding officers.

Meanwhile in Hollywood the Hope organization would be hard at work assembling a star cast, arranging its security clearance, and fixing an impressive and painful list of inoculations, ranging from cholera and typhoid in one arm to yellow fever and typhus in the other.

Bob always took a keen interest in the compilation of the troupe. His magic formula was two or three big names from show business, a major sports personality and a beauty queen, preferably the reigning Miss World, who was crowned – often by the man himself – only weeks before the tour kicked-off. He usually participated in the contest, thus ensuring that an agreement with the organizers was honoured each time.

Gag writers were busy for months before departure preparing enough one-liners to last a lifetime. Hope would only use a fraction of their efforts, but he liked to feel well-armed. One of their most important functions was to compose special material for each base from the advance party's information sheets. This would give every unit the feeling that Bob Hope was really there just for them.

By the time the comedian's cue-card expert, Barney McNulty, got around to writing up the giant four-by-four foot prompts, the operation would have set Hope back at least $50,000.

Mid-December would bring the entire company together at the Travis Air Force base just north of San Francisco. Stars, chorus girls, musicians, writers, volunteer film crews, producers, directors and Bob all piled aboard the huge air transport for the long flight across the North Pacific. Journalists would not be notified of their destinations until just a few hours before each concert – so worried were the USO chiefs about attempts on Hope's life by the enemy.

Twelve or thirteen days later they were back, often exhausted but always triumphant. As most joined their families for a belated Christmas and New Year celebration, Bob and his team got down to editing the 150,000 or so feet of television film that would go towards the two-hour Bob Hope Christmas Special which would be aired within a fortnight.

During those first years in Vietnam the television shows drew massive audiences. As many as seventy or eighty million Americans would watch tens of thousands of happy GIs holding placards hailing Hope as, among other things, 'The greatest American since George Washington' and hear roars of approval for his fast topical routines:

What a welcome I got at the airport – they thought I was a replacement.

And as we flew in today, they gave us a 21-gun salute – three of them were ours.

I understand the enemy's very close –with my act they always are.

I asked Secretary MacNamara if I could come here. He said, why not – we've tried everything else.

By the time the 1967 tour came round, the United States was having second thoughts about the conflict. There was no sign of an end to it and the casualties were steadily mounting. For the first time USO booking agents found stars hard to get; the growing anti-war mood amongst the nation as a whole had spilled over into the entertainment industry. Many artists suddenly discovered they had 'prior engagements'. Fortunately for the USO there were exceptions – and Bob was the biggest of them all. When he went other major personalities went with him. Raquel Welch backed Bob to the hilt. For her, that first trip was an enlightening experience.

'He was like the head morale booster,' she recalls. 'He kept reminding us all that we were there to spread cheer; we were people from home who still cared about them, because some of the guys obviously felt that they were on the wrong end of the totem pole and that they weren't really being supported.'

Raquel's first Hope troop show was at the Da Nang air base, close to the North Vietnamese frontier. 'It was almost like ticker-tape time,' she says. 'They had big signs out – "Bob Hope for President", "Raquel Welch for President"; crazy things like that. And I remember coming out on to the stage and thinking, "Where are all the people?" I couldn't see anything because it was still very foggy, even though it was mid-afternoon. You couldn't hear anything, but then I looked up and saw this great grey mass – I thought it was a mountain at first – and it turned out to be all people. Then this great roar went up. And Bob was just standing there doing his famous golf swing. It was a truly overwhelming experience.'

What made it more so was the revelation that they were not entertaining old veterans. In fact it was just the opposite. 'They were all kids,' says Raquel. 'They were all babies; they could have been my younger brothers, barely shaving ... fresh faced kids that were out there fighting that war. It was the first time that it dawned on me and I was overwhelmed.'

But the boys were growing up fast, if they lived that long, and many newspapers zeroed in on the sexual overtones of the Hope tours. Says Raquel: 'It was very frightening to me and some of the other ladies, because it was really like throwing raw meat to a lot of hungry lions. The press fantasized that this was a very licentious experience for all these boys. But it wasn't at all. I don't mean to make them out to be Polyannas, but really the expression was one much more urgent than a boy-girl kind of thing; it was like home ... Bob Hope, America ... and home.'

By 1969 the anti-war movement was reaching a peak. President Kennedy's successor, Lyndon Johnson, had been broken by the conflict and declined a second term in the White House. Richard Nixon replaced him in November 1968. He pledged to end it all and bring the troops home. It would be five more years before that promise was kept.

As the fighting went on, though, so did the Hope Christmas tours. For the first time in his career Bob faced hostility from American journalists – the same people who previously had called him the most accessible star in Hollywood.

Shortly before he hit south-east Asia for the sixth time – by way of Germany, Italy and Turkey – Bob took the, for him, unusual step of voicing his opinions seriously. 'The kids fighting in Vietnam know more about what they are doing than the people back home,' he told British newsmen during a stop-over in London. Then he accused the media of adopting 'a very provocative style of reporting the war'.

In the summer of 1970 Hope joined a move to make that year's 4 July Independence Day celebrations into a patriotic 'Honour America Day'. He told a June news conference in Washington DC that it was hoped half-a-million people would descend on the capital for an all-day rally – to show the world that 'Americans can put aside their honest differences and rally round the flag to show national unity'. He went on to stress that the festivities were not designed to garner support for the flagging war effort; nor were they intended to counter the 250,000-strong, anti-war protest held in Washington the previous autumn. 'We're not trying to answer a demonstration with a demonstration,' he insisted. 'We're trying to keep the war out of this ... to make this a celebration instead of a demonstration.'

In the event, Bob lined up with evangelist Billy Graham, Jack Benny, Dorothy Lamour, singer Glenn Campbell and heads of the Walt Disney organization before 400,000 'clean-cut' Americans at the Washington Memorial – wearing a bullet-proof vest. For, at the same time, an estimated 5,000 'hippies' were trying to disrupt the proceedings by holding a mass pot-smoke-in outside the White House. As riot police used tear-gas to disperse them, he joked: 'Just like Vietnam ... except there they had machine-guns over the stage ...'

Next year the going got even rougher. Many of his own countrymen called him a 'political hawk' and the Moscow newspaper *Pravda* dubbed him a 'Pentagon Clown.' Then the New York City Council of Churches, under pressure from a group of activist young clergymen, voted to cancel its previous decision to award him the 1971 'Family of Man' prize. Hope was disappointed, but unrepentant. 'I appreciate the Americans who have laid down their lives for our country,' he said. 'I won't change my views because of criticism. I'm not in favour of any war, but I'm also not in favour of surrender ... this is a tricky conflict. We're helping people maintain their freedom ... I'm not a hawk. I'm an owl.'

Anti-Hope campaigns were now becoming almost as commonplace as the anti-war movement and his popularity ratings were hitting an all-time low. Almost daily, it seemed, he was being forced to answer new attacks and criticism. 'I'm not a right-winger ... I'm middle of the road,' he countered, when students objected to their San Fernando Valley college giving him an honorary degree. 'I'm called a right-winger because I know the president and played golf with the vice president, for which I should get the bronze star. But I have known six presidents ... I believe in our country.'

Anti-establishment campaigner Jane Fonda assessed his yearly overseas trips as 'outmoded' and announced that she was going to put on her own show as 'an antidote to Bob Hope'. He replied: 'I don't want to get into an argument, but it's obvious from a jury of 80 million people who watched the television show of this year's trip that those kids laughing over there weren't from Central Casting!'

Apart from his well-publicized friendship with President Nixon, Bob's problems had been exacerbated by a statement he had made during one of his first Vietnam visits. Reporters had asked if he was against the war. 'No, I'm not anti-war,' he told them firmly. 'In this particular case I'm definitely a hawk. I think we're fighting for the right cause and that's the reason I go. If I were anti-policy I would never make the trip!' The remark stuck, no matter how hard he tried to explain that he had not meant it the way it sounded.

There was another disturbing development to come during the early seventies – the troops themselves were beginning to cool noticeably. He experienced his first rebuff in 1970, at Camp Eagle 400 miles north-east of Saigon. An audience of 18,000 were applauding his every word after hearing his newest line in topical material – the marijuana gag:

I hear you guys are interested in gardening here – our security officer says a lot of you are growing your own grass.

I think, instead ot taking it away from you soldiers, they ought to give it to the negotiators in Paris.

You ought to take up baseball. That's the game in which you can spend eight months of the year on grass – and not get busted.

But the laughter and cheers soon subsided when Hope introduced the South Vietnamese Vice-President, Marshall Nguyen Cao Ky, as 'a very great man'. When he went on to joke about World War II ' 'That was the one without the pickets!' – it raised only a ripple of laughter.

Pickets were again a source of embarrassment the following year, when Bob turned up at Long Binh on Christmas Day. Morale was at a low ebb: the whole army seemed to be drugged, depressed and unwilling to fight; 50 percent of all gunshot wounds were now being caused by GIs and not the enemy; over three years 500 cases of 'fragging' – attacks on officers with fragmentation grenades – had been reported. Against this background, Long Binh became virtually a political demonstration.

Outside the stadium where the show was being held Bob faced the pickets – 'THE VIETNAM WAR IS A BOB HOPE JOKE,' they challenged. And the atmosphere inside was not much better either. Officers and their wives were roundly booed and hissed as they took their seats, and television cameras had a job avoiding the plethora of placards: 'PEACE NOT HOPE', 'WHERE IS JANE FONDA?', 'MERRY CHRISTMAS NIXON. WISH YOU WERE HERE' and 'WE'RE FONDA, HOPE'. Even his normally successful jibes at the officers brought only mild reaction:

There's so much brass here the GIs sleep at attention.

A pair of jokes about homosexuals were greeted by a frozen, even embarrassed silence, and a routine pillorying Women's Liberation raised hardly a titter. One topical quip even inflamed the restless crowd:

You're off the front page back home – the Vietnam war is now tucked

143

away between Li'l Abner and Chuckle a Day.

Insult was added to injury near the end of the show – a group of military policemen clambered up onto the stage, unfurling a banner reading 'PIGS FOR PEACE'. Then, when a general mounted the boards to thank the troupe for the appearance and give Bob a 'Ho Chi Minh bicycle', scores of black dissidents in the audience – who had been giving clenched-fist salutes throughout the performance – got up and ostentatiously left.

Clearly rattled, Hope shouted after them. 'In my heart, you're the guys that are against war because you're the guys that are helping to end it. You've all listened to that garbage of the other cats ... what have they ever done for the world?'

The comedian was by then becoming enured to giving tough speeches at the end of his concerts. At the start of the 1971 tour, he got a standing ovation from 8,000 soldiers when he thundered: 'They think I come over here because I'm pro-war! Let me tell you something ... this is the 30th year that I've been doing this ... and there's nobody more anti-war than I am ... and there's nobody more anti-war than you are ...'

Bob was deeply wounded by the growing rejection amongst his beloved servicemen, more so than he was from the attacks by the media. They seemed to have forgotten that the stage shows were just part of the object of the USO tours. Behind the scenes there were literally hundreds of field dressing stations, hospital wards and gory operating theatres to visit.

For many of his first-time fellow performers it was a disturbing and shocking task. Raquel Welch says: 'We would go down these long corridors of beds, and Bob would always give out ball-game scores and things to the guys, and he would be very glib, very up, and very sort of energetic. A lot of the guys had injuries from grenades or mines; they had big metal sutures all down their fronts, because I guess they'd been hit from behind and you'd see lines of boys in these beds with the same sutures. But it wouldn't hit you until later ... what all the impressions were ... and then it was sort of overwhelming.'

To ensure that his young team were not too overcome by the sights of battle, Bob cast himself in the role of nursemaid. 'He wouldn't let you sit back and think, "God! This is a terrible thing! Why are we in this situation?"' says Miss Welch. 'His position was, "I'm here to do something good." And so he set the pace for all of us; if any of us started looking a little bit faint as we passed an operating room, or maybe fatigued or a little bit perplexed, he would be there with that smile and that sort of style of his. You couldn't ... you simply could not let yourself go down.'

Another unsung service performed by the Hope touring company, at the instigation of its leader, involved the collecting of telephone numbers and addresses. 'When we got back we made personal phone calls to the families,' says Raquel. 'It was really harder almost than the trip because it was real; it's so important to hear from somebody first hand. But in some instance they would say. "We've just received a telegram – he's not alive any more..." You never knew when it was going to be a telephone call like that!'

The main talking point of the 1971 tour was Bob's astounding personal bid to negotiate the release of 300 American prisoners of war, who were being held in Viet Cong jails. On his own initiative, but with unofficial State Department backing and the use of a US Army plane, he flew from Bangkok to the Laotian capital, Vientiane, to make a direct appeal at the North Vietnamese Embassy. First Secretary Nguyen Van Thanh met him and they talked cordially for 85 minutes. Bob explained that he wanted two things: a visa to allow his entire troupe to perform for the incarcerated men and their eventual return to the United States. In return, said the comedian, he was prepared to try to raise money for building hospitals and schools to aid North Vietnamese children. After some haggling they arrived at a figure of ten million dollars, but no agreement.

Said Bob afterwards: 'We talked about an exchange, with the children of America working up a fund to give to the children of North Vietnam. We also talked about a people-to-people fund. But it always came back to the regime's official statement that the prisoners would be released tomorrow if President Nixon would abide by the seven-point proposal advanced by the North Vietnamese last July.' That meant in effect the United States Government setting a date for a complete withdrawal from South Vietnam and Hope was forced to confess that 'the odds are very long'.

The boldness of the comedian's move confounded even his most severe critics. Many began to admit that maybe they had misjudged him. United States Senator George McGovern, the anti-war candidate for the Democratic presidential nomination, was in no doubt about the initiative, though. He pointed out that there had been a 'shocking escalation' in the bombing of the North and claimed: 'While Bob Hope acts as an emissary of the President in seeking the release of our prisoners, the Air Force acts as the true Nixon instrument in guaranteeing that the number of American POWs will be increased.'

Nixon reacted more calmly to the news. In fact he had not been told about the scheme in advance. 'I can only say,' he told reporters at a press conference, 'that the efforts that Hope makes, that anybody makes, are deeply appreciated.' The North Vietnamese never officially accepted or rejected the Hope plan, but no entry visa was ever granted.

A year later American involvement in Vietnam was almost at an end. Bob was able to explore a new line of topicality:

Now that the war is winding down, I want to say I do appreciate you fellows hanging around here – just for me.

Even before he left the States, Bob was hinting that his ninth visit to the Asian battle areas might be his last. History was to prove him right, but in the meantime he swung through a whirlwind 13-stop tour of his old stomping grounds, this time accompanied by his wife Dolores. The emotional journey, greeted once more by an enthusiastic and appreciative army (much to Hope's relief), ended at Anderson Air Force Base on Guam. The highlight of the final show was Dolores Hope's version of the Old Groaner's great hit 'White Christmas'.

On 8 January 1973 it was confirmed in Washington that Bob Hope had indeed undertaken his last Christmas show. The United States announced the suspension of hostilities in Vietnam – the boys were coming home.

But the tour finished on a note of controversy. During a concert in Thailand Bob cracked a gag that had international repercussions:

When I came out of a temple recently, I found two Thai families in my shoes who refused to evacuate.

Sensitive Thai newspapers reacted angrily to the joke and accused the comic of 'betraying Thailand's hospitality'. Bob was mortified, explaining: 'I had not realized that the Thai people were so sensitive about feet. Everybody knows how big my feet are and I was only trying to make a comparison.' Mr Leonard Unger, the American Ambassador in Bangkok, thought the incident serious enough to issue an official and formal apology to the Thai Government: 'Bob Hope is a very good friend of Thailand and the Thai people and he did not know all about Thai customs, and would never look down on the Thai people.'

Bob Hope's involvement in the Vietnam conflict gave him almost a decade of bitter-sweet memories. 'All I did was entertain in south-east Asia,' he said later, 'but I did witness some of the suffering and I didn't like it. And I hope it never happens again. Perhaps somewhere along the line we could have withdrawn with grace and honour on our part. I don't know...'

Time has brought a more realistic appraisal of his role in America's longest and most controversial war. Now many people are prepared to stand up and criticize those who critized him. Said former President Gerald Ford: 'Bob didn't argue about military strategy or the rightness or wrongness of the American commitment. He just went out to help the people who were sent there by the government. So any criticism of Bob was terribly unfair and certainly unwarranted.'

Veteran war and cowboy star, John Wayne, a close friend of Hope for more than thirty years, took an even tougher line. 'I hope to God he was supporting our side,' bawled the Duke. 'Nobody likes war, any war, but the kids were over there gettin' shot at by that flag that Miss Fonda finds the love of her life. I saw kids burned, beaten ... dead! So I see no reason for not backing our kids that were over there taking it on the chin for us.

'The only good I could be over there, was to wear a big hat – most of those kids had been to see those quickie Westerns and I represented a piece of America – but Bob could take all of the entertainment world to those kids and make something out of it ... give them something to write home about besides, "Mom, I've just killed two more Vietnamese." So Bob really brought warmth to them; so it was really an important, dedicated thing that he did; I don't think people realized how important it was.'

Raquel Welch agrees. 'I felt really antagonized by this attitude,' she says, 'because I felt that what he was doing was on a different level. It was never a question of political points of view when we were over there . . . it was strictly that those guys were stuck there at Christmas time; and he could get Les Brown and Raquel Welch, and a load of other people to show them some kind of appreciation and recognition for what they were going through.'

The Vietnam conflict was a confusing issue for Bob; along with most other Americans he had grown used to publicly supporting the president or administration in times of war or international crisis. And, again like the majority of his countrymen, he initially accepted the so-called 'domino theory', that if South Vietnam fell to the Communists, so too would other Asian countries. Throughout the war the comedian tried hard to avoid expounding his own opinions about American policy. Privately, though, he agreed with those who believed that, having got involved so deeply, the United States should have used its great military might to win outright long before the guerrilla warfare spread the way it did. Two years before hostilities were finally suspended, he admitted to the author that he realized America was fighting a battle it could not possibly win any more, and also revealed that his views on the bombing question had been formed at the very highest level.

'General Westmoreland [a former US Commander in Vietnam] once told me,' said Bob, 'that the Joint Chiefs of Staff were convinced that they could have ended it quickly by bombing the hell out of the North before they got properly organized. We had the capability, he said, but the politicians would not let them. It was politically unacceptable to the White House. Sure it would have been tremendously unpopular with the rest of the world, but what are wars about anyway? A speedy end would have saved countless wasted lives on both sides.'

Mel Shavelson, a staunch supporter of the Hope Christmas tours, feels that there was a time when Bob took a slightly hawkish line on the war in south-east Asia. But, says Mel, there was a good reason.

'Bob never discussed the causes of the war, or the operation of the war, with anyone below the rank of a five-star general,'

Mel explained. 'His viewpoint was completely warped. His friends are the presidents, the vice presidents and the generals. He entertained the privates, but had lunch with the generals; and that would colour anybody's viewpoint!'

It should be appreciated that, as early as the spring of 1970, Hope was made aware of how unpopular his continuing support for the USO tours was. He and Mel Shavelson had almost reached agreement on a film in which he would play an entertainer in South Vietnam who gets captured by the Viet Cong. But, on 30 April, President Nixon revealed that American troops had invaded Cambodia. Within hours of the announcement, Shavelson's secretary had threatened to quit if the film went ahead. 'I don't want to work on this film anymore,' she told her employer. 'I don't want to work with Bob Hope...' Mel called him right away and said, 'Bob, we'd better not do this picture ... it's wrong!' To Mel's surprise, Bob was sympathetic. 'You're absolutely right,' he said. 'I was just in Washington and I was outside the hotel putting my golf clubs in my car, when a car load of kids drove by. They stopped and one of them yelled out, "Hey Bob! We're going to bring them home to you this Christmas..." So I guess it'll be wiser to keep a low profile.'

The end of the Vietnam war almost saw the end of Hope's troop entertaining career as well. The man of whom it was once said, 'if there wasn't a war on, he would start one', had to think of a way to occupy his festive seasons in future. But in 1973, although managing to grab Christmas Day with his family for the first time in 25 years, Bob was back on the road touring military hospitals full of war victims. He went north to San Francisco, east to Bethesda in Maryland and south to the Long Beach Veterans' Hospital.

Over two thousand veterans call this place home – at least that's what they call it when the nurses are in earshot.

A nurse! That's a girl in a white uniform who can take your temperature and give you one – both at the same time.

To give you an idea how cute the nurses are in this hospital ... someone hung a bunch of mistletoe in surgery and they had to operate on one poor guy twice. Once to cure what was wrong with him – once to get his lips unpuckered.

In 1974 Bob wound up his regular winter troop excursions

altogether with visits to veterans' hospitals in Denver, Colorado, San Antonio, Texas and Tacoma in Washington State. The mini-tour marked the end of 33 years continuous service in the front line, years that had often brought him near to death or injury. One of his closest shaves came in Vietnam, when he only escaped being blown up thanks to the habitual tardiness of cue-card writer Barney McNulty.

Says show business writer James Bacon, who was also on the trip: 'We were leaving Seoul in Korea and flying into Saigon, and we had to hold the plane up for McNulty for fifteen minutes. Then we landed in Saigon and went to this hotel. We got there about ten minutes after it had been bombed and about 30 American officers had been killed by the Viet Cong.'

A few years earlier, again in Vietnam, an engine on the Hope Air Force transport stopped, giving the party an anxious time as it limped the remaining 900 miles on three engines. But when Bob was touring the Far East during December 1957, it was human error rather than mechanical failure that nearly cost the comedian his life. He was travelling in a jet fighter-bomber from Tokyo to Guam in the Pacific.

'They sat me in the co-pilot's seat with oxygen mask, crash-helmet and parachute,' recalls Bob. 'We weren't in the air long before I felt uneasy – a real claustrophobia. I started sweating. I took off the parachute, then asked the pilot if it was possible to make my seat go up so that I could see out. He told me to pull a little lever; I was a little groggy from lack of sleep and pulled at the wrong lever. The pilot screamed, "Get your hand off that!" It was the automatic ejection seat. We were a good 800 miles out in the Pacific...'

Over the years Bob came under fire many times. Although inwardly concerned, outwardly he would appear cheerful and confident in an effort to calm his co-stars. In Vietnam Raquel Welch found it an admirable quality. 'The helicopters we flew in were shot at,' she says. 'And Bob was always making jokes to keep us quiet while we were getting shot at. It was all like a joke at the time; then later it would dawn on you that it was really happening!'

Bob's sense of humour and coolness in the face of danger was not a product of long experience. He showed the same traits when he first set foot in the battle zones of North Africa. In

1943, after wrenching his knee during the bombings in Sicily, he went to see General Eisenhower in his Algerian villa to seek reassurance.

'Am I safe here?' he asked.

'Don't worry,' Ike replied confidently, 'nothing's going to happen here. The Germans are on the other side of the Mediterranean.'

The comedian went back to his hotel in the town, 'feeling very happy'; a short while later the Nazis began pounding the area and Bob spent four hours in the cellar.

The next morning he called the Allied Commander.

'What's the name of the fella who's in charge here?' he enquired tartly.   Recognition of the risks and extent of his services has been widespread. Bob Hope is the most decorated civilian in history, with more than a thousand awards and citations to his name. As far back as October 1952 President Truman called him to the White House to present a citation signed by himself and 31 dignitaries. Headed '*To Bob Hope The GI's Guy*', it marked his tenth anniversary of troop entertaining and read:

For the ten years of laughs he has brought over many thousands of miles to members of the armed forces of the United States and its Allies on every continent and island outpost;

For his unselfish giving of himself and talents at our camps and bases, our hospitals and our battlefronts, often at great risk to himself;

And, in this day of renewed crisis, for carrying on in bringing fun, relaxation and a bit of home to the GIs here and overseas;

On this, the occasion of the tenth anniversary of his first camp show at March Field, California, on May 6, 1941.

Thanks, Bob, from all of us.

(Although March Field was Bob's first official troop show, he had entertained the military a short while before that. When the US Government decided to form a conscript army, the numbers for the first draft were drawn in San Francisco. Bob heard about it and flew from Los Angeles to crack a few gags for the people waiting in the queue outside the hall where the draw was taking place. It therefore also marked his debut as a busker.)

Almost every American president since Truman has feted Bob's military exploits in one way or another. Eisenhower gave him the People to People Award and J.F.K. the Congressional Gold Medal. The latter has a significant place in the comedian's heart. President Kennedy presented it to him at the White House on 12 September 1963 and called him 'America's most prized Ambassador of Goodwill'.

'It's been one of the rarest honours given to Americans,' said Kennedy, 'and it's a great pleasure for me, on behalf of the Congress to present this to you...'

With Dolores by his side, Bob accepted with the usual wisecrack. 'Thank you very much, Mr President,' he said. 'Actually I don't like to tell jokes about a thing like this. Because it's one of the nicest things that's ever happened to me and I feel very humble – although I think I have the strength of character to fight it...'

John Kennedy's successor, Lyndon Johnson, honoured Hope, too, with the Medal of Freedom. Then in 1968 the American commander in Vietnam, General Creighton Abrams, gave him an 'Outstanding Civilian Service' medal for his work there. The following year President Nixon showed his appreciation by inviting the comedian to start his Christmas tour of that season with a show at the White House.

In 1971 a thousand sailors gave Bob a standing ovation in San Diego when Navy Secretary John Chafee pinned the Distinguished Public Service Medal to his lapel – the highest award the United States military can make to a civilian. Hope quipped: 'I can't tell you what a thrill it is to get this piece of gold back from the government. It's a good start...'

A year later, during his last Christmas tour, Bob received South Korea's Order of National Security Merit, Third Class, from Yu Jae Houng, the South Korean Minister of Defence. It was given for 'Mr Hope's contribution to morale since the Korean war'.

But above all his medals and awards, Bob values most his tributes from the fighting men. Whilst in south-east Asia he went out of his way to ensure that he kept the little prizes from the privates, like a pack of Vietnamese cigarettes and matches given to him by one grateful GI.

The seal was well and truly set on Bob's morale-boosting work in the summer of 1976, when Elizabeth II visited Washington as part of America's bi-centennial celebrations. She cited his services to British troops around the world during World War II and said he was 'one of the world's most beloved comedians and a favourite of the royal family.'

It was an honour that particularly pleased his *Road* partner, Dorothy Lamour, who had been with him for the first troop show at March Field. 'This man left his family at Christmastide,' says Dotty, 'when he had children growing up, and new grandchildren. And a lot of times I've gone to their house on New Year's Eve, to spend Christmas when he got home. I really had to hold myself back from getting on my hands and knees to kiss his feet, for coming back safe and sound, and taking the chances he did to give his all to those boys who were away from home. My son was in the United States Marines – and I know what Bob Hope meant. Bob was a god to all those boys overseas, and not just American troops.'

Bob sums up his 33 years on the military roads as 'gratifying'.

'When I started that thing,' he explains, 'I never believed I'd get hooked on it. And the gratification was tremendous, from both the parents and the boys. Today I can't take a trip anywhere without the pilot saying, "I saw you in North Africa," or "Germany," or "England". And it's a warm feeling. Of course, when we were at war you got the same feeling then; they let you know that you were doing something for somebody and that you were doing some good. It was a package of love so far as I was concerned.'

17

As the Christmas decorations and fairy lights were put away in the Hope mansion one warm January morning in 1970, the head of the household paused to reflect upon the coming decade. It looked decidedly promising. Despite continued rumblings about Vietnam, the early part of that year would see him on a 100,000-mile barnstorming tour of the United States. Then there was the news that negotiations concerning a pair of royal charity galas in London during the autumn were almost complete, after which he would crown Miss World, and a second grandchild was on the way (his first, Zachary, had been born the year before).

The 1970s certainly started well enough. The tour was a virtual sell-out, with only the occasional banner and heckler to disrupt the hilarity. And in July he was happily ensconced in London's Savoy Hotel talking to Lord Mountbatten about the November *Night of Nights* charity concert at the Festival Hall, which would star him with Sir Noel Coward and Frank Sinatra. Afterwards there was just time for a few words with Charlie Chaplin, who was staying in the next room, and a round of golf at Wentworth with James Bond star Sean Connery.

When he got back to North Hollywood, there was a letter of confirmation from the Earl signed 'Mountbatten of Burma'. Not to be outdone, the comedian penned a quick acceptance with the ending, 'Bob of Burbank'.

In August daughter Linda produced a long-awaited grandson – Andrew – and Bob handed round the cigars at his NBC television studio. A few weeks later he was celebrating again – the 10,000-strong American Guild of Variety Artists named him 'Entertainer of the Year'.

Bob was in fine form when he arrived in London for the autumn concert season and he came armed to the teeth with gags about his co-stars:

I asked Sir Noel if he'd do a number with me, and he said: 'My dear boy . . . there's only so much I'll do for charity . . .'

But, really, Noel Coward is a remarkable man. Playwright, composer, actor, and celebrated wit – it's encouraging to see an Englishman make it without a guitar . . .

You may have heard of Frank Sinatra. He's sort of an Italian 'Alfie' – part-time singer and full-time sex symbol . . .

Frank is known as a great admirer of women. He also sings – but then we all need an emotional outlet . . .

The Festival Hall evening, on 16 November, comprised two £50-a-seat performances – the first before Princess Alexandra, the second with Prince Charles and Princess Anne in attendance. All three were disappointed by the absence of Nöel Coward, who less than 24 hours before had been rushed to nearby St Thomas' Hospital with pleurisy. Fortunately the organizers were able to secure a last-minute royal deputy, Princess Grace of Monaco.

Bob filled the first half of each show, following a welcoming speech by Lord Mountbatten, who explained that the £100,000 they hoped to raise would be going to help establish a chain of international schools throughout the world to provide 'an opportunity for future leaders to get to understand each other'.

For some reason Hope was not at his funniest that night. Possibly it was the theatre that worried him; during the afternoon rehearsals he likened it to 'an operating table'. His hour-long act went down well, but not as well as he would have liked. Then, as he reached his finale, it all went very wrong. He had enlisted the aid of David Frost and the reigning Miss World; they were supposed to waltz slowly onto the stage, where they would become stooges in his last big routine.

Watching from the stalls was Bob's European gag writer, Denis Goodwin. 'This was the climax. This is where he got his big laugh,' said Denis. 'So obviously they were supposed to be fairly surreptitious. But David did this terrible dance; this dreadful, noisy, clumping dance, which got the wrong sort of attention. And he milked it for all it was worth...'

A thoroughly disgusted Hope hurried off to his dressing-room to try to bolster his material for the second house; closely followed by a hobbling Denis Goodwin, who had one leg encased in plaster as the result of an accident. They had just started discussing what should be done, when the door burst open to admit David Frost in euphoric form: 'Bob, that was fantastic ... that was super...'

Years later, shortly before he died, Denis Goodwin explained what happened next. 'It all came out,' he said. 'All those superlatives went on for a very long time and Bob, who is a very generous man – who was annoyed with himself, virtually turned his back ... he sort of turned aside from David. And David was looking around the room for someone he knew, because he was in full flood and he had to relate to somebody. He recognized me – but the words kept coming out: 'Super ... special ... marvellous ... wonderful ... hello Denis!' And because of the embarrassment of the situation I said, 'I broke my leg David...' and he said, "Oh good! How was I?"'

Prince Charles saw a slightly perkier Hope later that night. Among other things, he heard him joke about the M1 motorway and Crosby:

Bing nearly had a road accident last week. Fortunately he opened his legs wide enough to let the latest British sports car drive through. Just think about the headlines he might have made – little car with top down hits man with little down on top.

I like England – here the girls whistle back at you.

I know I was born here – when I cut myself I bleed tea.

And I'm glad to see you are getting the freeways here. You know we have the big Hollywood freeway in Lost Angeles, where you can drive for nineteen miles – without leaving the scene of the accident.

The next afternoon Bob was at the London studios of Thames Television, ostensibly to be surprised by Eamonn Andrews for a special two-part *This is Your Life* programme. The production team had been working on the project for a year under the apt code name 'Charity' (the comedian's press agent at the time was called Faith) and had secretly, or so they thought, flown in Dolores and the four children. Bob, however, had known of their plans for some time. Such surprises are not often tolerated in the Hope organization. But few – least of all Eamonn and his producers – guessed that he knew. When the host spelled out the magic words: 'Bob Hope ... this is your life!' he looked suitably astonished and said: 'Come on ... you're kidding?'

Twenty-four hours later Bob was on stage at the Talk of the Town near Leicester Square for his third charity show in as many days. The audience, which had paid between £25 and £500 a head, rubbed shoulders with half Europe's royalty, including the Queen, Prince Philip, the Prince of Wales, Princess Anne, Princess Alexandra, King Constantine of Greece, Prince Henrik and Princess Margaretha of Denmark, and the Grand Duke and Grand Duchess of Luxembourg.

On stage the cast was almost as impressive. The dapper Rex Harrison emceed; Glenn Campbell, Petula Clark, Engelbert Humperdinck and Millicent Martin sang; Rudolf Nureyev and Antoinette Sibley danced; Tom Jones left the stalls to holler 'I Who Have Nothing'; and Bob was a thousand times funnier:

Your Majesties ... Ladies and Gentlemen ... Peasants ...

Just to be here is a thrill; at this wonderful posh affair. I was just talking about it with my waiter – Harold Wilson ...

And I've never seen such royalty. I really never have. This whole thing looks like a chess game – live ...

And I'm flabbergasted by this crowd, really, because my mother always told me to be nice to my inferiors – but she forgot to tell me how to act when I didn't have any ...

The Talk of the Town cabaret raised over £100,000 for the World Wildlife Fund. Large sums of money were again at stake two days later at the Royal Albert Hall, though this time charity would not be the main beneficiary, when the 58 finalists gathered for the 1970 Miss World contest. The atmosphere was highly charged and all concerned were apprehensive. For days feminists had been criticizing the annual event and accusing the organizers of running a 'cattle market' that was demeaning to all women. On top of that, a few hours earlier a small bomb, thought to have been planted by the IRA, exploded near a BBC Television outside broadcast unit.

But on the night, in full view of a home television audience of about 33 million, it was the Women's Liberation Movement and a handful of Young Liberals who sensationally stopped the show in its tracks, and finally ruined Bob's six-day London visit. They had slipped past the supposedly tight security during the first part of the judging, while he was still in his Savoy Hotel suite frantically phoning New York and Hollywood for more topical jokes.

He arrived at the Albert Hall only minutes before compere Michael Aspel introduced his act – a monologue, during which the judges would whittle down the contestants to the last fifteen. Looking pale and drawn, but with the familiar lopsided grin fixed beneath the famous ski-snoot, he ambled on stage to face the music:

Thank you very much ... thank you, ladies and gentlemen. I'm very, very happy to be here at this cattle market tonight ...

Mooooo ...

No, it's quite a cattle market – I've been back there checking calves ...

No, but this is beautiful. But I wanna assure you about the bomb blast ... nothing is going to get blown up here tonight – they've checked every costume in the place ...

Minutes later, as Bob moved into a routine of gags about David Frost and Vietnam, the hall erupted in pandemonium as a cacophany of football rattles and whistles drowned his words. Up in the balconies scores of exploding fire-crackers added to the growing din. Then dozens of screaming demonstrators poured down the isles towards the stage hurling flour bags, stink bombs, rotten tomatoes, paint bombs and paper leaflets as they went. The barrage peppered the rostrum and all around it, spattering many guests in a colourful mixture of blue paint and white flour. As the missiles began to hail down, Hope stood firm on his allotted mark – looking down at Mike Begg, the BBC stage manager controlling his cue cards, who was crouching in a camera pit directly in front of him.

'He was above me by about six feet,' Begg recalls. 'He sort of paused and we gave him a keep going motion. Then I was suddenly aware, when this noise broke out, that a muslin bag had hit his shoe and a black sort of substance had hit him (later to be analysed as ink). He appeared to get very frightened about this, but he kept going for another couple of gags – then he went off stage ...'

One of the Miss World judges that night was Bob's *Road to Hong Kong* co-star, Joan Collins. 'They started to throw these stink bombs on the stage,' says Joan, 'and they exploded. But one didn't know they were stink bombs! It was quite frightening really. We ... the judges ... were sort of rooted to the spot, but we weren't in the direct line of fire – Bob was! And he stood there for a couple of seconds, and then made a rather swift exit. He didn't run ... but he walked briskly off!'

The comedian stayed off for five minutes, while security guards and police from outside the hall seized the struggling women and ejected them. When he returned, he delivered an ad-libbed broadside at the departing troublemakers and got tumultuous applause:

This is a nice conditioning course for Vietnam ...

I wanna tell ya ... anybody that would try to break up an affair as wonderful as this with these kind of proceedings, and with these wonderful people and wonderful girls from the entire world, has got to be on some kinda dope, ladies and gentlemen ...

After he had crowned Miss Grenada, 22-year-old Jennifer Hosten, Miss World 1970, Bob lashed out angrily at the protestors who had spoiled his performance:

'They said we were "using" women,' he thundered. 'I always thought we were using them right. You know, it's funny. I did a show in October about Women's Lib. They took over my programme and they took over NBC, and I had to go to work as a bunny boy. It was a very successful show. You'll notice about the women in the Liberation Movement – none of them are pretty, because pretty women don't have those problems. If a woman's clever, she can do just as well – if not better – than a man. Is there anything immoral about beauty? All it is, is that a pretty girl wins a competition; travels around a lot; goes on television; makes a lot of money. There's nothing immoral about that. They're exhibitionists, these people. They don't want to do things through Parliament or legal means – and they're always a danger. It's something you're not going to change; partly because they want the attention.'

Over the next few days Bob was roundly criticized in the British press for leaving the Albert Hall stage. They all but accused him of being a coward, which incensed contest organizer Eric Morley. 'Some people asked why he ran in the first place,' says Eric. 'Well he didn't run – he beat a very dignified retreat! Now a man like Bob Hope – who has been to every theatre of war where American troops have been, of his own free will – has got great guts. He's not afraid of anything. He wanted to find out what the hell was going on, that was all.'

In reality, though, Bob was indeed frightened by the on-slaught. The earlier bombing incident had flashed through his mind and, coupled with the fervent anti-Vietnam criticism he had been getting, he thought there was a distinct possibility of something more explosive than a bag full of ink being hurled at him. 'First I heard these bangs up in the balcony,' he said later, 'and then I saw these things starting to come down ... I thought it was safer to let the police sort it all out ... so I walked!'

Bob left for Chicago the next day, a sad and disillusioned man. On top of the problems during the Festival Hall concerts, the Miss World fiasco had been a major blow. It was to be seven years before he performed in Britain again.

Says his former gag-writer, Bob Monkhouse: 'He was deeply offended by the fact that the British public, to whom he had given his finest efforts for so long and who had returned that effort with love and affection, suddenly withdrew it because of one performance at the Miss World contest.'

Apart from the on-stage problems of which there were a number in the 1970s, it was very much a decade for saying goodbye to old friends. In September 1973 Bob opened his Toluca Lake home to give a surprise dinner party for 150 guests, with another 200 arriving later, to mark the retirement of Marjorie Hughes. She had been his private secretary for 31 years. 'During that time,' she said, 'I calculated that I've typed out about 7,000,000 jokes for Mr Hope – and never laughed at one!'

A year later Bob lost one of his closest friends and the world one of the all-time greats of comedy, when Jack Benny died at the age of 80. Benny had been part of Bob's life for more than 36 years and the only man to rival him as a stand-up comic. His death was a tremendous blow. Ever since Jack turned down the juvenile lead in the *Big Broadcast of 1938*, allowing Hope to es-tablish himself in films, the pair had vied with each other in all entertainment media. Surprisingly, though, their friendly feud

– although highly successful – never received the same worldwide attention as Bob's similar double-act with Bing Crosby.

Many people forget that for two decades Hope and Benny dominated the world of American radio comedy. Says Irving Fein, who managed both Jack Benny and George Burns: 'Jack was number one on radio when Hope started in radio, but Hope quickly caught up and then passed Jack. By 1941, Hope had become number one and Jack was number two. They went back and forth until 1948 – when Jack became number one again and Hope was number two or three. But they were both at the top practically all the time on radio.'

It is a little known fact that at one time, during the late thirties, executives at Paramount Pictures considered Bob Hope unlikely to make it big as a screen comedian, because they thought he was too much like Jack Benny. In retrospect, as Irving Fein is only too ready to point out, the very idea seems preposterous. 'They were different types of comedians,' he says. 'Jack Benny was a situation comedian, who would go along with situations and character to get his laughs. Hope would do the topical jokes always; Hope did fast jokes ... whereas Jack would build up a situation for ten minutes in order to get a big punch line in.' Bob agrees. 'Jack Benny was the slowest, most potent comic ever,' he says. 'I told ten jokes while he was telling one. I could milk a joke, but Jack got chicken fat out of it ... he just ripped it to pieces ... squeezed it until it hurt! A wonderful art. Jack had a great art.'

When television took over as the principal comic medium Hope and Benny continued their association to great effect on each other's shows. Said Jack, shortly before he died: 'We had almost a ritual of popping up unexpectedly. I would sit in his audience and make a few cracks and he would wander on when I was trying to tell a joke. It was great fun. But Bob has a very strong personality and not only did he produce his own shows – he directed, produced and starred in mine as well. In fact he was the star of both shows.'

The basis of many classic Hope gags about Benny was his legendary meanness:

I had dinner with him the last time I was here ... and we had a wonderful dinner, delightful conversation. When the check came, he ran and tried to hide in the washroom – but I wouldn't let him in.

A similar money joke was used for Benny's only screen appearance with Hope – an unbilled walk-on in the 1949 film *The Great Lover*. Jack played a ship's passenger who cashed a hundred dollar bill for Bob. As he examined the note with the jeweller's eye-glass, Hope snapped tartly, 'I don't want to hock it! I just want to change it.'

Then, as Benny strolled away, Hope looked perplexed. 'No! *He* couldn't be travelling first class.'

The pair were at it again when they each received an honorary Doctor of Fine Arts degree from Jacksonville University, in Florida, on 6 April 1972. First up was Jack, who could not resist weaving Bob into his acceptance speech:

'Bob Hope is surely one of the most dedicated and unselfish men in our industry,' he said. 'Each year Bob goes off entertaining our troops, while we sit at home with our wives and loved ones. Who else but Bob, while the rest of us are at home, would unselfishly go off year after year with Jill St John, Raquel Welch and Ann-Margret . . .'

Bob returned the joke during his speech. 'Jack's a great musician,' he told the students, 'and I'm a great actor – it takes a great actor to say Jack Benny's a great musician . . .'

But he was not in such jovial form when he rose to give the eulogy at Jack Benny's funeral. George Burns had originally agreed to do it, but when the time came he was so upset that all he could say was 'I loved Jack . . .' So Bob took over: 'How do you say goodbye to a man who was not just a friend, but a national treasure. It's hard to say no man is indispensable, but it is true just the same that some are irreplaceable. No-one has come along to replace Jolson, or Bogart, or Gable, or Will Rogers, or Chevalier. I think it's a safe bet that no-one will ever replace Jack Benny.

'Jack had that rare magic, that indefinable something called genius. Picasso had it, Gershwin had it and Jack was blessed with it. He didn't just stand on the stage – he owned it. For a man who was the undisputed master of comedy timing, you have to say that this was the only time when Jack's timing was all wrong – he left us much too soon. He was stingy to the end . . . he only gave us eighty years and it wasn't enough.'

1975 and 1976 were years which brought Bob another score of honours. He collected the Will Rogers Humanitarian Award

The stars of *Road to Morocco* (1942)

Bing and Bob on the perilous *Road to Utopia* in 1944

Bob and Shirley Ross, the original duo who sang 'Thanks for the Memory' in *The Big Broadcast of 1938*

The cast of NBC radio show 'Soldiers in Greasepaint' (1943). With Bob are Jack Benny (in front); Merle Oberon (on Benny's left); behind her, Andy Devine; Jerry Colonna (back row); John Garfield and Frances Langford (both at far right)

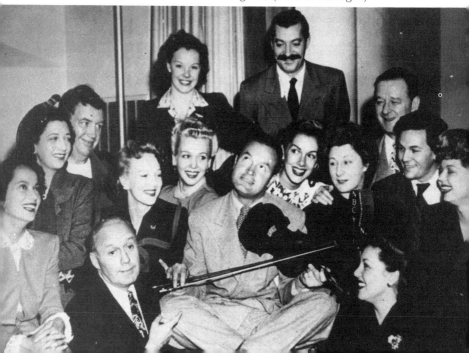

Bob presenting Princess Elizabeth with her wedding gift from Hollywood, 400 portraits of film stars, watched by George VI and Queen Elizabeth

Van Johnson, Jack Benny and George Burns with Bob in one of his early television specials

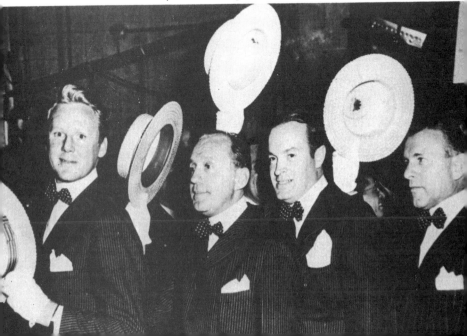

Bob and James Cagney in their famous dance sequence from *The Seven Little Foys* (1955)

Crossing Red Square, Moscow in 1958

Lucille Ball and Bob in *The Facts of Life* (1960)

A scene from *The Private Navy of Sergeant O'Farrell* (1968)

The world's leading troop entertainer hard at work

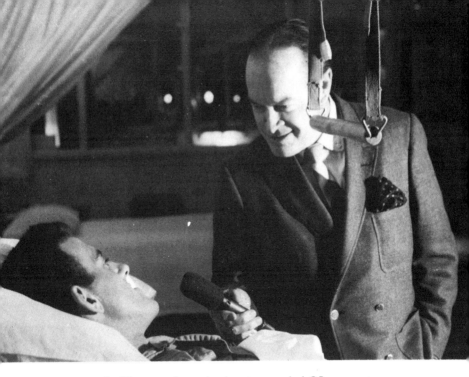

In Vietnam, interviewing a wounded GI

Facing the press while on tour (1971)

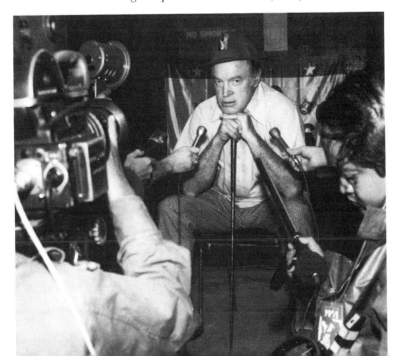

Frank Sinatra, Bing Crosby and John Wayne helped Bob celebrate
his 25th year in television (1975) with a special show

'I'm going to bore people for
the next twenty years...'

from his son; was initiated into the American Entertainment Hall of Fame; was voted the People's Choice Entertainer of the Year on each occasion and, on 25 September 1975, to mark his 25th anniversary on television, the United States Congress praised him with a special resolution: 'It is not only an historical milestone in the country's television annals, but a most significant achievement for a fellow American who already has achieved virtually every honour his nation can bestow.' On 17 March 1976, Frank Sinatra, Bing Crosby and John Wayne were just some of the stars who helped Bob celebrate his 25th season on the small screen with an impressive NBC special.

In July the same year, the comedian was called to Washington for a long-awaited accolade from the land of his birth. As part of the bi-centennial year festivities, the Queen made Bob an honorary Commander of the British Empire. He joined a list of thirteen other 'unusually distinguished' Americans – including Walter Annenberg, the former Ambassador to the Court of St James, and Dean Rusk, the former US Secretary of State. The then British Ambassador, Sir Peter Ramsbotham, hung the CBE insignia around Bob's neck at a British Embassy ceremony.

A week after the presentation Bob gave his new gong its first outing – in front of the Queen and Prince Philip at a White House banquet and supper show given by President Gerald Ford. 'I'll never forget the role that Bob played,' says Ford. 'He put the show together and did the whole job, and Her Majesty was really impressed.'

The highlight of Bob's act was a specially written version of his theme song 'Thanks for the Memory':

> Thanks for the memory,
> Of this dazzling affair,
> This gracious royal pair,
> Their presence at our birthday,
> Brought us joy beyond compare,
> And, we thank you so much.

The following year, 1977, should have been one of the best of the decade. And it should have been all fun with Bing Crosby. The pair had been invited to star before the Queen in the Silver

Jubilee Royal Variety Show at the London Palladium in November; a London-based record company wanted them to make a duet album; and plans had been almost finalized for the summer shooting of an eighth *Road* picture.

But a televised concert in Pasadena, 15 miles from Hollywood, changed all that. On 3 March Bing plunged 25 feet into a concrete-floored orchestra pit, severely crushing a disc in his spine, making him a virtual invalid for four months.

The show, at the Ambassador Auditorium, was part of the celebrations of Crosby's 50 years in show business. Moments before the fall Bob had stepped on stage to present him with a special 'Crummy' award. 'It's for performers who don't win anything else,' he explained to a laughing Crosby.

Bob was among the first to his side after the accident and he turned deathly pale when he saw his friend struggling to get up, with blood pouring from a badly gashed forehead. He had been sitting in his dressing-room beneath the stage when it happened.

'We heard this tremendous crack, followed by a horrible thump,' Hope told the author later. 'I don't know how he survived the fall. The stage was exceptionally high because a special platform had been built for the television people. The scenery must've slowed him up enough because it was a hell of a long way down.'

In hospital the next day Bing took a telephone call from Bob. 'I gotta change the act and get a new finish,' he told the worried comedian.

Hopes of starting work on the new film – provisionally called *Road to Tomorrow*, but later changed to *Road to the Fountain of Youth* – were dashed when it became obvious that Bing's injuries were more serious than at first thought. However, he was well enough to undertake his previously arranged autumn tour of Britain and a two-week season at the Palladium.

Bob, in the meantime, continued to crisscross the United States appearing at benefits and touring the college circuit with his stage show. On the afternoon of Friday, 14 October, he was in New York's Waldorf Towers Hotel preparing for a charity concert in New Jersey that night. Shortly before two o'clock the phone rang. Bob picked it up. 'Bing Crosby has just collapsed and died on a Spanish golf course,' a voice said somberly. 'It was a heart attack!'

Hope was stunned; the man he always thought indestructible was dead. Ashen-faced and near to tears, he could only mumble: 'I just can't believe it . . . I'm absolutely numb . . . I can't understand what happened . . .'

Later he told the author: 'It was the strangest feeling I've ever had. My head felt like someone had wrapped a steel band around it . . . it was an incredible sensation. Even when I lost my mother and brothers it didn't affect me in that way. My head was completely tight; it was a great shock.'

His first act following the news was to cancel the evening concert, saying, 'I just can't get funny tonight. It's just not in me.' He also pulled out of a personal appearance in Tucson, Arizona, scheduled for the next night and asked comedian Bill Cosby to deputize. He then flew home by private jet.

Later that same night he went out walking with his press agent, Ward Grant, to discuss the wording of the official statement he knew he had to make. The tribute read: 'The whole world loved Bing Crosby with a devotion that not only crossed international boundaries, but erased them. He was proof positive that you can replace a military uniform with a pork-pie hat, an Hawaiian shirt and a pipe.'

Bing's death made life doubly difficult for Bob – several days before his mother-in-law, Mrs Therasa Defina, had died also. She was in her eighties. And on top of all that he was in the final stages of a two-hour television special, which was to concentrate on his *Road* films with Crosby.

So, less than 24 hours after the fateful news from Spain, Hope was forced to temper his grief for discussions with his director, Howard W. Koch, President of the Academy of Motion Picture Arts and Sciences, on how they could best change their plans.

Koch said about that Saturday meeting: 'He seemed to be getting back to what he should be . . . where he was . . . but he still was a little off balance when we started to discuss what the show was going to be like. And we decided to switch the show from a *Road* show *with* Bing and Bob, to a tribute to Bing *by* Bob – which gave us a frantic ten days to get it ready for the air.'

The entire Hope production team – including Bob, Koch

and executive producer Elliott Kozak – worked until 3.00 each morning gathering and editing a mountain of material. The show contained highlights of the pair's 40-year association on radio, television and films. A score of writers, production assistants, tape editors and researchers toiled round the clock to get the extracts ready for Hope to accept or reject. Hope even enlisted the help of this author – Bing's authorized biographer – who had arrived in Hollywood on the Saturday evening to begin filming a 70-minute Thames Television documentary for airing in Britain on Hope's 75th birthday the following May. Bing had intended to be one of the main contributors.

Bob buried Dolores's mother on Monday 17 October and then, at dawn the next day, helped to lay the Old Groaner to rest in a hill-top grave near Hollywood. Accompanied by Dolores, he was one of only three members of the show business profession who crowded into the tiny Catholic chapel of St Paul the Apostle in Los Angeles with 38 other mourners (Crosby's will had specified a family funeral only). Rosemary Clooney and Phil Harris were the other two. Dorothy Lamour did not attend, despite a number of frantic phone calls to Bob asking him to persuade Kathryn Crosby to include her.

'How could I intervene?' said Bob later. 'It was none of my business. It would have been very wrong – Bing had made his wishes perfectly clear.'

The Hope-Crosby partnership was probably the most famous double-act since Stan Laurel and Oliver Hardy. It certainly was far more financially rewarding for the principals. Film producer Melvin Frank describes it as a 'highly ambivalent' relationship and likens it to a 'kind of marriage', with all the inherent problems of wedlock.

But in reality, the pair were never as close off stage or screen as their public imagined. Privately they were basically different types – Bing an introverted loner, Bob a natural extrovert. Joan Collins was one of many to be surprised by this, when she co-starred in *Road to Hong Kong*. 'They didn't spend too much time together,' she says. 'They didn't hang out in each other's dressing-rooms. Crosby was much lower key than Bob. He didn't talk much; he wasn't unfriendly, but he wasn't particularly friendly. Whereas Hope was always there, talking to the directors; talking to the gag writers; talking to the actors

166

– generally doing schtick . . .'

Bing's eldest son, Gary believes it was really a 'novel relationship' because they did not get too close. 'They both had fun at their work,' says Gary, 'but any kind of relationship you have with another person – if you are going to be with them, looking in their face 24 hours a day – will sooner or later bustup. These two men were very smart; they did not socialize together that much. Maybe two or three times a year we'd go to their house, or they'd come to our house, but the rest of the time they went their separate ways. So they always had new, fresh things to talk about and new bits to do for one another when they did meet. And it kept their relationship working, I think.'

Rosemary Clooney, Bing's long-time singing partner, feels the pair successfully 'skirted around the edges of a very close friendship' for nigh on 40 years. 'I think there was mutual respect, professionally,' she says, 'but I think they respected each other's privacy as well. I think they spent time together, but it was never enough time to get tired of each other or to hit on a spot where they would disagree . . . It was all the best parts of a good friendship, and a close friendship, with none of the kind of things that would get to be cloying or hard to live with after a while. They kept their identities separate.'

Another secret of their success was the vastly different pace at which they worked. Bing was always outwardly easy-going – 'lazy' is how he put it – while Rapid Robert often surpassed his nickname. It was something which always both impressed and astounded Crosby. 'He just amazes me,' he told the author in 1972. 'People ask me every place I go, "Hi Bing . . . where's Hope? What did you do with the old man?" And I only probably respond with maybe one or two wisecracks. But if they ask Hope, "Where's Bing?", he does about ten minutes – if he can get anybody to stand still that long! He's got a regular routine worked out.'

Says Gary Crosby: 'I think they kept each other interested that way. Dad could never figure out why Bob was always on the go. He'd say, "It would kill me, that kind of work is too tough, too tiring. I could never do it!" And yet, he'd look at Bob . . . and see it was keeping him going.'

Over the years a myth grew that Hope was often hurt by Crosby's refusal to join him in trying to attend every major

Hollywood show business function. This was not true. There were times when he was perplexed by Crosby's reluctance, but he was never hurt. Even when Bing failed to show for a charity dinner Bob had worked hard to organize, he ended up laughing.

'Why couldn't you make it, Bing?' enquired Hope a few days later.

'I wasn't hungry,' came the reply.

Only once did Bob show a trace of annoyance when Bing snubbed a big occasion: Paramount Pictures gave a splendid hundredth birthday party for Adolph Zuckor, the man who had given Crosby his start in films back in the thirties. Everyone who was anyone in Tinsel Town was there, including Bob and Dorothy Lamour. But Crosby gave it a miss, even though he had promised to be there. 'What is it with Bing?' Bob asked a friend afterwards.

He already knew the answer. He admitted to the author in 1978, 'I understood the way Bing was. He didn't like that sort of function, so he didn't attend. I knew that and he never hurt me once ... never once. It could be annoying, but that's the way Bing was ...'

A recurring question about the Hope-Crosby partnership has always been: would Bob have attained the heights he has without it? Gary Crosby believes the answer is a resounding yes.

'I don't think either of them had a need for one another,' he says. 'I think they found something that the two of them could do together and do well; I think both of them were giants. And just by having two giants come together, it worked great.'

The loss of Bing will have a lasting effect on Bob, more so even than the death of Jack Benny. For a start, as Melville Shavelson points out, it has made him realize that all men are mortal. 'I don't think it ever really dawned on Bob that he was included in that,' says Mel.

Bob has also lost a large slice of his stage act – around fifty Bing Crosby jokes have had to be retired, in Bob's view, prematurely. He was also deprived of the chance of hitting one final *Road* with Bing.

So too was Mel Shavelson, who conceived, wrote and would have directed the *Road to the Fountain of Youth*. He missed out on finally getting his name on the *Road* credits, after years of supplying unbilled jokes for the series when part of Hope's radio writing team. But could they have successfully recreated the magic after a gap of 17 years, when both stars were in their mid-seventies?

Says Shavelson: 'I felt, along with Bob, that the style of the *Road* pictures had been absorbed by some of the modern successful comedians. And that the things that Bob and Bing had done so well were now thought of to be something entirely new. But no one could do it better than the originals. Possibly, I felt, it was going to be the last *Road* picture; it should have been the last and the best – to show everybody that what made Bob, Bob and Bing, Bing was still there.'

The basic plot of the film, in which the pair would have played themselves, had them searching in vain for the Fountain of Youth. Lord Grade would have supplied the filming facilities in Britain, but very little money, and location work was planned in certain Middle Eastern countries. Dorothy Lamour had been promised a part, but the leading lady would have been one of the hot stars of the seventies, probably Farrah Fawcett-Majors.

'It was a gimmick picture,' says Mel Shavelson, 'and the joke was that the Fountain of Youth would work on everybody but Bob and Bing – because you can't expect miracles – and I think that we could have used their appearance as one of the jokes. It wouldn't have been simple; it wouldn't have been easy; but it would have been fun.'

Another piece of fun to die along with Bing was a proposed duet album with Bob to be made in London. British record producer Ken Barnes, who had been making albums in London with the Groaner for the three years prior to his death, had persuaded the Polydor company to finance such a project. The author had put the idea to Bob, who reacted favourably. Crosby, however, had not been so sure when it was first mooted to him. 'Oh no!' he said. 'That isn't going to sell two copies – who wants a record of Hope?' His reaction brought laughter from the record executives. And that produced a more positive approach from the crooner. 'Well, if you think you can get it together ... okay! Actually Bob isn't such a bad singer; he's a little limited, but he carries a tune,' joked Bing.

169

It had been planned to record the album during the Royal Variety Show in November, when the pair would be in London together for a week. Barnes had made arrangements to fly to California with arranger Pete Moore to finalize the deal on the very weekend of Bing's death.

Says Barnes: 'It's a shame that that album didn't take place, because it would have been almost a crowning achievement on both their parts. It's quite amazing that in all the years they had been together, nobody had thought of putting them in the studio together to do an album!'

Hope gave his first public performance since Crosby's death 10 days later before 7,000 people in Ganton, Ohio, 50 miles from the city of his youth, Cleveland. It was a nerve-wracking experience for him. 'But as soon as I heard the first laugh, I was on my way,' says Bob. 'And when I said to that audience, "You know what you've done for me tonight? You've made me feel awfully good!" they applauded like hell. Because they knew exactly how I felt about it. But what can you do? You just don't go on moaning about a thing like that – you just have to go to work . . .'

Before leaving for London, and the Queen's Silver Jubilee concert, Bob relaxed at his Palm Springs home while undergoing a thorough medical check-up. 'I worried a lot after Bing's death,' he says. 'I thought maybe I should ease up, but the doctor gave me a check and said I was completely fit.'

Bob flew to London in style. He stopped off in Washington to catch his first British Airways Concorde and at 50,000 feet above the Atlantic, at twice the speed of sound, he was like a child with a new toy. 'It's a great experience,' he enthused, before breaking into the inevitable joke routine. 'I have something in common with this aircraft – just look at our noses! I hope that when we get to London the runway isn't icy – because we could finish up in Oslo . . . I went over to England on the *Queen Mary* in 1943 and to think now that I'm flying up here at this speed is really something – I just hope my luggage is with us . . .'

When Bob stepped on to the stage of the London Palladium on 21 November to host the Jubilee show, he had more Concorde gags on his cue cards:

I am delighted to be here. I flew over on Concorde – I'm delighted to be anywhere . . .

Concorde is so fast – it gives you an extra couple of hours to look for your luggage . . .

And it flies so high – I swear I heard organ music . . .

But the sensation of the night came when the comic broke organizer Lord Delfont's ban on royal jokes. His target was Princess Anne's recent baby. First he congratulated the Queen on her new title – 'Royal Babysitter'. Then he swung into a routine that had Delfont squirming in his £100 seat:

You know I am over here on business. I am starting a nappy company – and I wanted to start at the top . . .

It is not easy to deliver a royal baby – while you are bowing at the same time . . .

Before they could smack its bottom – they had to wait for someone to dash to the Palace to ask permission . . .

The Queen wanted to have the baby at the Palace – but you know how difficult it is these days to get a doctor to make housecalls . . .

During the interval Lord Delfont hurried to have drinks with the royal family. 'I was very worried about all those royal jokes,' he admitted afterwards, 'but my mind is now at rest. The Queen has just told me that she thought they were absolutely marvellous and Prince Charles added that they were just right.'

The royal gala, which also starred Julie Andrews, Paul Anka, Harry Belafonte, Tommy Cooper, Shirley MacLaine and Rudolph Nureyev, raised a record one million pounds for charity. Most of the money came from television rights in the United States, where it was billed as *America's Salute to the Queen*.

Before returning to California – and a Palm Springs concert with Frank Sinatra – Bob spent a couple of hard days filming at the *Muppet Show* studios in Elstree, Hertfordshire. He recorded a guest spot for the British version of the show and then tapped a segment for a forthcoming American Hope special.

In February 1978 he did an 18-day concert tour of Australia and New Zealand, visiting six cities. The tour was filmed for his first marathon overseas television show since 1972.

He was made even happier by the Academy of Motion Picture Arts and Sciences, who informed him that they wanted him to play Mr Oscar again.

18

Bob Hope's long association with Oscar began back in 1940, when the prized gold-plated statuettes were handed out during an intimate ceremony at the Los Angeles Ambassador Hotel. Over the decades, he saw it grow into a national event – through radio – when it moved to the renowned Grauman's Chinese Theatre on Hollywood Boulevard. And then he helped the event come of age internationally – through television – when the yearly affairs were conducted at the Santa Monica Auditorium on the shores of the Pacific.

'That was very handy,' joked Bob, 'because the losers could walk right into the ocean . . .'

Now, 35 years later, after a record 22 show appearances – including serving as master of ceremonies 15 times (another record) and solo emcee on eight occasions, Bob was the unanimous choice to host the prestigious 50th Academy Awards Presentations at the huge Dorothy Chandler Pavilion in downtown Los Angeles.

On the evening of 3 April 1978, 70 million Americans switched on their sets to watch Mr Oscar unveil the Golden Jubilee affair. Academy President and show producer, Howard W. Koch, had promised to make it the most glamorous and star-studded of all. It was to be a night to remember. With the help of 50 past Oscar winners and Vanessa Redgrave he succeeded. Previous award-winners drew rapturous applause from the 3,000-strong audience as they crowded the stage just before Bob's entrance and their presence allowed him to be as topical as ever:

You're too kind ... maybe not too kind, but you're wonderful.

*Can you believe this group all on the same stage at the same time?
Looks like the road company of the Hollywood wax museum.*

*No, they're wonderful. They all have their Oscars – but are they
happy.*

*Some of the people here have won two or three Oscars each! Their
names have been taken – and they'll be getting their obscene phone calls in
due course.*

The laughter was long and warm, but in the back of everybody's mind loomed the spectre of Vanessa Redgrave – who had been nominated for Best Supporting Actress for her performance in the Jane Fonda film *Julia*. For weeks before the event Hollywood-based Zionists had been protesting about her involvement in an as yet unseen documentary film called *The Palestinians*, which they said was anti-Jewish. Fifteen hundred of them were at that moment wrestling with riot police outside the hall.

Bob appeared unconcerned about all the hullabaloo as he launched into his main menu of gags:

Welcome to the real Star Wars.

*When this event started out, I hadn't even started acting in films – and
throughout its 50-year history the Academy has maintained that attitude.*

*Coming into the theatre tonight, did you notice the ostentatious display
of national chauvinism? All the English stars arrived in Rolls Royces; the
Germans in Mercedes limousines; the Italians in Ferraris – the Americans in Toyotas.*

*And what crowds outside! When I arrived here tonight, my car was surrounded by packs of screaming women clawing to get at me! If you don't
believe me, just ask my driver – John Travolta.*

The biggest surprise of the year is young John Travolta in Saturday
Night Fever. *And I mean young – I have wine older than he is.*

Saturday Night Fever! *That's the movie in which John put on a
great white suit and then tried to wear it out – from the inside.*

*Fifty years ago in films, the boy got the girl. Today it's anybody – her
mother, father, brother, or cocker spaniel.*

Best Supporting Actress was the first major award of the televised section of the programme, immediately following Bob's monologue. 'We couldn't have moved it, even if we'd have wanted to,' explained Howard Koch afterwards, 'We have always had that particular award there and if we had put it somewhere else we would have been seen to have bowed to pressure from reactionary groups.'

Travolta, hailed as the hottest star since Elvis Presley, was making his Oscar show debut as the presenter of the hottest title of the night. And many held their breath as he announced that Vanessa Redgrave had won it. They did not hold it for long – having thanked the Academy voters for their 'tribute to her work', she reduced the proceedings to uproar by congratulating them on not being frightened by 'a small bunch of Zionist hoodlums, whose behaviour is an insult to the stature of Jews all over the world...' She got more whistles and cat-calls when she attacked McCarthy and Nixon for their 'world-wide witch-hunt against those who tried to express in their lives and in their work the truth they believed in'.

'I salute you,' continued Vanessa shrilly, 'and I thank you. And I pledge to you that I will continue to fight against anti-semitism and fascism.'

The next day Bob quipped: 'In one sentence she declared war on every country in the Middle East...'

1978 was also the year when actors again failed to collect their awards. Woody Allen, who won an armful with *Annie Hall*, preferred to play the clarinet in a New York bar. Best Supporting Actor, Jason Robards, did not even bother to explain why he could not make it. 'I think he's playing Bridge with Marlon Brando and George C. Scott,' joked Hope as he tried to move things along.

Bob was more upset by the non-appearance of the award winners than he was by Vanessa Redgrave's outburst. 'I suppose she felt she had to say it,' he told the author later, 'but it's a shame the event has become a political platform. She knew what she was doing. But I think the honour means just as much now as it did fifty years ago and these actors who say it doesn't... I think they have some kind of reason for it. It gets into a routine, where George Scott and Marlon Brando don't show up to get their Oscars... and then Woody Allen... who claimed he was "scared" to show up! He's worked in front of live audiences... I don't understand that, I really don't.'

With its massive 'live' television audiences the annual cere-mony is always easy meat for those seeking notoriety. And, in

1975, Bob was placed in the firing line for the first time when an Oscar winner, the film director Bert Schneider, stirred things up by including controversial references to the imminent 'liberation of Vietnam' by Communist forces in his acceptance speech. Angry viewers jammed the network switchboard and Master of Ceremonies Hope got a series of telegrams objecting to the remarks. He was furious and persuaded Academy Director Walter Mirisch to allow Frank Sinatra – who compered the final part of the show – to read out a disclaimer.

'We are not responsible for any political references on this programme,' stated Sinatra, 'and we are sorry they had to take place this evening.'

Such swift action pacified the viewing audience, but caused renewed unrest among the 3,200 celebrities sitting in the auditorium – including some heated objections from Shirley MacLaine, who has always considered Bob to be a right-winger.

Through the years, the Academy has recognized Hope's services five times – a silver plaque; the Jean Hersholt Humanitarian Award; a life membership (1945); an honorary Oscar (1953); and a gold medal (1966). In addition Greer Garson and Ray Milland were on hand in 1946 to laugh at his one-inch tall 'joke' Oscar. But Bob has always been piqued that his acting ability has never been rewarded with one of the famous statuettes. In fact he has never even been nominated for an award. He believes that this is due solely to a lack of appreciation of the art of comedy.

'You know Charlie Chaplin never won an award for comedy,' he says seriously. 'Or Cary Grant. I'm surprised at Cary Grant, because he did so many serious things too. And he's a fine actor. They finally gave him some kind of award a couple of years ago (as they did Chaplin) but you know, nobody did nicer work.' Publicly Hope has jokingly referred to the 'politics' surrounding Oscar, but privately he really believes that has had a lot to do with it. Three or four of his 54 major comedies, he says, deserved some sort of Academy nomination.

'But you have to go after a nomination,' he explains. 'They don't come after you. You gotta go ... and we've never done that. Panama and Frank, with *Facts of Life*, had a good chance of doing it, but they both left the set and went to England to make a picture. When they came back they said, "Oh! Nobody put it up for a nomination." That was the kind of picture that got a full page rave in *Time* magazine. And the *Seven Little Foys* for instance; that's the kind of a picture where you have a combination of drama and laughs. And even *Beau James*; there's another picture that could have won.'

Supporting Hope in his disappointment is the doyen of British actors, Lord Olivier, himself a past Oscar winner. 'One thinks of Hope more under the title of an entertainer than an actor,' he says. 'But he's quite right. He should be accounted an actor. That's what an actor is – to do what he does requires being a brilliant actor.'

Facts of Life director Melvin Frank, however, feels that Bob has never received a Best Actor nomination for one very good reason – he has never turned in a 'performance that was of Academy Award stature'. But, says Frank, that was not entirely the comedian's fault. 'They should in my opinion create a separate category for what was the best comedy performance of the year,' he says. 'It was terribly unfair for Bob to have to compete with Ronald Colman, or even Bing. But he never was given the roles that were Academy Award roles, because up until the time that he became independent, as all of us, he had very little choice about what he could do.'

In reviewing Bob Hope's career as a film actor one must bear in mind that it was his great success as a radio comedian which made him a film star in the first place. So it was therefore difficult for him to escape being typecast, both by himself and the casting directors. Very few of his 73 movies got overwhelming praise from the critics, but at the box-office he has been one of the most popular characters in the history of the industry.

Fellow comedian Frankie Howerd, who was born near Craigton Road in Eltham, considers Hope a much better actor than he has been given credit for. 'I saw a film of his once called *Critic's Choice* (1963) in which he played a drunk scene,' says Frankie, 'which I thought was brilliant. Because I don't think he does drink very much and it's not easy to portray a drunk. If you're supposed to be a comedian people want you to be funny – which is right, that is what they pay for; therefore it's dangerous to suddenly think, "I'll go into Shakespeare or

Othello or Hamlet." Because people say, "Leave it to some-body who's a great actor . . . do what you do best." And I think that Bob Hope is capable of doing more, but then if he were to appear as Othello or Hamlet people would say, "This is not the Bob Hope we know!"'

Writer-director Mel Shavelson believes that Bob is a much better actor than *he* cares to admit. 'He's a little embarrassed or ashamed about his own ability to act,' says Mel. 'In pictures like *Seven Little Foys* or *Beau James*, where he had to play dramatic scenes, he would always try to break up the camera crew during the shot by doing some bit of business or some joke.

'But the fact is, and I keep telling him and he doesn't deny it, that a comedian has to be much more of an actor – especially in a film – because he must carry the dramatic part and then he must also be able to get laughs. And I think because they are comedians they get very little credit for it. And Bob's dream with the Academy Award is true; he would love some day to win an Academy Award; the one thing that burns him the most is that Bing won it and he never did.'

Mel Frank, who also thinks that Bob has always underrated his own worth as a film actor, believes that the comedian has made one serious error during his movie career – not having grown to his 'fullest potential'.

'He could have done more with what he has,' says Frank. 'He has God-given gifts; he has for instance the most incredible sense of concentration. I used to be absolutely amazed as I watched him – I knew that he had a golf date on his mind, a real estate deal, a thousand different things – but it was like a doctor doing an important operation; it all vanished.

'My only beef with him as a performer is that I think he could have done more. He reached a certain level and has for years done too many of the same kind of jokes. I don't think we ever were quite able to bring out the work that he is capable of. I would love to see him play an older man and exhibit the sort of sensitivity of which he's capable. He doesn't necessarily have to tell the jokes all the time.'

According to Mel Frank, Bob himself once classically illus-trated his over-reliance on gags when they met at Paramount one night. He was soon to start a new film and held the script in his hand; when he caught sight of his former employee he waved it triumphantly in the air. 'It's all here!' he shouted glee-fully.

Mel says: 'He was like a little kid with a wonderful security blanket. What he really meant was, "It's loaded with jokes; it'll be fine; it'll be good; people will laugh." He was looking at me like a little baby who had just picked up his Christmas toys and said, "I've got all the goodies in the world right here ... I'm gonna be just fine today."'

Another former Hope gag-writer, Bob Monkhouse, differs slightly from those who consider the comedian to be simply the king of the wise-cracking movie stars. He admires the way Bob combined complicated sight gags with his undoubted vocal talents.

'Hope would have been a great comedian in the silent film days,' says Monkhouse. 'People remember those one-liners much more clearly than they remember all the sight material. He's a marvellous sight comedian. He had an innate sense of what would be comic when it got onto the celluloid. It hap-pened over the first few films; he grasped it almost at once. Nobody took him aside and taught him that, because nobody does that for you – they're looking after their own livelihoods. Hope had it already there within him.'

Monkhouse also disagrees with those critics who wanted to see more depth and real life in Bob's pictures. 'Hope never bothered about reality in films,' he says, 'When he appeared in a thriller – a perfectly sound 'B' picture like *My Favourite Brunette* or *My Favourite Spy* and added to it the fantasy of his per-formance, and the jokes – he wasn't worried about coming through to you truthfully. He was only concerned with making you laugh. I think the great quality about Hope's lasting ability as a comedian is that you will never doubt the fact that he is there with the prime objective of making you laugh.'

For his part, Bob – who claims never to have had any ambi-tions to be a 'straight' actor – believes that a large measure of his success on the big screen has been due to the long line of beautiful leading ladies he has been teamed with over the years.

'They've been very important to me,' he admits, 'because I need therapy at all times in my work ... but seriously, that's part of the thing; you get an attractive star and that's it. I had the good fortune of working with them. I was lucky; I always had a very beautiful gal; I worked with about every gal that's ever set foot in Hollywood; it just happened to me. The money was good too, although I think I'd do the same thing over for half...'

There is only one question about his extensive film career that Bob Hope really finds impossible to answer – what has been his best piece of work on celluloid? He 'likes' some of the classic bits of nonsense with Bing Crosby in the *Road* films and thinks his famous dance sequence with Jimmy Cagney in *The Seven Little Foys* was 'pretty good'. He is even 'fairly pleased' with his non-joking scenes in *The Facts of Life*.

But one man, at least, is absolutely certain of Bob's finest filmic hour – Melvin Frank. He says Hope hit the heights during the first piece of filming he ever did on his first Hollywood movie, *The Big Broadcast of 1938*, when he crooned 'Thanks for the Memory' to Shirley Ross. Mel unashamedly admits to weeping every time he sees it.

'It was the best thing he has ever done,' Mel insists. 'We did well with *The Facts of Life*, but although we tried hard we could not get him to that stage again. Perhaps it was the lack of songs ... I don't know. But there is something extraordinary about Bob in the way that he can work with music.'

And that is an amazing tribute to an entertainer who has never been highly rated as a singer. But, surprisingly, many people in the music business and a large number of his colleagues feel Hope is a far better vocalist than he has hitherto been given credit for.

Says Dorothy Lamour: 'Bob always wanted to be a singer, but everybody pushed him down on it. They said, "No ... you're a comedian, you're not a singer." But to me he was a singer and he still is a singer, and a very good singer, but the public would probably not accept him that way.'

Although Hope cannot claim to be a major recording artist in his own right, with only thirty or so discs to his name, it is not generally realized that he has been responsible for introducing a number of golden standards: 'Smoke Gets in Your Eyes', 'I can't Get Started with You', 'It's De-Lovely', 'Two Sleepy People', 'Silver Bells' and a pair of Best Song Oscar winners – 'Thanks for the Memory' (1938) and 'Buttons and Bows'

(1948). More recently, he was the first to popularize 'Tie a Yellow Ribbon', which Tony Orlando later took to the top of the charts. Originally the song was about a prisoner returning from jail; Bob changed the meaning and related it to the boys coming home from Vietnam and all but created a new anthem for them.

> I'm coming home,
> I've done my time,
> Now I gotta know,
> What is and isn't mine . . .

For over forty years Bob has held his own in duets with some of the biggest singing stars in the business, including Bing Crosby, Judy Garland, Doris Day, Eve Arden, Rosemary Clooney, Ethel Merman, Shirley Ross, Tom Jones and many others. And illustrious songsmiths like Cole Porter, Jerome Kern, Johnny Burke and James Van Huesen, Vernon Duke and Ira Gershwin, Leo Robin and Ralph Rainger, and Frank Loesser have supplied him with worthwhile original material.

Today he is still singing. During his 90-minute stage act there are usually about half a dozen songs – some his; some borrowed; some sung straight; some sung comically. 'It's Not Where You Start' and 'Tie a Yellow Ribbon' are supplemented with 'Applause' and 'Lazy'; 'Buttons and Bows' becomes a musical interlude interspersed with gags; 'De-Lovely' is sung with the female guest singer of the night; 'Thanks for the Memory' often stops the show, when first he bursts into a specially written country-and-western version and then really socks-it-to-them with a rock version.

The Old Groaner's last record producer, Ken Barnes, says of Hope the singer: 'As a man who can deliver a song with style and personality, Bob certainly fills the bill. Technically he's very good; he carries a tune very well; he harmonizes very well; there's a good musical ear at work there. I think Bob could have made it as a singer – he had an attractive tone and he was always good with timing.'

But like Martha Raye and Pearl Bailey, both superb singers in their own right, Bob has been inhibited by his comic success. Audiences are always waiting for the line that is going to make them laugh and that makes creating the right mood in which to deliver a serious song difficult, if not impossible.

Another medium in which Bob might be forgiven for feeling aggrieved at the level of recognition he has received from the award-givers is television. Throughout his 29 years on the box the coveted Emmy trophy has passed him by personally – astoundingly, he has never been named Best Comedian. However, he can draw some consolation from the fact that his 1966 Christmas show got an Emmy as 'The Outstanding Variety Special of the Year'.

As a comedian, though, Bob Hope has been showered with honours a-plenty from just about every other quarter. His name has become synonymous with the meaning of comedy. Not everyone by any means laughs wholeheartedly at his jokes, but almost without exception he is universally admired as the most professional and durable of comedians.

In analysing the secret of his great success as a stand-up comic it is very easy to hark back to his unique quick-fire de-livery and choice of the topical quip. But the reasons are far more complex than that; his longevity is due to something else entirely. For, after more than 56 years in show business, Hope stands virtually alone as guardian of an apparently dying breed – the monologist. Only he and George Burns remain as sole perpetrators of the art of American vaudeville comedy. Modern equivalents have followed in their footsteps, like tele-vision star Johnny Carson and funny-man Alan King, but they yet have to prove they can stay the course. Bob has already done so. Faced with an overwhelming television trend away from the monologist in favour of the situation comedy and a change in public taste towards comedy of character, he stuck stubbornly to his tried and trusted routine. 'That does not mean the wisecrack is dead,' he has said many times.

Despite all the sophisticated comic developments of recent years – *Monty Python* for instance – Bob still stands by his belief that letting an audience discover a joke is the greatest form of entertainment. Or that perhaps his cleverest trick is in telling the gag which lays an egg – the one he deliberately lets fall flat:

A man goes into a psychiatrist with a rasher of bacon over each ear and three eggs on top of his head. He says, 'I wanna see you about my brother . . .'

The secret lies in the telling. Hope delivers it too quickly, thus killing the laugh. Then he accuses his audience of not getting it. He cracks other successful gags, but keeps coming back to the supposed 'dud';

A rasher of bacon over each ear and three eggs . . .

'Even critics are fooled by this,' says Bob. 'But it wins me just the sympathy I need. The greatest danger for a comedian is walking on cake – loading an act with too many laughs. The audience needs relief. If everything is funny it is like too much ice-cream.'

This fellow was out hunting ducks and he shot this duck, and it landed on the water, and the dog walked across the water, picked the duck up and brought it back. And the other guy said, 'Don't you notice something strange about that dog?' He said, 'Yeah – he can't swim . . .'

That's it . . .

You see, the dog walked across the water . . .

Oh my God! Start the motor, this may be it . . .

Says former Hope writer, Bob Monkhouse: 'The cleverest thing he does is to make you like him through self-denigration; by setting himself up to be pompous and then bursting the balloon. He continually used that; and I think it's one of the reasons why we love him. He shows himself as frail as all of us, right in the middle of appearing to be cleverer than anyone.'

Monkhouse is just one of many comedians who have based their careers on the Hope technique. 'He was the greatest influence in my comic life,' admits Monkhouse.

But who influenced the master? Who did he borrow from? Apart from silent-screen geniuses like Chaplin and Harold Lloyd, Bob reveals that his basic groundings came from vaudevillian Frank Fay. He was a monologist who never achieved the immortality of humorist Will Rogers, or even Hope, but he was the one who a young Bob considered the top.

'He was the sharpest I've ever seen in working to an audience,' says Hope. 'I can't work as slow as he was. He would economize on material so much, by slowing everything down; he'd get a laugh just on the mood and motions. I remember once seeing him at the Palace in Chicago. He was in a spotlight and there was a piano on the stage with somebody sitting at it. He was very grand, what you'd call a distinguished bum. "Tonight," he said, "I'm going to play the piano." And he walked very slowly over to the piano, saw someone was there and walked very slowly back to the front centre of the stage again. "There's somebody there," he said. That was all ... and the place broke apart.'

Whatever the comedian took from artists such as Fay was soon lost when he introduced the quick quip. He became the first comedian to master the popular one-liner totally. It made him unique – no one had preceded him in a big way – and assured him a place in history.

'There were comedians doing one-liners,' says Bob Monkhouse, 'but none of them did it with the impact, the vitality, the veracity, the appeal that Hope had. He looked good and he sounded good. No comedian looks into a mirror and adjusts his tie, and says "You're too beautiful for comedy!" without paying tribute to Bob Hope. He was the spearhead and still remains the number one comedian in the art of getting over a complete comedy idea in the fewest possible words.'

Hope's *Roberta* co-star, the tap-dancing former Senator George Murphy, believes much of his success was founded on his naturally attractive personality. 'When you walk out on the stage,' says Murphy, 'It's the first impression that counts – they either like you immediately or they dislike you immediately.'

Veteran comic George Burns considers that it was the impact of Hope's material which made him noticeably different. 'Bob is sort of a Peck's bad boy,' says George. 'He'd hit the audience with some shocking line – he was always very local, very full of politics and big personalities – and then he'd look at 'em in that little way. He'd cock his head and look at 'em, and he always looked like he didn't mean it – but he did!'

Bob Monkhouse is amazed how unclown-like his former employer is. 'The astounding thing about Bob Hope is that he has no discernible hump. He has no great fat belly; he is not four foot high; he has no stammer; he doesn't have crossed eyes, like Ben Turpin; or a deadpan, like Keaton; or a weird series of mannerisms, like Groucho. He's a perfectly normal looking guy – except for his ski-snoot!'

For more years than he cares to remember, Hope has been criticized as a comedian for relying too heavily on joke writers and cue cards. 'Hope?' said an ageing Groucho Marx in 1972.

'Hope is not a comedian. He just translates what others write for him.' The remark was, of course, unfair and tinged with more than a touch of senility, but it indicates the kind of sniping he has had to endure.

George Murphy thinks such criticism was often made in ignorance of Hope's innate ability. 'I don't think that you learn timing and you certainly don't learn the handling of comedy,' he says. 'Comedy is much more delicate than tragedy on the stage. And I think Bob had this sensitivity from the beginning.'

To a man, past and present members of the gag-writing team insist that the Hope reputation was enhanced by good joke writers, but never created by them. 'Nobody made Hope's career except Hope,' says Melvin Frank. 'Hope was the architect of the comic structure and great edifice that is known as Bob Hope. He is responsible for what's good about it and I think he is responsible for what's bad about it. Some of us helped, some of us hurt it occasionally. When you get down to it, it's the selection of material and taste; my own feeling is that Bob – who is an incredible deliverer of material – often settled and opted for the sure thing, rather than take a chance on a new formula.

'Even though he has made millions out of it, and seems to be still constantly operative and successful, I personally feel that he should have tried a wider range of material.'

Bob is absolutely sure that he was right to run the show himself. 'That's a business in itself,' he says. 'It's a matter of editing and knowing what the audience wants. Somebody has to know, and if the comedian doesn't know you're in trouble. And that's been my business; I've edited everything ever since I started.'

The Hope editorial capacity, like his work rate, has always been impressive. 'He can look through forty pages of new material from writers and spot the gags that will play for him faster than a computer,' says Bob Monkhouse. 'And he also spots the gags that are no good. He whisks down the page, almost speed-reading.'

Bob's secret is to look first at the tag-line of a joke – to see if it is snappy – and then he examined the construction of the words leading up to it. If it meets his requirements, he puts a cross or tick against it and it is more than likely to make his act.

Comedy writers and comedians are often a difficult mix. Many careers have foundered because the mouthpiece cannot come to terms with the fact that he or she is not the originator of the words. And many writers resent comedians, because they wish they could present their own material. But Hope is one of the fortunate few who does not suffer from that. He works with his writers easily and happily, and he likes them.

Says Mort Lachman, a former head writer of 22 years standing: 'He did it without any neurotic feelings. He didn't have to kill writers. Like Red Buttons who drove himself out of the business – he had a successful show, but hated the writers so much that at the end of the first year of success he got rid of all the writers – he never made it again.'

Most Hope writers say they gave their star much more than just an act-full of snappy gags. They presented him with a raw material as precious as the gold he made from them.

'The actual art of writing gags is one of the sharpest forms of creation that I know of,' says Mel Frank. 'It's like writing novels in terms of telegrams. Gags are stories; you have to use the right words, the right thoughts, and in a very small period of time say things that are going to make people laugh. But having written them, you must have someone who can say them – and say them well. And Bob Hope fulfilled that part of the contract for all of us for many, many years in a way for which we all owed him a lot of gratitude.'

In doing so, though, Bob gets value for money from his people. When you work for Bob Hope, you work hard. 'He drives them like Simon Le Gree drove Uncle Tom and the rest of the people on the plantation,' says Bob Monkhouse. 'When Denis Goodwin and I were working for him he drove us hard. He would come to the hotel room where we were working, and if you were in the lavatory, he'd rap on the door and shout "You taking a vacation? There's paper in there ... write!" He once woke me up ... shook me awake, "Are you thinking?" He expected you to be on the ball every minute of the day that he was paying for you – or someone else was paying you to write for him! He was a slave-driver ... yes. But it was fair, because he drove himself just as hard. And where else could you get a training like that, but working for such a perfectionist?'

The Hope writers' club endorse that statement almost unanimously. Mel Frank echoes their sentiments: 'I personally will have an everlasting sense of gratitude for the discipline that he instilled in me as an artist.'

Bob's writers are intensely loyal, as indeed he is to them, but they are also reasonably objective about his faults as well as his abilities as a comedian. One of his longest serving gag-men, British-born Charlie Lee, will view a Hope television show and fearlessly inform the boss, 'What a load of rubbish!' if that is what he thinks. Bob listens without rancour, although seldom agrees.

When Mel Shavelson was part of the team he always complained that the comedian understood little about comic plot or character. 'He understands what jokes are better than almost anybody in the world,' says Mel. 'And he enjoys jokes more than almost anybody else. But he feels the more laughs the better and he's usually wrong about that. Bob never realized that what went before a joke sometimes had more influence on what the laugh was than the joke itself.'

One of the questions most asked about Bob and his writers is – why so many? Why an army? The army is a myth; today he employs only half a dozen full-time and at his peak the maximum reached was thirteen. The six are necessary because, with so many engagements to fill, you can never rely on the best joke writer in the world to come up with the right joke at the right time. 'It's like producing automobiles,' explains former radio writer Carroll Carroll. 'You gotta keep 'em coming. And there's gonna be some bad ones; there's gonna be some with Coca Cola bottles in the doors.'

Not all Bob's jokes are written, though; beneath the cue cards and scripts lies an able ad-libber. But his use of such tools of the trade has tended to cloud this aspect of his talent. For those privileged to have seen it, Hope without specially prepared material can be very amusing indeed.

Says Bob Monkhouse: 'I have seen Bob ad-libbing on the Jell-O Show, which was a fifteen-minute daily show recorded at the Palladium. A mike like an umbrella was turned on the audience and they would shout out questions, and Hope would rattle back answers. Now, there was a tremendous back-log of material in his head – there is in the mind of any comedian who is retentive – but the speed at which he came back with a series of answers impressed me deeply.'

Monkhouse is not so complimentary about Bob's reliance on the idiot boards, however. He accepts their necessity for last minute topicality, but deplores the way they have become a way of life on television and believes passionately that they have 'robbed the greatest technical timer of comedy in our lifetime of much of his edge'.

'Sometimes he is putting more effort into reading the words than into thinking about their meaning,' says Bob Monkhouse. 'So that frequently, you're getting a reading instead of a performance. I don't believe that he can be watching his own performances as acutely as once he did, because I think if he watched them closely he would spot the number of times his eyes are lifelessly reading; rather than having that little sparkle that having to remember puts into your eyes.'

Criticism such as that does not pass Hope by. He avidly reads his reviews and notices, and thinks carefully about what is said. Sometimes it hurts. 'Of course it does,' he admits. 'When I am criticized, I examine my conscience to see if there is an element of truth in the criticism. Let's face it, occasionally there is. Then I try to remedy matters . . .'

Bob also listens to what his fellow-performers have to say. He is eager to adopt their ideas if they will benefit the overall performance, as David Kossoff discovered when he made *The Iron Petticoat* with him in the mid-fifties.

'There was a funny sequence,' recalls Kossoff, 'where somebody took a karate chop at him as he came out of a night club. And he took it on the chest. And I said, "If you were to have a cigarette case in that pocket and you took it out, and it was bent, you could hand it to somebody saying – 'Get this pressed for me!' Would it be funny?" He not only thought it was funny, but it was in the film. There was no "Please David, my writers handle all this." We worked it out and it was in the film.'

Some of the most impressive tributes to Bob Hope the comedian have come not from critics, writers or fellow artists, but from presidents of the United States. However, there has been one exception, until very recently.

19

Jimmy Carter was the first president for thirty years not to lean heavily on Bob Hope when he moved into the White House. For once, in January 1977, the comedian's name was not topping the bill at the ball celebrating the new president's inauguration. And to make matters worse, Jimmy was not sending out golfing invitations either – he played tennis. Bob was greatly dismayed and hurt by this lack of acceptance by the tenth president to serve during his career. He had grown used to his role as court jester to the White House.

But that did not stop him from weaving the one-time peanut farmer into his act. The President's beer-swilling brother Billy, young daughter Amy and controversial advisers like Bert Lance offered a wealth of satirical material:

Jimmy Carter's a very religious man. I know, because every time I eat a peanut – I feel immortal . . .

I love Billy Carter. I had an uncle just like him. He drank so much that when he died and they cremated him – his liver burned for three months . . .

Billy's got a new book coming out – with or without crayons . . .

When President Carter set America buzzing by signing an agreement handing the Panama Canal back to the Panamanians, Bob was ready with the repartee:

I hear we're not going to give it back until the year 2000 – so I guess they're going to mail it to them . . .

I think they ought to fill it with sand – and let Amy play in it . . .

Or fill it with beer – and let Billy play in it . . .

Or fill it with money – and let Bert Lance play in it . . .

The estrangement ended in May 1978, when Jimmy and Rosalyn Carter gave a reception in honour of Bob's 75th birthday. A personal note from the President to mark the occasion amused the comedian greatly. 'It began *Dear Mr Hope*,' says Bob, 'but was signed *Yours Jimmy*. Isn't that great . . . him calling me Mr Hope!'

On Wednesday 24 May Washington DC opened its doors to an entertainer as never before. In the early evening President and Mrs Carter welcomed Bob and Dolores on the steps of the White House, and they reminisced about the last time they had met – in Atlanta, Georgia, when Carter was still governor.

Later the same night a limousine sped the Hopes the five miles to Alexandria, Virginia, where Elizabeth Taylor was waiting to greet him with a huge private birthday party in a restaurant owned by a distant Hope relative. 'He is one of the most unique people in the whole world,' said Taylor, as she and Bob posed for photographers. The room was so packed with celebrities that one show business wit was heard to observe: 'Somewhere in Hollywood there are two tourists from Alexandria wondering where all the stars are . . .'

Noisy carousing went on until the small hours, but Bob was up early the next morning for a date he was to describe as 'a high spot in my 75 years'.

At 10.00 a.m., flanked by Dolores and his grandchildren, Hope was escorted by the Sergeant-at-arms of the United States Congress into the House VIP box in the Capitol building. 260 Congress members were gathered for a rule-breaking special session to pay tribute to, as the House Speaker Thomas P. O'Neill Jnr. put it, 'A fine American; a great American; and an all-American.' The members rose for a standing ovation, the first of many during the one-hour salute. Then both Republicans and Democrats took turns to praise and poke fun at him. 'The first time Bob Hope entertained Washington,' joked Texan Majority Leader Jim Wright, 'he said – "George . . ."'

'Bob Hope has proved that while it's nice to be important, it's more important to be nice,' commented a Congressman from the comedian's home state, Ohio. A Democrat from Massachusetts latched on to the lack of food during President Carter's reception: 'It seems that with Republicans you have feasted, and with Democrats you have fasted.'

But the undisputed show-stopper of the morning was Illinois Republican Robert H. Michel, who crooned his own version of Bob's 'Thanks for the Memory':

> Thanks for the memory,
> Of places you have gone,
> To cheer our soldiers on,
> The President sent Kissinger,
> But you sent Jill St John,
> We thank you so much . . .

Hope, who had sat impassively through the proceedings until then, joined in the enthusiastic applause and cheering. Later, at a private reception in the Speaker's room, he told Michel: 'You could afford a singing lesson – put it on my taxes . . .'

Although genuinely moved by the politicians' outpourings, the comedian was in mischievous mood afterwards. 'Sitting up there I was thinking no man can be that great – but you finally convinced me,' he quipped

That evening the familiar strains of 'Thanks for the Memory' were echoing across the Potomac from the splendid Kennedy Centre Theatre. But for once they did not herald his imminent appearance on stage – he was audience-bound as 250 stars gathered to pay homage during a three-hour televised gala for the United Services Organization. Lucille Ball, Sammy Davis Junior, Angie Dickinson, Elizabeth Taylor, Pearl Bailey, Telly Savalas, Dorothy Lamour, Danny Thomas and Farrah Fawcett-Majors were just some of the the celebrities present.

The performance, which was transmitted in the US on the night of his birthday – 29 May – included film clips of Bob's career and a special taped salute from John Wayne, who was recovering in California from surgery.

Actor George C. Scott spoke for most of the 2,000 guests when he opened the show. 'Who in the world has not been touched in one way or another by a man named Bob Hope?' he asked. 'Just for once you are going to receive our love, our respect – and a massive gift of creative performing talent. We salute you! Happy birthday, Bob, and thanks for the memory . . .'

In Britain the occasion was marked by a host of reflective newspaper features and a 70-minute ITV documentary produced by the author and Thames Television's Terence Dixon. Amongst those taking part were George Burns, Michael Caine, Joan Collins, Perry Como, Rhonda Fleming, ex-President Ford, Dorothy Lamour, Fred MacMurray, Bob Monkhouse, Jane Russell, John Wayne and Raquel Welch. BBC Radio Two also ran a four-part tribute, written by the author and narrated by entertainer Danny Kaye.

Breaking the ice in Carter's White House was an important culmination to an amazing career in presidential comedy. As Hope told the author, 'They're very important to me . . . most of them are monologue subjects. The White House is always *the* place, because one of the greatest formats of comedy is turning down dignity. So we always work on the White House and whoever is in it.'

Over the decades Bob has not only worked on the White House but has also got to know many of its incumbents intimately. He knew and kidded Presidents Roosevelt and Truman, and has been friends with five successive presidents since; Eisehower, Kennedy, Johnson, Nixon and Ford. All have been subjected to the joke, 'Who's that up there with Bob Hope?'

Golf has played an important part in these friendships. Eisenhower initiated him into one of the most select golfing circles in the world – the presidential foursome. Nixon and Ford later repeated the honour and indeed Ford still partners Hope in charity matches. Golf with presidents has not only given Hope much pleasure, but also more material for his act.

President Eisenhower has given up golf for painting – it takes fewer strokes . . .

The last time I played a round with Vice President Agnew he hit a birdie – an eagle, a moose, an elk and a Mason . . .

Ex-President Ford plays wonderful golf – for a man wearing skis . . .

He draws a big crowd – you know how people gather at the scene of an accident . . .

It's a very eerie thing with all the Secret Service men around him. It's hard to keep score the way I do – with a guy peeking over your shoulder . . .

And you never know where they are. I hit a ball under a tree. I walked over – and the tree moved . . .

He hit a ball in the rough – and a cactus clump threw it back on the fairway . . .

In 1965 President Johnson made a surprise appearance at the 25th annual USO banquet, which was honouring Hope. Johnson presented him with a plaque commemorating his long service to the United States. Then he got in a dig at Ronald Reagan and his presidential ambitions. 'You are unique,' he told Hope. 'You are an actor. And you are an actor who isn't running for office!'

Johnson then pointed out that Bob was one of the few frequent visitors to Vietnam not to have been called before the Senate's Foreign Relations Committee. 'At least not yet,' continued the President slyly. 'I understand he was planning to testify – until he discovered that there was live coverage on only one network . . .'

Johnson's predecessor, John Kennedy, was Hope's favourite raconteur. 'He was marvellous,' says Bob. 'He had a great sense of humour; loved jokes. I once did a routine about Kennedy – we had a little depression at the time – and I said, "The stock-market's so bad . . . I put a dime in the phone today – and this voice said 'God Bless You!'" He invited me over to the White House after he heard that . . . just to talk. And then he started putting material in his speeches. I met him so many times; he just loved to hear jokes.'

J.F.K. was gifted enough as a storyteller and jokester to be able to hold his own or even to better the master of the wisecrack. Once Kennedy topped him after hearing a Hope after-dinner routine full of gags about the nation's first Catholic President and jibes at younger brother Robert's nomination as Attorney General.

'What's wrong with his getting a little legal experience before he goes into business for himself?' quipped Kennedy as Hope sat down.

When Richard Milhous Nixon beat Hubert Humphrey in the 1968 race for the White House, he openly courted the support of old friend Hope – and got it. Bob remained a staunch Nixonite throughout the six troubled years of his administration. They first compared ski-snoots for the campaign when candidate Nixon turned up at a 1967 Boys Club dinner in Pittsburgh to give Hope the annual Herbert Hoover award and remind him of his 1960 advice to debate Kennedy on television.

Bob had another close friend in the Nixon White House – Spiro Agnew. The pair had first met while Angew was still Governor of Maryland and found they had much in common: the same sense of humour and a love of the sort of jokes that Hope could rarely use in his stage act. Often they exchanged gags during late night telephone calls between Washington and Hollywood. Publicly, though, Agnew was a prime source of comedy for Hope; Bob ribbed him unmercifully at every opportunity. When President Nixon gathered the nation's governors together for a 1971 White House party, Bob was there to advise him to send Spiro to Laos with a 'number three wood':

He's a wonderful athlete – he's got a black belt in golf.

But at least he can't cheat on his score – because all you have to do is look back down the fairway and count the wounded.

But it's hard for him to concentrate on his shots – because the entire gallery is there reciting the Lord's Prayer.

Mid-way through Nixon's first term Bob helped the President raise a record five million dollars for the Republican Party. First he joined Nixon at a $500-a-plate dinner in New York's Americana Hotel, where they ate the hors d'oeuvres, and then they flew to Chicago for dessert at a second banquet. Both functions were linked by closed-circuit television to 18 other dinners, involving 7,000 Republicans, across America.

January 1973 saw Nixon talking the oath for his second term of office and Bob was amongst the show business personalities helping him celebrate the occasion. On the face of it, the four-day inauguration festivities went well – they should have done, being the most lavish in American history at a cost of almost $4,000,000. But behind the scenes there were rows.

Bob arrived for a concert at the Kennedy Centre to find that emcee Frank Sinatra had pulled out at the last minute. The singer was upset about the vetoing of a comedian friend from the bill. Hope was furious too, but at Sinatra. His humour was not improved when an over-anxious stage manager lowered the curtain while he was in full flood.

Nixon's resignation in 1974 sent most of his former friends scurrying for cover. But not Hope. In February 1975 he was one of 24 guests to be present at Nixon's first social appearance since his fall from grace. The lavish party was held at the Palm Springs estate of Walter Annenberg, the former American Ambassador to London. Shortly before the party broke up at midnight, the ex-President gave an emotional speech and talked about the value of friendship.

As Nixon left, Bob gave a brief account of the party. 'He didn't talk about the past,' he told waiting reporters. 'He said friends are very important when you are at the top, but more so at a time like this ... he had people in tears ... I'm sure he enjoyed the evening. I hadn't seen him since he left office. He looked to me as if he needed a lot of rest. Pat (his wife) looked good and she seemed in better spirits ... We were all trying to make it as jovial and as light-hearted as possible, but he was only in fair spirits...'

Bob's continued support for Nixon amazed many of his friends and confounded his critics. They saw a new side to him – no more could he be accused of being a political opportunist.

Says Zsa Zsa Gabor: 'That's one of the things I admire him for – he's really loyal. I like to think the White House has human beings too and just because you're in show business, and you make your money through show business, doesn't mean that you have to be just a puppet who goes with the winner. Nixon is the biggest loser in America and I'm proud of Bob.'

Even today Bob has nothing but kind words for the former president: 'The man had one of the finest minds of any president I've known. And I've known a few. Also, he's a friend and I stand by my friends.'

Bob also made friends with Nixon's successor, Ford. They are now near neighbours in Palm Springs, and spend a lot of time together playing golf. Their association goes back a long way: in 1936, during a pre-Broadway tour of *Red, Hot and Blue!* Bob arrived in New Haven, Connecticut, and one of those who congratulated him backstage was a young Yale law student called Jerry Ford.

In October 1977 Ford told the author how he felt about the support he had received from Hope during his short time in the White House: 'He was a tremendous asset. The things he did for the country, not only in the United States but overseas, you couldn't measure in dollars. But I don't think that Bob, in the strict partisan sense, gets involved in politics – although he will raise funds for a certain candidate or for certain individuals. But I think that's honourable on his part.'

Rosemary Clooney, herself a committed Democrat, agrees with him. 'He is non-partisan,' says Rosemary. 'His humour is that way too; it's so topical. The things that are going on right now are the things that he talks about and a great deal has to do with politics. I believe that anyone who spends time with Bob Hope has a little bit of his lustre rub-off on them. And that doesn't get past many politicians; they would like very much to have some of the acceptance that Bob has all over the world.'

Many Americans are highly sceptical about entertainers who support political candidates, and some would even like to see show business divorced from politics altogether. Bob believes this to be wrong and has been supported by a large number of fellow artists, including the influential John Wayne.

'We are representatives of responsible citizenship,' the Duke told the author shortly before he died. 'We believe in responsibility rather than irresponsibility and we haven't got a United States to back us up – if we go, the western economy is gone. So I suppose we are a little more interested and hope that our people will be less careless with the values that we have if we are involved. I think it is normal for top entertainers to be recognized by high level officials.'

A question most asked of Hope is who was his favourite president. Although it is clear that Eisenhower was the one he loved most, Kennedy was the one he laughed at most, and Nixon was the one he supported most, he is always diplomatic with his answer. 'I have fond memories of them all,' he says.

It has often been suggested that had Bob Hope not been born in England, he would have forsaken comedy for politics and tried for the White House. Nothing could be further from the truth. He has never harboured such ambitions and anyway, as he says himself, 'I couldn't work for that kind of money . . .'

20

For more than three decades speculation has been rife about the true worth of Bob Hope – that he is a millionaire there is no doubt, but how many millions does he actually have? The question has fascinated media and public alike for years. In 1952 his attorney Martin Gang let slip that he thought his client was good for about four million dollars. Sixteen years later *Fortune* magazine computed his assets at between $150 million and $500 million, and named him as one of the fifty richest men in the United States – the only show business representative on the list.

Bob has always played down the press guesstimates. 'I think their computer drinks,' he said of the *Fortune* estimate. 'If I sold my land today, I'd be worth no more than $100,000,000 – well maybe $100,000,001 . . .'

But even his own 1969 figure must be taken lightly. A year earlier he told reporters in London that 'the last time I saw a bank statement', the amount was about 'Twenty-five million dollars'. The fact is that Hope hates talking about his money, unless it was jokingly in association with Crosby's or Benny's wealth, and refuses point blank to be drawn on the actual amount. 'Ask my tax man – he knows' is a favourtie quip when pressed.

However, shortly before his 75th birthday in 1978, he did discuss the speculation seriously with the author. 'I tell you I would have done a lot of things if I'd had half a billion dollars,' he said. 'I never even came close to that and never had anywhere near that kind of money. I am a rich man, but I don't have that kind of money . . . and I actually have to work to pay my taxes.'

Currently Bob pays at least a million dollars a year in property taxes alone – a result of astute land purchases back in the late thirties and early forties, when he first moved out to Hollywood.

His first coup was in 1938 with an $18,000 plot near the Lakeside Country Club down the road from his home. For 25 years he ran it as a golf driving range, before selling out to the giant Music Corporation of America – the owners of Universal Pictures – for a million dollars.

At one time the comedian was probably the biggest single landowner in California. With brother Jack at the real estate helm, he moved into the arable wastes of the San Fernando Valley and picked up around 16,000 acres of bean fields for between ten and fifty dollars an acre. As Hollywood boomed and the studios moved into Burbank on the edge of the Valley, the farmers gave way to property developers who enticed more than a million people to live there. Bob parted with just over half of his acreage for almost forty million dollars; the remaining 7,500 acres are now said to be worth in excess of a hundred million.

After buying up the San Fernando Valley, Hope expanded west to Malibu, now a fashionable movie stars' colony, but then site of the Paramount Ranch where most motion picture exterior scenes were shot. Says Herb Polesie, producer of *Don't Look Now*: 'We were at the Ranch one day making a film with Dave Butler directing. He wanted a particular shot with long shadows – which wouldn't be possible till around 4.00 p.m. So Bob was told he had some time off; he went and never came back. Later we learned that he had gone out and bought 1,500 acres in Malibu and the surrounding canyons.'

When the Hopes sought a winter retreat in the burgeoning resort of Palm Springs, 120 miles east of Hollywood, Bob bought more than another house; he added 8,000 acres of prime undeveloped desert to his land folio. Supplementing his real estate profits was the insatiable appetite of the big studios for western locations. They paid handsomely for his rolling hills and mountain canyons.

Bob Hope Enterprises Incorporated was formed not only to handle his film and television business, but to control his growing investments in a wide range of interests. When the Old Groaner became a major shareholder of the Pittsburgh Pirates baseball team, Rapid Robert bought himself a slice of the Cleveland Indians. Later he extended his sporting interests by acquiring part of the Los Angeles Rams football team. He also put some money into Bing's racetrack at Del Mar near San Diego. The crooner always awarded Hope the laurels in the money-making stakes – 'a pretty good businessman,' he called him – perhaps because one of his most lucrative financial involvements was in association with the comedian, and black gold.

A big wildcat oilman from Texas, who used to play golf with the pair from time to time, agreed to cut them in on his next deal – provided they continued to play with him. Each put up $150,000 initially, but before the first well gushed oil they were nearly a couple of million lighter. For two years, though, they played golf with the Texan and collected steady returns from the field. Then a major oil company stepped in with a bid and Bob got out with a clear profit of a million and a half dollars. Twelve months later the oilman arrived in California and rang Bob for a game. 'Imagine!' said Hope to Crosby. 'This guy still wants us to play golf with him!'

Oil was about as speculative as Bob was prepared to get with his money. He remembered well the years of poverty in vaudeville and was not about to risk returning to them by entrusting his hard-earned cash to the whims of the stock-market. The only real gamble he took was in buying shares in a soft drinks company and RCA records.

Hope wears the trappings of his wealth well. He does not drive a Rolls Royce, unlike many of his movie-land compatriots, preferring to use a sponsor-supplied Chrysler instead. Home and clothes are comfortably expensive, but not ostentatious. And in all matters relating to the running of Hope Enterprises he is the undisputed boss.

The corporation was set up towards the end of World War II, aimed primarily at making a rich man richer. But others benefited too. Writer Carroll Carroll had just finished ghosting two books for Bob – *I Never Left Home* (1944) and *So This Is Peace* (1946) – and during dinner at the Hope mansion one night the comedian asked him to send $1,500 to brother Jack. This he did.

Two days later Mrs Norma Carroll, master of the family finances, asked, 'Why are we sending money to Hope? Does he need it more than we do?'

Carroll had never even thought to ask Hope what the money was for, 'that's how much I trusted him', so he phoned to find out.

'Didn't I tell you?' said the comedian with a chuckle. 'I've formed a company called Bob Hope Enterprises and that fifteen hundred dollars is worth ten shares of stock in it.'

Family, close friends, agents and even Bing Crosby also got ten to fifteen shares each from the magnanimous Hope.

After six years Carroll Carroll was understandably getting a little edgy about his investment. Dividends had been non-existent and Norma persistently inquisitive. All was saved by a call from Bob's attorney, Martin Gang, who instructed Carroll to authorize the sale of a quarter of the shares. No argument was brooked and in November they were sold.

Says Carroll: 'At about ten thirty or quarter to eleven on New Year's Eve the doorbell rings and there's a registered special delivery letter with a cheque for $10,000 inside...'

The sale was enforced by the introduction of a new partner into the organization: NBC purchased a 25 percent holding. From then on Hope Enterprises was known affectionately as 'Son of NBC'. Carroll got abother $10,000 for another two and a half shares, after another six years.

As the Hope film career faded the Enterprises became more and more involved with NBC and television. Bob has been with the network ever since his first television show. In the early years company business was handled by James Saphier, whom many claim was responsible for putting Hope on the television map. When he died, his assistant Elliott Kozak took over the reins.

A tough, stocky New Yorker, Kozak ran the comedian's television and business affairs for 18 years until his resignation in 1979. Although he was responsible for dealing with the Hope sponsors, and the multi-million dollar television specials they supported each year, in the final analysis it was the star who made the decisions. Elliot may have booked the talent – producers, directors, writers and guest stars – but Hope approved everything in advance. 'I think I can get Bob to buy that...' was more often than not Elliott's final negotiating posture.

In all matters of business, and that includes his comedy, Bob Hope has one simple philosophy – divide and rule. Every member of his staff is placed in his own little box and is rarely allowed to operate outside it. Writers write and publicists publicize, but Bob is always the boss. He is also the unquestioned producer of his show. As one unfortunate free-lance producer who tried to change the system found out: 'When I'm around I produce and you help,' thundered Hope witheringly. 'When I'm not around you get to do the producing.'

Many executives would find working for such a demanding employer difficult, and many of the Hope people do. But Elliott Kozak had few such problems. 'Because Bob knew what he wanted,' he explained. 'And I had so much respect for him, and we had a mutual admiration for one another; he respected my judgement at times and I went along with his. He was very, very easy – because he knew what he wanted.'

In almost everything, though, Hope is firm but fair. Even when it comes to advertising and promoting the television shows. Says Kozak: 'One of the great things about Bob is that he approves the ads. His attitude is, "Hey! They know me ... they know what I look like!" And he makes sure that the guest stars are there all the way. He doesn't want his picture bigger than anyone else's.'

Many Hope specials are all about debts – either owed or due. Sometimes Bob must be made available for another star's programme, because that artist is guesting on a forthcoming Hope show. On other occasions a recipient of a Hope guest shot is persuaded to repay the favour on his show.

While such delicate bargaining is going on the Hope negotiators are peppered with calls from the man himself. A change of mind about a guest star; new ideas for comedy skits; more possible guest artists. Then the long arm of the Hope organization must reach out far and wide: 'Has Olivia left Sydney yet? Is Lief still in London? What time does Frank's plane leave Chicago? Is there a phone on board?'

Without the telephone the comedian's operating style would

be vastly different. Much of each day is spent on it and his staff are expected to be available for calls at all times. 'But the thing that is marvellous about him,' said Elliott Kozak, 'is that *he* can always be reached too.'

When Kozak left Hope Enterprises to take up a position as Head of Television at International Creative Management in Los Angeles his place was filled by Linda Hope.

After her marriage failed she 'drifted' into her father's company as a producer of non-Hope television products. To begin with she used to admit that her position was due to 'nepotism', but now feels that she is making a real contribution.

'I am able to get into doors because of his name,' admits Linda, 'but once I am there I'm really on my own. People in fact look a little more sceptically and say – "Can you really do it?" And – "What have you got there?" I am finding that in fact I am able to hold my own and come up with things that are very credible, and are in fact different from the kind of things people associate with Bob Hope,' said Linda, referring to her efforts to develop programmes other than her father's comedy specials – movies of the week and situation comedies for the American networks. 'So, while I am still very attached to him in a certain way, I feel I am doing my own thing in my own way.'

Hope Enterprises has two office centres, both within minutes of Bob's Toluca Lake home. The nearest houses Hope press agent Ward Grant and two secretaries. Linda Hope is based a few miles farther on in a medical building on Riverside Drive. A staff of six occupy a ground-floor suite of as many offices, which are comfortably but not lavishly furnished. Gigantic photographs adorn the main corridor walls – featuring Bob and Lee Marvin; Bob and Barbara Streisand (who got her first national television break on a Hope show); Bob and Jack Benny; in fact, Bob and just about everyone . . .

The comedian has an office of his own in the suite, but has never used it. He prefers to meander in and out of other people's. Upstairs in the same building works another important cog in the Hope business machinery – Mark Anthony. It was he who recently gave his boss a major new source of income.

Mark, who has been with Bob since 1949 and now carries the

title of business manager, put together an advertising deal with a local savings company – Cal Fed – worth half a million dollars. The first series of television ads featured Hope with a camel called Clyde – he became almost as big a personality on the West Coast as Hope. 'It's really a great deal,' says Hope, 'because we get all that money just for commercials that are only shown here in California – just think, if we could repeat the deal in every state!'

According to Anthony, though, he is just a figurehead in Bob's world of business. 'Business manager is just the title I have,' he confessed. 'Bob Hope is his own business manager. I just follow the details.'

Although Bob has proved his business acumen beyond doubt, he does confess that he just hates office-work and all the paper that goes with it. Each day hundreds of letters, from fans and businessmen alike, pour into his home. Most have to be dealt with and replies dictated, a chore which displeases the boss greatly. 'It's a mess,' he admits. 'I run out of the office and the secretary chases me down the drive. She says, "What about so-and-so?" I say, "Check with me after golf..." I run right out – right to the golf course!'

The shambolic paper-work is the least of Linda Hope's worries. One of her biggest headaches is running the other side of Bob's career – his charity work, for the Hope organization is not only concerned with making money for itself, but in raising millions of dollars each year for worthy causes. Over the last five decades he has made literally thousands of cash donations to needy people all over the world. Some have been publicized, most have not. But it is with his time that Bob is most free. It would be impossible to calculate the sums of money he has helped raise by turning up at functions in person. Many of his stage shows support a cause of one kind or another – either national or local. Often his $25,000 appearance fee at a college date will go to the scholarship fund or a medical research centre. And, at many Hope benefits, it is not only Bob who appears. He persuades a host of stars to give their time as well.

One of his biggest money-raising events, and one of the most complicated to arrange, is the annual *Bob Hope Supershow* in Cincinnati, Ohio, which benefits a little-known local charity – the Bob Hope House Incorporated. The trust was set up in

1962 to care for delinquent and under-privileged boys and now has a two-storey house with room for thirty inmates. Since its inception more than 900 young men have been sent there by the Ohio courts. The motto of the home is, 'If you treat a human being like a human being, he will act like a human being.' In the driveway leading to the house stands a sign that heralds, 'The Road to Hope', and embellished on it is the famous Hope profile.

Says project director, John Schern: 'There have been many kinds of young men at the Bob Hope House. Some have exhibited minor behavioural problems, while others were more serious. Some have been in need of strict external controls, and others merely needed shelter, care and a feeling of being wanted ... only a small percentage have required placement in facilities with stronger controls.'

For each *Supershow* Bob tries to get at least a dozen headliners. In November 1977, at the Riverfront Coliseum in Cincinnati, he paraded a glittering array of stars for the three-hour concert (which almost 18,000 people paid to watch): Buddy Rogers, Gordon MacRae, Joey Heatherton, Jane Russell, Mark Hamill (from *Star Wars*), baseball star Johnny Beach and – topping the bill – 'The advance man for Ovaltine' Perry Como.

During the interval Bob spoke to the current year's intake of Hope House boys. For once his remarks were devoid of wisecracks.

'A lot of these people you see here tonight,' he told them, 'started in the same spots that you got in – me for one! This is all done for you guys; it's done so you all get a chance to really get out and get moving the right way ... think about that. It's something when people are thinking about you and want to help ... and I hope you enjoy that house out there ...'

But Bob not only frequents the big arenas. Often he will make surprise appearances to aid the smallest of efforts. Once when the author was on tour with him, he dropped in on a tiny local television station in Fargo, North Dakota (population 53,365), to help along a $90,000 telethon for disabled children. For an hour he cavorted on camera and answered phone calls off, asking viewers to 'pledge whatever you can afford to help these kids'. Later he went back, shortly before an evening concert, to 'finish the job'. At the end of the day the organizers were just a few thousand short of their target.

Another major part of his charitable work involves attending scores of religious benefits. And, as he points out in his monologue for such auspicious events, he is not choosy about the denomination:

I do benefits for all religions – I'd hate to blow the hereafter on a technicality . . .

It's getting so my golf game needs all the help it can get, so I never say no to any religious groups. I did that once several years ago – and my best writer turned into a pillar of salt . . .

But I believe in both Christianity and Judaism – I have ever since Danny Thomas and Sammy Davis did a dance number on my swimming pool together . . .

And it doesn't matter whether one is Catholic or Jewish. We all believe in one God – George Burns . . .

No, I don't mind kidding about religion. If God let George Burns play him in a movie – he's gotta have a sense of humour . . .

According to John Wayne, who was another tireless fund-raiser, Bob's greatest gift to the charities he supports is in getting that little bit extra out of the givers. 'They probably would have raised a lot of that money anyway,' he said, 'because of the charitable feeling of the average American person. But I think Bob needles them into giving a little more here and there than they normally would.'

The reasons behind Bob's compulsive urge to give so much of himself to others have perplexed show business observers for years. He had been hitting the charity road since his earliest days on Broadway, and he has no intention of stopping now.

'You do the charity work for your own feeling,' he says simply. 'When you're lucky enough to be able to help it's wonderful. All artists are the same. God! I don't think there is anybody in our business who doesn't really want to help somebody.'

Such generosity is only made possible, though, because the comedian can earn such vast sums of money for his non-charity performances. Otherwise it might be a different story altogether. It is expensive to run three offices, two homes, a full-time staff of thirty and a 251-day-a-year career. So on top of his million-dollar property-tax bill, Bob has to find at least the same amount again. To make ends meet he must net at least two million dollars a year. And that means grossing a far higher figure – possibly as steep as three to four million. The alternative would be to start selling off assets to pay the bills and, as any good businessman knows, that can be the start of a very slippery slope indeed, no matter how rich you are.

However, as Bob is the first to admit, there is enough work around to ensure that the bills are paid and to allow a fellow to spend a little more time on the golf course.

21

Bob Hope caught the golfing disease during his earliest days in vaudeville, when he was touring the towns and cities of middle-America, 'where you didn't have anything to do in the mornings'. And it has inexorably grown on him ever since.

'You know, golf is my meal ticket,' he is fond of joking. 'Entertainment is just a sideline . . .'

He first learned the rudiments of the game whilst hauling clubs for the rich as a youngster in Cleveland, but these days other people care for his custom-made set of irons and woods. Although Bob denies ever having a lesson as a child, expert tuition through the years from the golfing greats – Ben Hogan, Sam Snead, Arnold Palmer, Jack Nicklaus and others – has made him one of the top players in show business. At his peak he was down to a creditable four handicap and even today, despite the reduced vision caused by the haemorrhage behind the left eye, he can play off 15 shooting consistently in the low eighties.

Many high golfing honours have come his way, including an American PGA medal – as 'one of the three men who have done most for golf' – and a silver *Sports Illustrated* cup marking his fifth hole-in-one, achieved at a 220-yard hole in Oak Brook, Illinois.

During his long career Bob estimates that he has played on more than 2,000 courses around the globe – from 'chilly' Alaska to 'simmering' Australia, as well as 'a few wet ones in between'.

Each year he forks out around $50,000 for the privilege of belonging to some 20 country clubs throughout the United States, including membership of the exclusive Lakeside Country Club just minutes from his front door. And if he is feeling really lazy, he only has to step out into the grounds of his Toluca Lake mansion to practise on his own 190-yard hole (which has yet to be conquered in one). He also has a water hazard hole at his Palm Springs complex.

Bob is also a competitive golfer who plays at his best when 'there's a little action at stake'. Said Crosby of him: 'I'd rather have him as a partner than an opponent. The first thing he does is to try to talk his opponents out of their rightful handicaps!'

Kings, presidents and dukes have all won and lost side-bets with Hope. Usually they are not huge, maybe five or ten dollars, although Bob laughingly recalls one famous match with the late President Eisenhower, shortly after he had approved a massive long-term loan to a South American country, when the stake was limited to a dollar.

'It's a funny thing, Bob,' explained Ike. 'I've just lent Bolivia millions of dollars, but I only have one buck on me to pay with . . .'

The Hope clubs are probably the most travelled set in history; even the leading professionals have many miles to go before they can catch him up. They go wherever Bob goes, and that has been a long way. Often they get used at the strangest of hours. Irving Fein, the late Jack Benny's manager, will never forget a Florida benefit when it was well after dark when Hope and Benny – and clubs – even reached the hotel.

'The rooms were facing on to a park-like setting,' remembers Fein, 'and Hope was outside with his clubs practising. And Jack said, "Bob, we're going in for a bite of dinner. Do you want to join us?" He said, "Oh no! I'm going to hit some golf-balls at a driving range." We said, "It's ten o'clock at night!" He says, "Oh, I've found one . . . it's about half an hour from here – I'm waiting for a car to pick me up." There he was, at ten o'clock at night, being picked up to play golf for an hour. Then he came back and went to sleep.'

Dolores Hope is a keen golfer too, with a double-figure handicap, and is often seen out on the links with her husband. But rarely are their sessions gentle knockabouts; Bob still smarts at the mention of her one and only victory over him, in France. 'I was a little off-colour that day,' he says by way of excuse.

Says Dolores: 'I beat him fair and square, but he is embarrassed about it. We don't joke about it much and he still refuses to pay me the dollar I won!'

Through the years Bob's most famous golfing partner was Bing Crosby. 'A sensational golfer for a fellow playing with wooden-shafted clubs,' jokes Hope. 'I really had a lot of fun playing with Bing.'

Between them Hope and Crosby raised millions of dollars for charity while tramping the fairways of the world. They were the biggest single cash draw in the history of the game. Not only could they play golf well, they were witty and clever with it too. Both had their own fund-raising tournaments as well, the Crosby at Pebble Beach on the Monterey peninsula near San Francisco, and Bob's pride and joy over 300 miles south in Palm Springs. He started the annual Bob Hope Desert Classic Pro-Am in 1959, and now it is one of the richest events on the professional tour – and the longest, with 90 holes over five days. Each year around 110,000 spectators turn up to watch their favourites golfing and show business idols compete for big cash prizes, and big laughs.

'Dean Martin plays every year and if he wins anything we always tell him,' says Hope.

In recent years the profits from the Classic have helped build a hospital – Bob's pet project, the Eisenhower Medical Centre in Palm Desert. Over six million dollars have already gone towards it and more is undoubtedly on the way. Dolores heads the fund-raising committee and Bob is continually insisting that special fees for his services go the Centre's way. (When the author proposed the Thames Television documentary to mark his 75th birthday, he agreed subject to $25,000 being donated to the hospital. It was.)

The Eisenhower also stands on Hope land. Says Bob: 'When we were getting the whole thing up I knew Dolores would have trouble finding a site. And she did. After a while she came to me; eventually I gave her an 80-acre parcel of real estate I'd had for some time and everyone was happy but my accountant. The Inland Revenue Service allowed us to deduct tax only at the value I bought it at – which wasn't all that much – and not the huge amount they had been charging property taxes on. And that ain't show business . . .'

It is fitting that the Hope Classic should have spawned such a memorial to Dwight Eisenhower. In February 1967 Eisenhower supported the event by presenting the winner's trophy to Tom Nieporte. Recently former President Ford has appeared every year to lend his weight to the cash drive. And when Nixon was in the White House he too helped the fund with a 1971 benefit match with the comedian.

Nixon was lucky to make the date. The year before, while partnering Bob in another contest with actors Fred MacMurray and James Stewart, there was almost a fatal accident with an electric golf-cart. 'Fred and Jimmy nearly changed the course of history,' says Hope. 'They almost ran Nixon down and in front of all those Secret Servicemen. It was a very close thing and would have been very nasty indeed – expecially for the President!'

Another Hope golfing campaign was launched in January 1975, when he headed a venture to encourage blind people to take up the sport. In view of his own particular sight problems, it is a cause with a rather special significance.

In 1980 the Bob Hope Desert Classic concept was picked up by the land of his birth. The first Bob Hope British Classic, a £100,000 pioneering pro-celebrity spectacular, was held at the RAC Club at Epsom, Surrey, in September. Hope became the first entertainer to have his own golf tournament in two countries. The British jamboree was the brainchild of London businessman John Spurling, who also runs the Kenyan Open in Africa, and comedian Dickie Henderson. 'John and I had been trying to get the idea off the ground for four years,' says Dickie, 'but always there was a snag. I almost gave up, but John kept on going and eventually he pulled it together.' Hope's American charities got $75,000 from Spurling for his services and the event was a smash hit. 50,000 fans poured into Epsom to watch stars including Burt Lancaster, Sean Connery, Telly Savalas, James Garner, Efrem Zimbalist Jnr., Don Rickles, Bob Newhart, Bruce Forsyth and Eric Sykes, compete in the four-day 72-hole event. The tournament cost £700,000 to stage, but in the end £62,000 went to two British charities – the Stars Organization for Spastics and the Bob

Hope Theatre of the Arts Foundation at Eltham.

Bob had become involved with the theatre project as long ago as 1970, when he agreed to be the first patron of a trust set up to build a new entertainment complex based at Eltham. Although a few thousand pounds were raised, the plan never really got off the drawing-board – until Spurling, Henderson and Hope put the British Classic together. Now Hope's dream of having a theatre named after him in his birthplace could become a reality.

22

Home for Bob Hope is a fifteen-roomed mansion set in six acres of plush grass and thick shrubs just off Moorpark Street in North Hollywood. Protected from prying eyes by an ivy-covered 20-foot brick wall and electronically-operated wooden gates, it is basically the same place he purchased in 1938. But in 1957 Dolores took advantage of his prolonged absence – making *Paris Holiday* in Europe – to remodel the two-storey interior.

A heavy oak front door opens into a spacious hall, from which a wide staircase winds up to the sleeping quarters. Off the hall is the kitchen, a library stacked from floor to ceiling with Bob's fifty-year book collection and the 'family room' – a massive lounge. At one end a huge oval bar is set into an alcove, while facing it is an impressive stone fireplace surrounded by easy chairs and sofas. Against one wall stands a diminutive ivory upright piano, which Bob cannot play, and above it hangs a Norman Rockwell portrait of a baggy-trousered comedian at play on the golf course.

A big bay window looks out on to a patio and the gardens, which harbour the one-hole golf course and a swimming pool. Sitting in the window is a white round table surrounded by matching wicker chairs – where Bob most likes to take his breakfast. Off the lounge is a small pool-room, a broom-cupboard before Dolores got at it, complete with table and rack full of cues. Attached to that is the two-car garage, above which are a pair of luxurious guest suites.

The main bedrooms in the Hope House, as it has been dubbed by the staff, are situated in the west wing. Each principal has a master suite comprising three rooms and a bathroom.

Bob's bedroom, the only part of the mansion where the maid 'fears to tread', has a dressing-room and a study, overlooking the lavish grounds, off the bedroom. The walls of the two-foot square dressing-room are lined with fitted-units bulging with clothes. One houses a row of suits; in another hang hundreds of shirts; a third is stacked with scores of sweaters and cardigans – Bob's favourite casual apparel. In the centre of the room stands a square chest of drawers, the top of which is littered with hats of all types. Against it lean an assortment of joke golf-clubs: one with a flexible shaft, one with a banana for a putting-head and even one with a diamond set in the putting-face.

Next door, the comedian's bedroom would bring joy to the heart of any teenager. The double bed is conventional enough, but on the shelves which circle the walls are a host of souvenirs and momentoes from all over the world. Dominating them is a colourful Mickey Mouse telephone. There is also a small stereo record player and, next to the bed, a cassette player. When Bob is at home the room always has a lived-in look about it: newspapers lie on the bed and chairs; his travelling cases are usually open on the floor – either being unpacked or repacked – and recent presents from fans, more often than not boxes of sweets, are dotted everywhere.

The house is kept clean by a daily maid and the Hopes also have a live-in cook to prepare their meals. The large gardens are tended by a stocky Mexican, who also doubles as the electrician and handyman.

Skirting the front and side of the mansion is a sweeping tarmac drive watched over by one of the original walnut trees. Adjacent to the garage is the single-storey office block, which is really the heart of the Hope organization. Bob's private secretary works there, as does Dolores's. They are backed up by a couple of general secretaries who try to cope with the mountain of fan mail and business correspondence. All phone calls aimed at the Hopes are routed through that office as well – anything up to two or three hundred a day.

An outstanding feature of the building is Bob's special joke vault. 'That's more valuable than the United States Treasury,' says former Hope gag-writer Mel Shavelson. 'That's Fort Knox in laughter!'

Although exaggerated, Shavelson's definitions are astute. The bank-like, walk-in steel safe contains every joke that has ever been written for the comedian, about seven million in all, as well as around 1,400 discs and tapes of his radio programmes and copies of his films and records. Each one-liner is first filed by date and performance in rows of metal cabinets, then it is carefully cross-referenced in a master index under subject title. The contents are irreplaceable and worth millions of dollars. No one is allowed in the safe without specific authorization from the boss and he has never allowed it or the contents to be photographed. Mainly, though, the joke reservoir is useless for the comedian's day-to-day activities.

'We hardly ever go in there,' admits Bob. 'We nearly always have fresh stuff written. Sometimes I go in and look at the material and at the style, because maybe it'll remind me of something that we did or something good that we can repeat.'

Near the safe is Bob's own office – called the 'play-room' by his writers. A massive oak desk dwarfs the huge room, with its big sofa and soft armchairs (so soft that he has to sit on a pile of thick telephone directories when doing television interviews) and a long polished mahogany table that would happily grace any company's board-room.

Much to the chagrin of his staff, Bob uses the inner sanctum infrequently, preferring to work from his bedroom from the end of his phone. He personally will make and take around 200 calls a day, seven days a week. 'I prefer to work on the phone,' says Bob. 'I can get much more done that way.'

When he does venture down to lean back in his high-backed swivel chair it is usually to tape some audio messages or commercials used to support his forthcoming stage shows. He has had a full-track tape recorder, complete with extension microphone, built into one of the cupboards.

But the show-piece of the office is a ceiling-high, wall-long, glass-fronted display case containing many of his awards and trophies, as well as hundreds of special gifts. Gold and silver medals nestle alongside rows of cups, Bob's honorary Oscar and the Medal of Honour presented by the late President Kennedy. Also on the shelves are some of the scrolls he has picked up from the more than forty honorary academic degrees given to him since 1958. 'Not bad for an uneducated lad from Eltham,' says Bob. Doctor Hope has them in Humane Letters, Laws, Fine Arts, Humanities and Humane Humour. His first was awarded at Quincy College, Illinois, in June 1958. One of his most recent – and most valued – came in March 1978 from Bing Crosby's former university, Gonzaga, in Washington State.

Although the comedian's Moorpark office show-case is bursting at the seams with his awards and trophies, it contains just part of a vast collection of memorabilia. For more than half a century he has kept almost every important scrap of paper, and some not so important, and all awards. Most of the Hope bric-a-brac is stored in a North Hollywood security vault – 'The Morgue', Bob calls it. But eventually he wants it all on public display in a special museum. If he finds a suitable site, the Bob Hope Museum could be the first venture of its kind by a show business personality.

With so many priceless possessions, and an equally valuable occupant, security at the Hope House in North Hollywood is tight. Shifts of uniformed guards operate round the clock, and every visitor is carefully logged in and out. And at night, after the office staff have gone, the security officer notes every phone call too. Yet, unlike so many of his fellow Hollywood super-stars, Bob Hope is not security mad. Careful – yes. But over-protective – no. He does not have a bodyguard and firmly rejects efforts by well-meaning associates to give him one. 'People don't bother me,' he says. 'I like people. And I like meeting them, and talking to them.'

The security services at Moorpark are supplemented by a pair of guard-dogs, which double as household pets. For many years they were Shadow, a black Doberman Pinscher cross, and Steele, a white Alsatian named after the British enter-tainer. He was given to Bob as a puppy during an English visit and travelled to Hollywood on his lap. Shadow still roams the grounds of Moorpark, but now he has a new companion – Steele was destroyed after an astonishing attack on one of the Hope staff. A personal secretary, who was leaving after many years service, went to say goodbye to Steele as they had been very close. As she stroked him, he seized her savagely by the hand cutting right through the ligaments. The woman may never fully recover the use of her hand.

The third canine member of the Hope family does not have to perform guard duties – Tobe, a French poodle. He is Dolores's constant companion.

Moorpark is worth millions of dollars today. When the Hopes first occupied it in 1938 there was nothing but farms for miles around. Now, however, it is surrounded by the sought-after suburbs of Burbank. But neither Bob nor Dolores will profit from any sale. In the mid-sixties the comedian donated both mansion and grounds to their local Catholic church, St Charles'.

The Hopes own two other homes in Palm Springs, where the summer temperatures soar to around 120 degrees. Moorpark is very much a working base these days; Bob and Dolores prefer to relax in their eight-roomed ranch-style bungalow, which is flanked by a string of sun-drenched golf-courses.

Soon, though, they will be ensconced in an even more luxurious holiday mansion. Costing $5,000,000 and covering 29,000 square feet of wooded hilltop overlooking Palm Desert, the space-age home has taken six years to complete. Construction started in 1972, but since then the project has been dogged by misfortune. The Hut, as Bob called it, was to be the most palatial and futuristic residence ever built in the exclusive desert oasis, which boasts hundreds of millionaires per acre and a golf course for every 600 of its 21,000 residents. The roof alone – a sweeping, mushroom-like dome with a 60-foot living-room skylight – would set the comedian back half a million dollars.

'When the house is finished, it is going to make Bing Crosby's look like an outdoor privy,' joked Bob in May 1973 as he approved plans for a pair of lake-sized covered swimming pools and a dining-room that would comfortably seat 200 people.

Exactly two months later the Hope dream house went up in smoke when a spark from a welder's torch set the partly-built edifice alight. In January 1978 the Los Angeles Santa Monica Superior Court awarded the Hopes $300,000 damages against the welder's employer and a number of other construction and insurance companies. The bad luck continued: the chief designer and his associate were killed in a car accident in Palm Canyon minutes after leaving the blackened site. Hut Mark Two rose from the ashes under the personal supervision of Dolores. Work finally finished early in 1979. The lay-out and design is similar to the original Hut, but the mushroom roof has now been replaced by one resembling a space-helmet from *Star Wars*. Dolores, who spent many months commuting between the resort and Moorpark with colour charts, carpet samples and architects' plans, became the seemingly ill-fated project's third casualty. On 1 December 1978, while making final checks on the near-completed building, she fell heavily, badly bruising a number of ribs and breaking two fingers.

Successful Hollywood marriages are commonly thought to be a rarity, but Bob and Dolores Hope are among the few show business couples who have made it work. Theirs has lasted for more than 45 years with only the occasional 'communication problem' to disrupt the bliss. 'It's possibly one of the most ideal combinations,' says long-time family friend George Murphy. 'Bob understands Dolores and Dolores understands Bob. It's as simple as that.'

According to Dolores, her 'abiding memory' of their married life from 1940 onwards is of 'Bob always being someplace else.'

'People keep asking me,' she says, 'whether I resented all the times he was away, but knowing how much good he was doing helping to keep our troops entertained, how could I possibly object...'

Her husband is less forthcoming about the secret of their success. He is much happier using it as part of his act:

Marriage is a great institution – no family should be without it...

I took her for better or worse. The only trouble is – she was worse than I took her for...

After marriage I got to know her true character – the only time I got to open my mouth was when I yawned...

They say a single man has no buttons on his shirt. Well – the married man has no shirt...

Despite all that Dolores says her husband is easy to live with – just so long as everything goes smoothly. 'He's just like your average man,' she reveals. 'The one thing that really angers Bob is incompetence. Otherwise, he's pretty even-tempered.'

Says Bob: 'We have a lot of fun. We have a lot of mutual likes. And then she does her own things, while I do mine. We play a lot of golf together – she's always been a great golfer. We just have a lot of fun . . .'

This is confirmed by their jokes about Bob's prolonged absences from home: 'I've been married 45 years and I've been home two months.'

'If you see Bob – say hello!' is Dolores's favourite.

Her children and charitable activities obviously helped Dolores combat any feelings of loneliness over the years, but her religion has been the greatest source of strength. She is one of the most devout of Roman Catholics and, unlike Bob – who is a sporadic church-goer, she goes to church every day, and sometimes twice a day, whether at home or abroad. She has even had built into one of the footings of their Palm Springs home a tiny chapel, with pews and an alter.

Dolores Hope is tough and has insulated herself well. But, although Bob does not take her along on his whistle-stop tours of the United States – 'because she hates that one-nighter thing' – he does want her around for the longer trips. And when she started singing again it gave him extra comic scope:

Those audiences have a way of inflating your head. By about the fourth show, I was standing in the wings as she walked off. And she said – 'Don't clutter up the exit, boy . . .'

Then, when we got home, she had the nerve to sit in my spotlight at breakfast . . .

Dolores laughs heartily at such jokes, just so long as they are for a paying audience. 'I'd hate to be married to a walking joke-book,' she says. 'Fortunately he doesn't pepper his conversations with gags and one-liners – and I'm very grateful.'

Bob describes his wife as 'a very funny lady – who can't tell a clean joke . . . nor remember a dirty one,' but admits that she is probably his greatest source of material and someone who really makes him laugh. When the annual Christmas tours came to an end, and Bob was feeling lost, it was she who stepped in with a timely joke. 'I've invited all our friends to the house for Christmas,' she told him, 'and they are all going to be dressed in camouflage uniforms – so you will feel at home . . .'

Recently, Dolores Hope has spent much more time on stage with her husband. She virtually retired as a singer to bring up

217

her family and run their home, but now she joins him in the spotlight to sing 'On a Clear Day' and 'I Love You Just The Way You Are'. It is a supporting role she enjoys immensely.

'When I think back on it all,' she says wistfully, 'I have to admit that there were times when I wondered whether I'd made a mistake not pursuing my own career as a singer and spending all my time and energy raising four kids. But that's the way things were and I just accepted it! Being married to a famous star had nothing to do with my responsibilities at home ... and that was that.'

One of Dolores's greatest joys comes from surprising her husband. For one birthday treat she organized a 'shotgun golf match' at a local course, where she knew he would be stopping off for a late afternoon nine holes. On each of the nine tees stood three close friends. So, when Bob arrived he found Fred Mac-Murray, George Murphy and another buddy waiting at the first.

'What are you guys doing here?' asked Hope.

'We're just going to play nine holes before dinner,' replied a nonchalant MacMurray.

'Mind if I play with you?' asked the still unsuspecting Hope.

Says George Murphy: 'We said, "Oh, that'll be fine." And the shotgun went off and we played one hole. Then he moved on to the next three-some and so on. Afterwards there was a big spaghetti dinner at the club-house.'

Along with his marriage, Bob has also managed to maintain a close relationship with his four adopted children. Despite his great fame and constant roamings they feel as near to him as they would to any nine-to-five father. The eldest, Linda, speaks for all when she says: 'As a father he has been very present in my life. He has been physically absent on a lot of occasions when I would have wished that he had been there. But basically he has been a real presence. The psychologists and psychiatrists say it is not the amount of time that you spend with your children, but the quality of the time you spend with them. And I think certainly, qualitatively, that we have had an exceptional growing up period.'

As young children Linda and her brothers and sister had the benefit of a dad who entertained them as well as exercising parental authority. His morning departure for Paramount would often be a performance in itself.

'What kids going off to school have "shuffle-off-the-buffalo" and the little dance steps outside the window?' says Linda. 'He used to do that when we were small children and we were delighted; we were getting ready to go to school. He would hum a few bars of something that he may have been working on in the picture – a song or something – and then he would dance off...'

Bob's antics used to amuse and perplex his children at the same time. One of his favourite night-time games, while they were having dinner, was to open the curtains slightly and pretend to carry on a conversation with falsetto-voiced Bessy, the little orphan girl.

'He would talk to her,' says Linda, 'and they would have this conversation back and forth. And then every time my brother or I would run to the window, to look and find Bessy – who we thought would be friends with us – Bessy disappeared. And it took us a long time to finally figure it out; and even when we figured it out, because it was so delightful, we were reluctant to tell him that his secret was out. There are things like that, that are very warm memories. That he was gone, we accepted ... just like someone, I'm sure, who is the son or daughter of a plumber or doctor who is always on call. I don't feel really that I was cheated, or that I got any less of him than I had a right to have.'

Linda was almost a teenager before she first became aware that her father was an international celebrity and very famous indeed. 'I always remember seeing people come up and ask him for autographs,' says Linda. 'But I never realized why somebody would want my Dad's name on a piece of paper. I don't think it really hit me until I was much older. I always realized he was different from fathers of friends of mine, but I was not ever really that impressed, in a sense, with who he was. And I think that our mother also made an effort to keep it more or less natural, and as much like a family as possible. I think I was ten or eleven when I realized that Bob Hope was something special...'

Younger sister Nora had her first inkling at the age of nine, following a visit to Madame Tussaud's in London, where she saw her father's waxen effigy.

'Oh! It was terrible,' she told her mother afterwards. 'I didn't like it. That's how he might look in fifteen years time!'

Being the children of well-known entertainers has always been difficult. The pressures are enormous. The list of off-spring who have fallen by the wayside, because they cannot stand the constant references to their famous parent or parents, grows longer by the day. Even the benign Groaner had endless troubles with his first family of four sons. But the Hopes have escaped such trauma. The only problem they ever had concerned the elder of the two boys, Tony. He once lived under the assumed name of Marsh to get away from the stigma of the Hope surname. Happily he has now overcome the need for it and proudly bears the family name.

Many of the Crosby boys' problems were caused by an attempt to emulate their father in show business. With the exception of Linda, who is involved in a different area of the business anyway, the Hope children have mostly managed to steer clear of the grease-paint.

Tony, who for a time did toy briefly with a career as a producer at Twentieth Century Fox, is now an attorney living and working in Washington DC. During the administration of Gerald Ford he acted as a presidential legal adviser. He and his wife Judy have given Bob and Dolores two grandchildren – Zachary, aged ten, and Miranda, aged eight.

Nora Hope, the youngest of the four adoptees, is content to be a housewife in San Francisco, where she lives with her husband Sam McCullagh Junior and their young daughter, Alicia. Number two son, Kelly, also lives in San Francisco; he works at a local museum, but has not yet added to the Hope collection of grandchildren.

According to Linda Hope, their father did them all a great favour by not trying to push them into show business and allowing them to find their own careers. She ended up working for the family firm only after separating from her husband. But before marrying she had already gained some experience as a maker of documentary films.

'Then I was married and produced a son (Andrew, now almost nine) and very little else,' says Linda. 'After my divorce I was looking for something to do. I knew that he had this production company and asked if I could have a chance to get involved in television production. He said yes; so I have been developing properties and things for his company. I have found it extremely helpful; I would not be where I am now, in the short amount of time that I have been doing it, if it was not for the fact that Bob Hope is my father. And I certainly accept that.'

Although Bob admits that he would have been proud to see his children follow him on to the stage, he confesses to being relieved that they did not. The business has changed greatly and these days it is much harder to get started than it was when he was a young would-be star.

'They don't have the set-up in the studios today like they used to,' he explains. 'because they don't make that many pictures. One studio used to turn out maybe forty or fifty pictures a year; the same studio today will turn out ten. And there's a lot of talent around now, because they all work in television; that's where the stars are really made today. So it's really tougher . . . Whereas you used to be able to bring a girl into a studio, and if she was exceptional-looking and she passed the talent test, why, they'd go to work on her; then she had a good chance of becoming a big star.'

Apart from his immediate family, Hope has a stock of relatives on both sides of the Atlantic. 'They're all over the place,' he says. 'Every time I lift a few rocks, I keep finding Hopes. They're always happy to see me – but they're just as happy getting it by mail . . .'

In Ohio there are around fifty Hope nieces and nephews, while in Hertfordshire the Hope band has shrunk to about twenty cousins. Bob's last British uncle died in 1976, leaving first cousin Frank Symons – a retired joinery works manager – to organize clan activities in England.

Throughout his career Bob has maintained close links with all his relations. But, despite his jibes to the contrary, they are not a bunch of scroungers. When in England he always tries to arrange a big dinner for them at a London hotel. He pays for the food and drink, but they bear the cost of getting there. Says Frank Symons: 'We usually hire a coach to travel down to London and have a collection for the fare – it's a couple of pounds or so a head normally. There is always someone who asks why Bob isn't paying for it. But I think it would be wrong

221

to ask; we never ask him for money.'

Mr and Mrs Symons, who have three married daughters and eight grandchildren, live in Brampton Park Road, Hitchin. Although Bob has visited them many times, they have never had enough money to accept his invitations to spend time at the Hope mansion in North Hollywood.

'He likes to come to us for tea,' says Frank, 'but insists on no fuss or special treatment. If we're having kippers, he'll have one too. It's a bit embarrassing really, because he's always asking us to visit him in California. But we just haven't the fare; and I would never tell him that in case he thought we were hinting that he should pay it.'

When he is at home in Toluca Lake the usual Hope day starts late. But then it finishes late too. Bob usually wakes around eleven o'clock to read the morning papers in bed. By mid-day he has showered and dressed, and breakfasted on stewed fruit, toast and coffee substitute.

Lunch is often a series of phone discussions with booking agents, journalists, radio show hosts, his writers and publicist Ward Grant. By early afternoon he is ready to meet television producers and directors, or some of the many businessmen with whom he is involved. But always there is the constant buzzing of the telephone (he has one in every room) and he rarely refuses to take a call personally.

Sometime during the afternoon, business schedule permitting, Bob will drive himself down the road to Lakeside for a quick round of golf before returning to work in the early evening. Whenever possible he tries to finish any late television taping or writers' meetings in time to dine with Dolores at around nine o'clock. But such quiet tête-à-têtes are rare; more often than not the couple have a charity dinner to attend somewhere in Los Angeles.

Wherever the meal, though, Hope is still raring to go afterwards. And, unless there are friends to entertain at home he is frequently to be found burning the midnight oil. 'Bob loves working at night,' says Elliott Kozak, his former business manager. 'He's a night-owl. And while putting together some of the shows we were often editing until three in the morning. Many times he's been with us till four or five in the morning, making sure that everything is cut properly.'

Says Bob: 'After being in Hollywood for forty years, I'm still on Broadway hours. I stay up until at least one o'clock; I very seldom get to bed before that. If I'm doing a picture, they have to pound my head so I go to sleep at ten-thirty. But I find I do my best work at night ... office work, I mean!'

Bob's nocturnal habits not only affect the home lives of his long-suffering staff. When Dorothy Lamour lived across the street from him, she was never safe. 'He'd knock on the door at all hours,'' says Dorothy. 'One night he came to the front door – my husband and I were in bed, sound asleep, but it didn't make any difference ... Bob knocked on the door. My husband opened the little peep-hole we had, because you didn't know who it was at that time of the morning, and Bob's nose came through the hole. And he said "Come on, Willie, don't you recognize the nose?" Then another night he did the same thing to us. He had a big press party at his house, and he wanted Bill and me to go, but we couldn't, so Bob brought five or six of them over to us. And I looked terrible, but they came in and we had a big conversation for a couple of hours.'

Select dinner evenings are more Bob's style than parties. But he does like pushing the boat out on special occasions – he gave one of the biggest parties Hollywood has ever seen when Linda married Nathaniel Lande in 1969. Fifteen hundred guests, from old pals like Bing and Dotty to political VIPs such as Vice President Spiro Agnew, ate and drank the Hopes' health under five acres of towering marquees. As the wedding party roamed through the grounds the bride's father was heard to remark: 'Rarely do I do a benefit in my home.'

Dolores, however, feels there is all too little time for a truly private life. The Hopes' moments together are genuine scarcities, to be savoured to the full. 'You can't imagine what a luxury it is to talk to your husband alone for an hour or so,' she says, 'We have so much to say ...'

Says Bob: 'Dolores is my best friend and sternest critic. She is very strict and religious. She is a barometer for me. I check everything with her. If she says something is not in good taste, I think very seriously about doing it ...'

23

He glides into the spotlight with all the grace and cockiness of a man who has been doing it for more than fifty years. The ski-slope nose juts proudly. The lantern-like neanderthal jaw wears the familiar broad grin. Bob Hope is following his favourite road – getting out on stage and making the folks laugh. As the young rock stars of today call it a day in their early thirties, the lad from Eltham, now in his late seventies, keeps rolling along – travelling a staggering 250,000 miles annually and averaging at least twenty live shows a month.

'I've been living out of a suitcase for half a century and I am not about to stop now,' says the effervescent comedian. 'I love it. I book the work myself and if I didn't like it I wouldn't do it. I just have to get out there . . . crack a few gags and meet a few people. I just love people and a comedian has got to be out amongst them all the time, if he's going to be any good. I'd rather wear out than rust . . .'

There is little danger of that happening to Hope. If he is not cracking jokes at a charity dinner, or guesting on a television show, or preparing one of his own specials, he is out pounding the same gruelling American college one-nighter tour as the top rock groups. His 90-minute, one-man, song-and-gag show still thrills audiences of all ages almost as much as it does its star. 'Laughter is his life,' says Mel Shavelson. 'He doesn't want to stop. He doesn't really have another life; he lives by the laughs; he lives on the stage; he lives with the public attention. Without it, he would deflate and become somebody else.'

Mel Frank believes that Hope is essentially a seductive human being. 'He must seduce that audience,' says Mel. 'There is a deep inner reason why Hope must perform every single night – it's a challenge to say, "God damn it! I'll make you love me!" And he does. When you're in the dressing-room of a comedian who has just had an incredibly successful engagement ... he is all perspired and worn out; he is exactly as a man spent after a bout of love-making – relaxed and euphoric, from that wonderful ecstatic moment of release from tension.'

Frank also takes the view that in all great comedians there is a strong element of sadism; an element of reducing an audience to a state of helplessness; of saying, 'I killed them!' or 'I had them in the aisles!' And Bob Hope, he says, is no exception: 'They have to get audiences completely under their control. That is what a certain type of comedy is all about. It's certainly the school of comedy from which Bob originated.'

Bob Monkhouse agrees: 'There's an engine inside every great performer which is usually a need to satisfy, a need to please, a need to hear applause – in terms of either clapping hands or cheques through the post. It's probable that Bob Hope's engine is not only a need to succeed, but quite a naive need to succeed ... a childlike enthusiasm for what he does ... which remains unaffected and never world-weary. I think Bob, if he stopped being Bob Hope, would wonder who to be. Because it keeps him young.'

Actress Rhonda Fleming thinks that compulsive performers such as Bob must have a very special kind of a mind to survive for so long. 'The mind of a superstar like Bob Hope has to have a sub-conscious seed planted there that takes over and will not let him quit. He must be the best. He must make people laugh, or whatever it is that God gave him the talent to do. It's like a law – the more you give, the more you get back. The show must go on.'

Joan Collins feels that there could be a slight trace of insecurity at work – even in such an established entertainer as Hope. 'I think all actors are insecure,' she says. 'Even Laurence Olivier is supposed to be sick to his stomach in the wings before he goes on to play King Lear. I've never met an actor or performer who wasn't – although they love it, that tense, nervous, tight knot in the stomach. It's sort of looking for love in a way

225

. . . it's wanting approbation.

Bob's pre-show nerves are rarely evident to others before he walks on stage. His supremely confident manner usually sees to that. The only outward signs are a constant pacing, as though a caged animal, and a continual humming and ba-ba-ba-boo-boo-ing. But he does admit to feeling 'better after a show than I do before'.

'In our business,' he says, 'it's a great thing when audiences can keep you so exhilarated that they fool you – they make you think you're young; it's just a wonderful thing. And that's my business. There's 24 hours in a day and I can only play golf for two or three hours; then you have to sit around. So when you still feel great and you still have the desire to do jokes, which is fun, you carry on.'

His long-time friend, actor Douglas Fairbanks Junior, concurs: 'I think he'd go crazy if he had to give it up. He just loves to work for its own sake. He's not a very good gardener and I think if his work were denied him, he'd go climbing up the wall. He'd go berserk . . .'

Off-stage, and out of the limelight, Bob Hope is a far less brash individual than his public image suggests. But he is a natural wit and disproves the oft quoted theory that behind every comedian's mask there is the sad face of the clown. 'He's very modest and quiet, and pleasant,' says Douglas Fairbanks. 'He's always got a story on the tip of his tongue, because he's got a marvellous memory and one joke reminds him of another. But he can be very quiet; very serious; thoughtful and interesting.'

American comedian Don Rickles, now a major television and Las Vegan draw, finds it hard to comprehend why people expect comedians to be *on* all the time. 'Comedians when they get together,' he explains, 'are like anybody else. A lot of us kid around, because that's our living and we're always looking for new thoughts, and we are stimulated by other performers. But when I'm at home with my family or when I'm with Bob Hope we're serious. A comedian can't walk around in a clown suit 24 hours a day.'

Daughter Linda, who believes her father to be basically the same man publicly and privately, makes a surprising admission about the real Bob Hope. 'I remember as a kid,' she says, 'growing up feeling intensely disloyal, because we would listen to the radio shows ... and I always thought "Gee! I don't think he's nearly as funny on the radio." I don't know why people want to sit and listen to this man, because at home he was so delightful and funny with his spontaneous humorous observations of different events and people. I thought him, and I still do, a much more amusing and humorous man in person than he is on stage. And that may be the end of my job at Hope Enterprises for saying that!'

John Wayne, who confessed to being 'in love with comedians', was another who laughed heartily at the off-screen Hope. 'I turn on every time he's around,' said Wayne. 'I love to meet him, because he always has two new stories. You just can't walk in on Bob and find him down. I snarl when I get up and look around, but I've never seen Bob anything but light-hearted.'

There are times, though, when Bob does show a tougher side to his character. Being a perfectionist he expects the same high standards from others that he demands from himself.

Says Jane Russell: 'I've never seen him lose his temper, although I've seen him get annoyed, but he pulls back ... thinks it over ... and then goes very quietly to that particular person, and tells them what it is that's bugging him.'

Miss Russell recalls one of the rare occasions when the comedian allowed his frustration to surface for all to see. It was during the making of *The Paleface*. 'The shooting hadn't gone too well. I think he had a hang-over or something and he said, "That's enough of that!" And he walked off the stage...' Director Norman McLeod, who spoke in a stage-whisper at the best of times, shouted after his star, demanding that he return. 'Bob was at the other end of this forty-foot stage. He couldn't even hear him. But it wouldn't have made any difference anyway,' says Jane.

Normally Hope manages to contain his annoyance until such time as he can vent it privately. He makes a point of trying never to chew members of his staff out in public. Former head gag-writer Mort Lachman felt the lash of the comedian's tongue many times, but usually discreetly.

'He can get angry,' says Mort. 'He doesn't repress it. But he's only angry at that moment – and then it's on to the next thing. He doesn't live with it. He's not a neurotic person; he'd never make a psycho. When he's in pain, he's in pain – you can see it on his face. When he's happy, he smiles.'

Hope's underlying toughness and obvious strength of character have stood him in good stead over the years. He has worked closely with just about every major star in all entertainment media, yet his career is not littered with spats and incidents like those of his more temperamental fellows. In fact he has had a distinct calming influence on virtually every difficult artist he has come into contact with. He has proved that he is neither impressed by star stature, nor afraid of sheer physical size.

This was graphically illustrated in 1976 during a television show featuring World Heavyweight Boxing Champion, Muhammed Ali. The comedian was emcee and Zsa Zsa Gabor was to present the 'Greatest' with a 'Sportsman of the Year' trophy. But Ali was having none of it.

'I don't want a white woman to give me the award,' he told Hope sourly during rehearsals.

'I'm sorry, but she is going to give it to you and nobody else,' replied Hope.

'Then I am not goin' to do the show,' retorted Ali.

'Well,' drawled Bob, 'it is entirely up to you. If Zsa Zsa can't give you the award, you are not going to get it at all ...'

Gabor recalls: 'After about ten minutes Muhammed was like a little boy; he accepted the award and he adored me. You see, Bob was so nice and so gentlemanlike, and so firm.'

There are few people who believe in the adage, 'I don't care what they say about me, just so long as they spell my name right,' and to Bob Hope, like all superstars, image is and always has been of vital importance. Throughout his career the comedian has worked hard to ensure that his persona has been projected in the right manner. Public statements and actions have always been carefully guarded, and a permanent media relations spokesman has long been part of the Hope retinue. Today he still employs a staff press agent, as well as a couple of part-timers for special projects. For the most part their efforts have been highly effective; no hint of scandal has touched him – even though he readily admits to 'not having been an angel' – and the only occasion his reputation was ever slightly tarnished was during the Vietnam conflict.

But unlike many show business stars, whose official images often differ greatly from reality, Hope has never tried to put forward a dual personality. Despite the fact that many people consider him to be simply a fast-talking smart-aleck jokester with a streak of ham a mile wide, the Bob Hope the world sees is the very same man his family and friends know.

'I think in the course of his lifetime the man and his image have blended together, so you cannot separate the man and his image; the image that the people see is basically the man himself,' says his press aide, Ward Grant.

Mel Shavelson agrees that the comedian is true to his image, but claims that it has manufactured origins. 'In 1938 we created the character that is now Bob Hope,' says Mel. 'We had to create a character, because at that time Bob had done nothing but monologues. We created a character who was egotistical, who chased the girls ... a few other characteristics. Bob thought they were fictitious, but of course they were exaggerations of some of his own characteristics. And over the years he's grown into the character we created for him. He's still playing the same character; he can't change, or he won't change, because that's his lucky charm. Maybe it's that familiarity that's kept him where he is. I don't know of anybody else who's managed to do it.'

One of the great truths on which the Hope personality is built is an underlying natural exuberance. Many performers who give the impression of being outgoing on stage or screen are actually introverted or loners. But not Hope. 'He loves the laughter he generates, the cheering, the applause, the attention. He loves meeting and talking to all kinds of people,' says Geoffrey Clarkson, his musical director for the past thirty years.

While other artists shut themselves away behind closed doors or armed guards, Bob parades himself normally before his public. In Hollywood he spurns a chauffeur, preferring to drive himself around, but he usually switches to a chauffeur-driven limousine when away from home.

When flying within the United States, which he does almost daily, Hope likes to travel with the minimum of fuss. On tour he is normally only accompanied by M.D. Geoffrey Clarkson and either his road manager Mark Anthony or his press agent Ward Grant. Unless he can borrow the twin-engined jet of his close friend Alex Spanos – a builder from the San Francisco area – Bob flies the commercial airlines just like any other passenger. If there is no first class section on the plane his only claim for preferential treatment is in asking for the front two left-hand seats in the forward cabin and a chance to board first.

Otherwise, he is content to turn up at the airport and wait with the rest of his fellow travellers. Autograph hunters are cheerily dealt with and those who linger to converse get a warm response. Says the comedian: 'I can go anywhere I want. I don't need protection. It seems to me that it is only when you hide behind other people that things get difficult. No one ever attacks me. In fact they come up and say the funniest things. I was in Dallas, Texas the other day and this little old lady walked up to me. She must have been at least 85. She said, "Bob Hope! I've been watching you forever!" I guess she has too!'

Although he enjoys being a free agent, Bob does like to have the company of people at all times. In his book the world now revolves around him. If he wants his golf clubs from Lakeside there is always someone on hand to collect them. If he wants to know the time he has to ask, because he never wears a wristwatch.

'Bob cannot stand to be alone,' says Mel Shavelson. 'He must have an audience, even if it's only one person. I can remember in the early days of the radio show driving back east in a bus scheduled to hit some place to do another show. We were going through the Mohave Desert and we came to an old dusty crossroads ... there were three Indians standing there. And Bob stopped the bus, took the whole cast off, and we did an hour's show for three Indians in the middle of the Mohave – he just couldn't resist the opportunity.'

Says writer Carroll Carroll: 'When he's in a room with any number of people, he's Bob Hope the comedian; if he's sitting talking to you, he's Bob Hope the other fellow. You can be talking to him, but when a couple of people walk in the room you can feel the climate change.'

There are times, though, when Bob wants to be alone – he loves to watch sport on television. Wherever he goes the nearest set is always tuned to the sports channel. More often than not he is checking the results to see how much money he has won – for he is a compulsive gambler. He bets on everything: football games, baseball, his golf matches and even jokes.

Many of his writers have found to their cost that if they say a joke will work and Hope disagrees, he will bet them it won't get a laugh. 'And then he will go out, and give it the worst possible delivery in order to win five dollars,' alleges Mel Shavelson with a laugh. 'He'll win the five dollars, I'll guarantee you.'

Over the years Hope has gained a reputation for being careful or even mean with his money. He is certainly careful with it, you do not become a multi-millionaire by throwing cash around, but suggestions of tightness are wholly refuted by friends and staff alike. They admit that he does have a habit of borrowing the odd dollar to tip caddies or waiters and then 'forgetting' to repay. But that is all. When *Time* alluded to him being 'cheap' an angry Bing Crosby, no waster of a dollar himself, fired off a letter to the editor complaining about the offending article. 'A man who gives away $20,000 a week each year could not, in fairness, be called cheap,' argued Crosby.

Bing's eldest son Gary, who says Bob 'saved' his life by hiring him for an overseas troop show in the mid-forties when he was going through a 'bad time' with the US Army in Europe, backs up his late father's rebuttal. 'He always paid top dollar,' insists Gary. 'That story about him being cheap is not true. I went to Africa with him and also one time I went to Alaska and he always paid top dollar. Of course, you had to show up and work hard for your money – but that was fair.'

Gary also reveals that, in Hope's case, generosity with money began at home. 'In the eyes of small children he was very generous,' he says. 'I remember we used to sing Christmas carols together, the four of us and Dad, and we always made a stop at Hope's house on Christmas Eve. We always made the most money there ... even more than from any of our relatives ... so he tips big, I know that.'

For half a century Bob Hope has given of himself to others. But his least praised charitable attribute has been his services to fellow performers such as Gary Crosby. And it has not only been the lesser-known artists who have benefited. When

Milton Berle, one of America's most famous comedians, was trying unsuccessfully to make a come-back on ABC television it was Hope who helped him.

'I remember the day Milton got cancelled,' says show business writer James Bacon. 'He read it in a trade paper. He said, "Now I know how to end the war in Vietnam – put it on ABC and it'll be over in thirteen weeks!" And it was amazing how many big comedians he asked to guest on his show; they all had excuses ... Bob Hope was the only major comedian who guested on Milton's show. With no questions asked. He did it between benefits – flew in and did the show, flew out and did another benefit that night.'

Another star to get a helping hand, from both Bob and Dolores Hope, was Broadway's Mary Martin. 'When I would get really down I would call them,' she recalls. 'They would say, "Come on over and have dinner with us tonight." Or, "Whenever you feel really upset – please call us." So he was at the beginning of my career in Hollywood; long before I ever became involved in pictures.'

Hope has long been one of the most prolific and astute spotters of new talent in Hollywood. And he still searches for it, as Phyllis Diller – a self-confessed discovery from years back – explains: 'He's constantly on the go. When he hits a town, you think he'd be exhausted, but he goes out and sees if he can find people who are working – new people – and watches them.'

Raquel Welch was a relative newcomer to show business when she first experienced his expert tuition. 'He would always tell me, when I had skits and things to do with him, how to read my lines; and when I was supposed to pause after a laugh line, because I would never pause after I had said it,' says Raquel.

In his yearly travels around the United States Bob employs around a dozen young inexperienced singers for his stage shows and all receive the same treatment as Raquel got. Each girl has her own solo spot, but must duet a comedy number and a routine with him. Often they work with him only once every few weeks and, because Bob always arrives at the last possible moment, most rehearsals are hasty affairs in cars, hotel rooms or backstage.

Says Hope: 'A comedian knows just how to feed somebody and I can take a girl who's never been on before, and I can get her laughs just by working with her and in my reactions to what she says. When you're on my show, it all counts.'

Loyalty is one of Bob's great character strengths. Most of his staff have been with him for years and one writer, Norman Sullivan, has been supplying gags since 1939. And for a joke-writer that is about three life-times.

When the late Denis Goodwin left London to write for Bob in Hollywood, he needed all the loyalty the comedian could give – and he got it. Denis was a gentle and vulnerable man, and found it virtually impossible to get along with the hard-nosed team of resident writers. Eventually he cracked up under the strain.

'I feel excluded,' he wrote his former partner Bob Monkhouse in Britain. 'They seem to have formed a ring around Hope. I can't get to him...'

Bob knew nothing of the desperate letter, but he realized Goodwin was having trouble and took steps to try to make things easier. Denis was invited to dinner at the Hope House, introduced to other writers, given special assignments and even taken to meet Hope's film star friends.

'It wasn't done to get more work out of him,' says Bob Monkhouse. 'In fact, eventually, towards the end of the period that Denis was living in Hollywood, he was doing virtually no work. He was so demoralized that he had stopped producing comedy material. But Hope never stopped the pay cheque; he kept supporting Denis because he liked him and I think he saw in Denis what he saw in so many of the people that he has always supported, and helped – that childlike quality that he knows is right inside him too.'

Others who have been supported by the comedian include an invalid wardrobe girl, who worked from a wheelchair, and the widow of a long-serving press agent. He has also seen to it that old radio buddy, Jerry Colonna, who was semi-paralysed by a stroke, gets plenty of work.

At the height of his success in films, when 135 million Americans flocked to the cinema every week, Bob Hope was regarded as one of the screen's most handsome leading men – a rare honour for a comedian. Dolores found him 'almost handsome' when they first met in the thirties, but his leading ladies are more enthusiastic. Rosemary Clooney thinks he was a 'terrific kisser'; while Dorothy Lamour confesses to believing him to be 'one of the sexiest types of men', ranking him alongside Clark Gable and Tyrone Power. 'Bob had something about him,' she says. 'It appealed to me and I'm sure it appealed to a lot of women.'

Says Edith Head, queen of the movie costume designers: 'He was always kissing somebody. But he always did it with a little bit of humour. It was never ever just plain sex – it was always sex with charm. He isn't the traditional handsome hero like Valentino and he wasn't a sex-symbol, but he has the ability to make people love him.'

Raquel Welch looks at Bob in a different way. 'He's synonymous with so many things that I've experienced over the years,' she explains, 'that maybe it's a sort of paternal thing that keeps me from thinking of him as a sexy man. But I think personally – his vitality and the way he looks – that he still has what the French call "Le Class" and I think that's sexy!'

Today Hope still attracts the girls in droves – many of whom are young enough to be proud granddaughters. Physically he looks more like a man of fifty than someone in his late seventies and mentally he is, if anything, even younger. True, the light brown hair is a little thinner now, the sideburns grayer, the face slightly more lined and the waistline thicker, but his non-stop energy puts men half his age and more to shame. But it is not only the performing that keeps the Hope looks intact. He does not smoke and only rarely takes a drink. 'The last drink I had was a glass of white wine at a Liz Taylor bash. I mean, you can't turn a woman like that down,' quips Bob.

'I used to smoke and drink,' he continues. 'When I was on Broadway I smoked so much my throat would close shut. I went to a doctor and he stuck the whole office down my throat trying to get it open. He told me he wouldn't be responsible for it if I continued to smoke. My mother had just died from cancer, so I cut it off right then and there. I wouldn't be alive today if I hadn't stopped smoking forty years ago.'

Alcohol went after he contracted a bladder infection. The occasions when he takes the odd glass of wine are becoming less frequent. 'Because who needs yellow tennis shoes,' jokes Bob.

Eating is another thing he watches carefully. Meals at home are invariably light and healthy, with lots of fruit, although he does have a chronic weakness for ice cream. Usually Dolores controls it by refusing second helpings, but on tour or on the golf course she is helpless. In Palm Springs he has a favourite local ice cream parlour where he sneaks double helpings after golf. But on the road he can celebrate with hamburgers and milk shakes as well as the ice cream. He loves to pick up a take-away dinner at a handy hamburger drive-in following a show. Once, with the author in San Diego, he sat outside the city's airport terminal in the back of a vintage Rolls Royce munching away as autograph hunters clamoured around the car. 'Isn't this great!' he enthused, with all the pleasure of a teenager enjoying a midnight feast.

On another occasion, in London, Bob, a group of writers and the author were on the way to a meeting with Lord Grade at his office near Marble Arch. As the car pulled up outside, the comedian ordered the driver to go around the block. 'I've spotted an ice cream parlour – let's get some,' he said gleefully. The ice creams were still being eaten as the party arrived on Lew Grade's floor. But Hope, with impeccable timing, managed to finish his by the time the impresario arrived to greet him. The rest of the group juggled with half-eaten, melting cones as they shook hands – much to the amusement of both Grade and Hope.

Dietary excesses are quickly dealt with, though. For the famous frame is kept in trim by regular vigorous massaging, even while on tour. Many a frustrated masseur has kicked his heels in an hotel lobby until the early hours waiting to get at his illustrious client. Bob also makes sure that he gets at least eight hours sleep a night – no matter what time he eventually climbs into bed. However, his real keep-fit secret is walking; not while playing golf, because he rides around the course in an electric cart, but last thing at night. His North Hollywood neighbours often see him striding out at 2:00 am as if he has a train to catch.

Says daughter Linda: 'He always walks a mile or two. There's one French poodle in Palm Springs that will attest to that fact. Then he has massages almost daily and I think all of that combines to keep the circulation going, and allow him to do the things he likes to do.'

Mort Lachman believes the comic's apparent agelessness is

due to the same constant activity that gained him the nickname Rapid Robert. 'Motion has kept him young,' explained Mort. 'His whole body is always moving. He can't even walk around a golf course; he has to drive around it to get there faster, so he can get on to the next thing. His need to move has always been the most fun part of him.'

Dolores gives the recipe for her husband's longevity in two words: 'Hard work.'

'Don't ever be fooled by his relaxed, easy-going manner,' she says. 'Underneath that smooth, unruffled exterior is one of the hardest working guys you have ever met. It's been that way ever since I've known him and it'll be that way until the day he dies. We both feel half our ages, because we're happy, fulfilled, contented people who enjoy the day-to-day challenge of being alive.'

Although Hope seems to be indestructible, there have been indications that the years are beginning to tell. In November 1977, following a taping session with the ATV *Muppet Show* at Elstree, he fell asleep in the back of his limousine – while giving a radio interview. 'I've fallen asleep while others were talking before,' admitted Bob when he awoke outside his West End hotel, 'but never when I was talking . . .'

A year later, in a television studio in Ohio, he worried everyone by complaining of chest pains after four hours of rehearsing a complicated tap-dance routine with Sammy Davis Jnr. A doctor was urgently summoned, but pronounced Hope fit following a thorough examination.

But since then old ski-snoot has showed little sign of slowing down. On 21 March 1979, he arrived in London to prepare for his first variety season at the London Palladium for 25 years. He arrived a happy man – millions of American teenagers, readers of the magazine *Seventeen*, had just voted him their 'Most Admired Man' ahead of heart-throbs John Travolta, Robert Redford and Burt Reynolds.

A little over 24 hours later the familiar strains of 'Thanks For The Memory' heralded a surprise Hope appearance at the British Academy of Film and Television Arts awards ceremony at the Wembley Conference Centre in North London. After announcing *Julia* as the winner of the Best Film award, Bob had a five-minute private meeting back-stage with the President of BAFTA, Princess Anne. With them were the author, who was handling press and media relations during the visit, and Captain Mark Phillips. While the Princess and the comedian chatted, the author made small-talk with Mr Phillips. On the way out to the car Bob inquired: 'Who was that guy you were talking to?'

'Mark Phillips. Her husband,' replied the author.

'Oh! I thought he was her private detective,' admitted Hope.

Another amusing incident occurred earlier that same evening. Pacing the corridors in the bowels of Wembley was Lord Olivier, who was to give a special BAFTA honour to Lord Grade. 'Bob's here,' the author informed him. 'I'm sure he'd like to see you.'

'Oh no! I'm sure he's got far too much on his mind,' replied the actor.

Minutes later the author told Hope about Olivier's presence a few yards away. 'Not now,' said Bob. 'I'm sure he's got much on his mind . . .'

The pair did meet though – just before Hope was due to go on, in the award-givers' ante-room back-stage. The embrace was warm and emotional – prompting actor David Janssen, also about to make an appearance, to quip, 'Those two should get married!'

Hope's day did not end at Wembley. After a light supper in his hotel room at Claridge's, and a chance to watch himself on the BBC telecast of the awards ceremony, it was off to the nearby Hilton Hotel for a paid cabaret show at a Datsun motor dealers' dinner. Comedian Dickie Henderson was the compere and Petula Clark the supporting singer. She had flown in from Geneva specially for the evening. Backing Bob was Syd Lawrence and his Orchestra. Although it was a very private affair and the Hope presence was kept secret from the press, it was lucrative. Hope's bank balance was improved to the tune of £15,000 for his hour's work. The money was earned, however. It was well past midnight before Henderson announced him. He awaited his cue amidst the slops and grease of the hotel kitchen trying to avoid getting his tuxedo dirty. 'Ah! This is the life of a star,' mused the comedian. 'I've seen more kitchens than any chef!'

It was 3:00 am before Hope clambered into bed at Claridge's

– for his second sleep of the night. He'd managed to catch forty winks at the Hilton earlier. Bob took the opportunity to stretch out on the bed and make a 'phone call to his Moorpark home to have some new material read to him. Private secretary Lee Barnes took the call and went in search of the jokes his boss wanted. By the time he'd found them, Bob was fast asleep with the receiver lying against his ear on the pillow. Fortunately, the cost of the 6,000-mile call was down to the organizers of the Datsun show, because Bob Hope does not like wasting his own money on the telephone. When calling long distance he always makes person-to-person arrangements through the operator and keeps it short, though he'll run through a whole routine of gags if you call him.

His system broke down at Claridge's, however, much to his chagrin. Twenty minutes after making a call to Los Angeles he picked up the receiver to dial locally, only to discover he was still connected to the States. 'We'll have to speak to them about that,' he said with great feeling. 'They're playing around with my bank-roll!'

The days before the Palladium opening were hectic: a photo-call outside the famous theatre halted traffic as hundreds of journalists and photographers fought to get a story; then came a British Captains of Industry lunch at a Knightsbridge restaurant honouring the 16-strong MCC cricket team which beat Australia the previous winter. Hope exchanged ties with captain Mike Brearley and raffled a cricket bat to raise cash for the Gunnar Nilsson Cancer Treatment Campaign – a million dollar target set by the Swedish Formula One racing driver as he lay dying from cancer in London's Charing Cross hospital. To the comedian's amazement, the 200 industrialists – many of whom were the bosses of Britain's leading companies – were less than generous with their bidding for the bat, which was signed by every member of the triumphant team. Hope put an end to it by buying it himself with a personal cheque for one thousand dollars.

The Palladium season got off to a grand start on Monday, 26 March, before a packed house which included a host of celebrities, Raquel Welch, Lew Grade, David Janssen, Les Dawson, Mike Brearley and the Chinese Ambassador Mr Ke Hau. Ke Hau's presence had been carefully engineered. The

238

comic was in the middle of negotiations for a televised tour of China and was anxious to become the first Western entertainer to perform there since the Communists brought down the Bamboo Curtain. Although Bob did tour China later in the year, he wasn't the first – Shirley MacLaine beat him to it. But, fond memories remain from Ke Hau's Palladium visit; he sat in the stalls with his wife, with an interpreter between them, translating and explaining every Hope joke! 'With my act I bet he needed one,' quipped Bob when he was told about it.

Variety took a different view. 'The first night house, which included a fair smattering of local showbiz celebrities and captains of industry, accorded the comedian a fittingly lusty welcome,' wrote its reviewer. 'With some opening references to the strike here by public employees ('I haven't seen so much garbage since vaudeville"), Hope, embarked, in traditional vein, on some 15 minutes of topical material to a delighted response... His famed rapid delivery and precise pausing notably gratified an audience so well disposed that it might well have settled for less.'

Hope's seven Palladium shows were seen by a capacity audience of 16,500 people, who paid a record £110,000 at the box-office. According to theatre-owner Lord Grade, it was 'the busiest week we have ever had with any single artist.'

Said Bob: 'For an entertainer there's no better stage or better audience than the Palladium. I intend to keep coming back as long as they'll have me...'

He was back at the Palladium even before he had really left, for a television special with Richard Burton and Raquel Welch. The show was an Anglo-American co-production between Lew Grade's ATV and Sentry Insurance of the USA. It did not go smoothly.

Final rehearsals were held on Saturday, 31 March, and they proved to be frustrating for everyone. Bob spent much of the day in his Palladium dressing room either waiting to be called on stage or else trying to make peace between Raquel Welch and Richard Burton. The problem was the main comedy sketch of the show – an *Upstairs, Downstairs* – type skit set in Buckingham Palace – based on the song 'The Waiter and the Porter and the Upstairs Maid'. Both Burton, who surprisingly was making his debut at the Palladium, and Welch were unhappy with the material. And in truth they were both right; it was not the funniest ever written. However, Hope was determined it would stay in. First he would call Richard, who was staying at the Dorchester on Park Lane, and satisfy his demands and objections. Then he'd call Raquel, who was at the Savoy overlooking the Thames, and try to get her agreement. 'I feel like Henry Kissinger!' commented Hope.

Eventually Raquel, who had ended up in tears at 1:00 on Saturday morning when an ambitious production number she was taping went wrong, pulled out of the sketch altogether. 'I won't do it,' she said. 'I just can't!' By lunchtime on Saturday the Palladium was in uproar: rehearsals were chaotic and everyone was frantically searching for a replacement for Raquel. Susan George, back in England from Los Angeles for a working holiday, was chosen. But where was she? 'In Liverpool, watching the Grand National at Aintree,' said her agent.

'Ger her paged,' ordered Hope. 'We need her!'

'I took the call just behind the Tote, so you can imagine the background noise. We had this amazing conversation with me trying to grasp what they wanted me to do. If it had been a day later – April the first – I'd have been convinced it was an April Fool's joke . . .' Susan recalled.

Having been convinced it wasn't a joke, Susan George dashed back to London for late night rehearsals with Hope and Burton at the Dorchester. 'I didn't even back a winner at the Grand National,' she told them, 'but I feel pretty good all the same!'

By Sunday evening, when the show was to be taped before an invited audience, feelings at the theatre were running high. Richard Burton was far from pleased with Miss Welch, who felt unable to share her dressing-room with Miss George, but remained cheerful as he and wife Suzy welcomed the latecomer into their room. 'If we have to do that sketch again, I'll try it in Welsh,' he said laughingly.

Throughout all the turmoil Hope worked away at his monologue material impassively. Until, that is, technical hitches delayed the start of the show. 'What the hell's going on?' demanded a perturbed comedian, when it became obvious that the audience were getting restless. 'These people have come here to be entertained.'

Lew Grade was angry too. He left his seat in the Royal Box

and headed back-stage. 'Get the show on the road ... or else!' he ordered.

Meanwhile, Hope was out in front of the curtain getting a tumultuous round of applause. He explained what was going on and why it wasn't, and then launched into an ad-libbed routine of jokes. All was going well until Barney McNulty, who was setting up a huge stack of idiot boards with the show script on them in the middle of the stalls, dropped the lot with a crash which silenced the theatre. The Hope riposte got the biggest laugh of the night:

He's just dropped my ad-libs ...

Many hundreds of the invited guests didn't stay to see the end of the show and a river of people poured from the Palladium during breaks in the taping. For the first time in many decades Bob Hope was subjected to the indignity of an audience walking out on him. They had trains to catch and beds to go to. Monday was a working day. It made a mockery of one of his favourite gags:

England's a great place for a comedian to work. It's an island, so the audience can't run very far ...

Bob was philosophical about the show when he saw the video tape the next day at Lew Grade's office: 'It's not the best show I've ever done, but it'll be all right when it's edited and we sweeten it up a bit.' The reviews following its American transmission in May proved him right. 'An enjoyable soufflé of a special,' said the *Hollywood Reporter*. 'Hope gave ample evidence of his invaluable mastery of every comedian's crucial commodity – timing.'

Variety was much cooler, but still complimentary: 'Burton and Hope worked best alone together, with the experienced laugh-getter coaxing the dramatist, who got off a solid chuckle noting that the one thing they shared was that neither ever won an Oscar.'

Despite the traumas of the April Fool's Day show, it was a day to cherish in other respects – the Queen had Bob and Dolores to Sunday lunch at Windsor Castle. Also there were Prince Philip, Prince Andrew and Prince Edward. Bob was delighted. 'She was so nice to us,' he told the author afterwards, 'and was pleased with all the royal jokes that I had been using in my Palladium act. I told her a couple and she laughed almost as much as Prince Philip ...'

A few days after meeting Princess Anne, Hope was at Sandown Park racecourse with the Queen Mother. Dolores was pleased too – she won £25 by picking two winners.

As he packed his bags and prepared to fly back to Los Angeles, Hope was able to reflect upon a successful but eventful trip. Apart from everything else, he had managed to sleep through the first act of a top London musical and engage in some long-distance sparring with actor Marlon Brando.

'It's the best musical I've ever slept through,' joked Bob as he went back-stage to congratulate the cast of *Evita*. 'But seriously, Joss Ackland was wonderful as Peron. I knew both Eva and him, and Joss had the mannerisms just right. What an actor. And boy, can't that little girl Elaine Paige sing! She could wake the dead. Well, almost . . .'

The clash with Brando followed an interview the actor gave to *Playboy* magazine, in which he called Hope 'pathetic'.

'He's like a junkie – an applause junkie,' said Brando scathingly. 'Bob Hope will go to the opening of a phone booth in Anaheim, provided they have a camera and three people there.'

Bob hit back. 'It made me sad for a moment,' he said, 'and then I thought of the man – and you've got to *know* Marlon Brando. I think Marlon is a great actor. But you don't know his condition at the time of the interview. I understand he did it in Tahiti – he might have had a little too much of that Tahiti apple juice . . .'

Hope even agreed with the phone booth jibe. 'If it's a benefit, I will,' he said. 'I probably give away more money to charity than he makes in a year – even when he is playing in *Superman*,' referring to the actor's massive million-and-a-half pound salary for only 12 days work on the film.

Brando also accused Hope of being ' a man who has an ever-crumbling estimation of himself'. That brought a chuckle from the comic: 'A lot of other people say it's the other way around – that I do think too much of myself. Which I do . . .'

Back in California Bob had hardly time to unpack before the news came through that his trip to China was on. The adrenalin surged as he realized that at last he had the chance to cross another frontier; to get at an entirely new and fresh audience. Dolores, who was going too, caused much amusement amongst the Hope staff by insisting that they took with them a plentiful stock of American food. Later, most were to thank her for doing so. For, as Bob put it, 'China was boring and the food was uninspiring.'

The tour, though, was a great professional challenge. An NBC-TV special, *The Road to China* was being taped along the way and with the Hopes were ballet star Mikhail Baryshnikov, singer Crystal Gayle and Big Bird from *Sesame Street*. Laughs were hard to come by, because the Chinese audiences needed interpreters to explain the Hope jokes and also the comedian was not known. 'It was really weird,' said one of the television production team, 'we'd drawn huge crowds when we were taping segments for the show and we'd think, "Gee, this is great! Bob's really pulling them in." Then we realized it wasn't him – they didn't know who he was – it was the cameras they were interested in!' If this was a blow to Hope's ego, he never showed it. In fact he turned street photographer to keep the atmosphere going. Says Bob: 'I'd got this Polaroid camera and took some pictures of some Chinese to take home. When I showed them how they developed they went crazy. They'd never seen anything like it. Soon they were all lining up to have their pictures taken with the Polaroid. I could have made a very good living in China...'

The following year Hope was back on Communist soil again, this time in Russia. On the way to launch his first British golf classic he made his long awaited return to Moscow to entertain the embassy staff there.

1980 was also the year when Hollywood went to Washington. Ronald Reagan produced the political shock of a lifetime when he unseated President Jimmy Carter to become the 40th American President. Reagan scored two firsts: he was the oldest man to reach the White House and the first actor to become President.

Surprisingly, Hope did not actively campaign for Reagan in the way he had done for other presidential hopefuls, even though they were old and close friends. During the campaign the comedian had hoped that ex-President Ford could make a come-back and win the nomination in Reagan's place. 'He left it too late,' admitted Bob. 'It was a great shame.'

President Reagan, though, will provide a wealth of political barbs for the Hope tongue in the coming years which could once again establish Hope as America's leading satirist.

Postscript

This, then, has been the story so far of the life and times of Leslie Townes Hope. The lad from Eltham who, having dreamed of stardom in a Cleveland pool-hall, reached out and earned it the hard way. The young man who became a comedian by chance, but a personality by design. The senior citizen who has won the love and respect of his adopted country by example.

It is the story of an Englishman who has risen higher in his chosen profession than any entertainer in history and of a performer who has met more people face-to-face than any other artist anywhere.

An admiring public has rewarded Bob Hope by paving his way with gold. But he has amply repaid the debt – by paving millions of roads with laughter.

And the journey is far from over . . .

Laughter is the only tonic I need to keep young and right now I feel 45! I can only play golf once a day – then I have to hear some laughs. I have a laugh machine which gets me up in the morning . . . then I turn on the applause . . . just to get on my feet . . .

I'm never going to retire. I like what I'm doing. I do every show like it's my last one – my last chance. As long as I feel good, I've got big plans to go on and on, and on!

I'm going to bore people for the next twenty years . . .

Index